Reverence for Life

Reverence for Life

*Albert Schweitzer's Great Contribution
to Ethical Thought*

ARA PAUL BARSAM

OXFORD
UNIVERSITY PRESS

2008

OXFORD
UNIVERSITY PRESS

Oxford University Press, Inc., publishes works that further
Oxford University's objective of excellence
in research, scholarship, and education.

Oxford   New York
Auckland   Cape Town   Dar es Salaam   Hong Kong   Karachi
Kuala Lumpur   Madrid   Melbourne   Mexico City   Nairobi
New Delhi   Shanghai   Taipei   Toronto

With offices in
Argentina   Austria   Brazil   Chile   Czech Republic   France   Greece
Guatemala   Hungary   Italy   Japan   Poland   Portugal   Singapore
South Korea   Switzerland   Thailand   Turkey   Ukraine   Vietnam

Copyright © 2008 by Oxford University Press, Inc.

Published by Oxford University Press, Inc.
198 Madison Avenue, New York, New York 10016

www.oup.com

Oxford is a registered trademark of Oxford University Press

Library of Congress Cataloging-in-Publication Data
Barsam, Ara Paul.
Reverence for life : Albert Schweitzer's great contribution to ethical thought /
Ara Paul Barsam.
    p. cm.
Includes bibliographical references and index.
ISBN 978-0-19-532955-1
1. Schweitzer, Albert, 1875–1965—Ethics.   2. Schweitzer,
Albert, 1875–1965—Religion.   I. Title.
B2430.S374B37 2007
170.92—dc22   2007009458

9 8 7 6 5 4 3 2 1

Printed in the United States of America
on acid-free paper

Preface

The figure of Schweitzer has shadowed me since childhood. Amidst the medical accessories in my father's study, pride of place was given to Le Grand Docteur's photograph above the mantelpiece. As a child, I recall being awed by Schweitzer's fierce countenance, notably his bushy moustache and piercing eyes. Only later could I begin to read, let alone understand, the words which appeared below: "Reverence for Life affords me my fundamental principle of the moral."

Little did I know that years later, when I moved to Mansfield College, Oxford, I would inhabit the small study where Schweitzer penned those very words. It is there he delivered the Dale Lectures on "the struggle for the ethical conception of the world in European philosophy,"[1] later published as *The Decay and Restoration of Civilization* and *Civilization and Ethics* (parts I and II of *The Philosophy of Civilization*). Schweitzer used this study to compose his scripts in German, which he later delivered in the lecture room, across the quad, in French. Thus Schweitzer's ethic of *reverence for life* was first publicly articulated in an academic context at Mansfield College.

During the subsequent five years, I pored over Schweitzer's work and followed his footsteps to Europe and Africa—aided, I should add, by occasional interludes provided by the organ in Mansfield Chapel (which Schweitzer himself played during his visit in 1922). In the process, Schweitzer became an indispensable companion and mentor.

As I immersed myself in Schweitzer, I became increasingly dismayed by the range of misunderstandings both of his life and of his thought—misunderstandings, it must be said, that continue to characterize supposedly scholarly as well as popular judgments. Whatever Schweitzer's limitations are—and I have made no attempt to disguise them—it has to be said that what emerges after the misunderstandings have been put to one side is a remarkable human being, one who still has every right to be called a moral giant of the twentieth century.

Schweitzer was also an intellectual in every sense of that term. True, his scholarship was often marred (or improved, depending on one's standpoint) by apologetic purposes, specifically, his desire to commend religious and theological insights. But the range of his work encompassing inter alia philosophy, theology, music, and medicine makes him one of the few genuinely Renaissance figures. All this should be enough to justify serious intellectual study, but there is more. And the more, namely, his conception of reverence for life, continues to be of increasing ethical and practical importance. Schweitzer would have been well pleased, for he regarded reverence as the capstone contribution and the one for which he wished most to be remembered.

In my journeys, I have accumulated many debts. Keith Ward was an insightful critic who supported the project over many years. Andrew Linzey's intellectual companionship was greatly appreciated throughout the process, and helped to make this book a reality. Shortly before his death, Peter J. Wexler critically reviewed the entire manuscript, and gave me the benefit of his immense erudition both logical and linguistic. His painstaking work enabled me to think though Schweitzer's legacy from a new vantage point and to be made aware of Schweitzer's shortcomings as well as my own. He will, unfortunately, not know where his influence has led.

I wish also to record my appreciation to my family for all their support and to my grandparents, whose journey for peace in a new world has spawned my own.

Contents

Introduction

Schweitzer maintained that the idea of *reverence for life* came upon him as an "unexpected discovery, like a revelation in the midst of intense thought." He describes how in a small steamer ship, slowly creeping upstream and laboriously navigating a long journey on the Ogowe River in the dry season, he was

> struggling to find the elementary and universal concept of the ethical that I had not discovered in any philosophy. I covered sheet after sheet with disconnected sentences merely to concentrate on the problem. Two days passed. Late on the third day, at the very moment when, at sunset, we were making our way through a herd of hippopotamuses, there flashed upon my mind, unforeseen and unsought, the phrase "reverence for life." The iron door had yielded. The path in the thicket became visible.[1]

Whether it was, in fact, that simple, and whether Schweitzer found what had hitherto been undiscovered in any philosophy, are moot points. But what is not debatable is that he did uncover and articulate an idea that has had an increasing resonance in ethics and society since his death.

Ideas do not come from nowhere. What was revealed to Schweitzer on the Ogowe River may have felt like a direct moment of illumination, but behind the idea stands a complex intellectual history, both philosophical and religious. The argument of this book is that in order to have a firm grasp of the concept of reverence for life, we need to wrestle with this intellectual heritage. Schweitzer is case in point that all great thinkers stand on the backs of giants.

Others, in turn, have stood on his back. The publication of Rachel Carson's *Silent Spring* in 1962 is frequently regarded as the beginning of the modern environmental movement. It was to Schweitzer that Carson dedicated the work, and she opened her text using his words: "Man has lost the capacity to foresee and to forestall. He will end by destroying the earth."[2] When Carson received the Schweitzer Medal in 1963, she summed up her work in Schweitzerian-like terms: "What is important is the relation of man to all life." An inscribed photograph of Schweitzer (together with a letter of thanks for the dedication of *Silent Spring*) were encased, center stage, in her study. According to Carson's housekeeper, Ida Sprow, it was her "most cherished possession."[3]

It is unsurprising that Carson, and others, have found in Schweitzer an inspiration for a wider ecological ethic. He was a pioneer of *life-centered ethics*—to use the modern phrase—and prophetic of contemporary environmental and animal concerns. He repeatedly drew attention to the inadequacy of humanocentric thought as a rational critique of the world and sought to widen the scope of ethics to incorporate concern for all manifestations of life. It is wrong, then, to telescope Schweitzer's legacy into a sole focus on any one current concern. His life-centered ethics is broader than these concerns and traverses a wide range of life issues from euthanasia to animal experimentation to nuclear testing.

The reason that we bother with Schweitzer is because by throwing light on the origin and development of his thought, we are led to a closer appreciation of the contribution that reverence for life makes to contemporary ethical concerns. Life-centered ethics—in the broadest sense—has continued to flourish on the moral agenda, though Schweitzer's pioneering contribution to it is often overlooked. Not only did he help put the issue on the agenda, but—most significantly—he also offered philosophical and theological foundations for such insights. The point to be grappled with is that there is an ineradicably religio-philosophical, nay mystical, dimension to the whole notion of reverence that Schweitzer expresses both in his writing and actual experience.

One of the many problems with Schweitzer, however, is that he defies easy conceptualization. He was a polymathic figure: biblical scholar, musician, physician, philosopher, and theologian. He is remembered in theological circles for *The Quest of the Historical Jesus*, or more broadly for his medical mission in Africa or for his interpretations of J. S. Bach's music. But Schweitzer considered his most meaningful contribution, the one for which he most wished to be remembered, to be his ethic of reverence for life (*Ehrfurcht vor dem Leben*).

In this book, we will journey with Schweitzer through the various intellectual worlds he inhabited—philosophical, theological, religious—that were critical to the genesis of reverence for life. Some of these worlds, it must be admitted, are more foreign, even esoteric, than many readers might imagine. But Schweitzer was not an occultist; all his journeying really did lead to that decisive moment on the Ogowe River.

Schweitzer's ethic has equally excited varied and contradictory reactions. His thought appears trapped between the acclaimers who tend to gloss over inconsistencies and the critics who see his pith helmet as symbolic of his outdated ethical thought. Magnus Ratter, whose book the biographer George Seaver deemed "undoubtedly the most informed and penetrating study of Schweitzer's life and thought that has yet appeared,"[4] passes entirely into adulation when he goes so far as to claim:

> To anticipate the verdict of posterity, to enhalo a living man, is to challenge the world: and we challenge it.... Reverence for life will deepen the spiritual life of the individual and has power to create an ideal society.[5]

Such romantic heroism has prevented serious engagement by publicizing his public image while ignoring the roots of his thought and some of its inconsistencies.

At the opposite end of the pole, the extremes are more striking. Contemporary theological and philosophical literature abounds with rejections of Schweitzer as an ethicist. Reverence for life has been said to involve ad hoc decisions (Charles Birch and John B. Cobb, Jr.), to uphold the moral inviolability of all life (Emil Brunner and Paul Tillich), to be untenable and impractical (Brunner and Hans Leisegang), insufficiently theological (Karl Barth), purely philosophical (D. E. Rölffs), unbiblical (Oscar Cullmann and Peter Vogelsanger), inconsistent (Cullmann and Vogelsanger), pantheistic (Brunner), un-Christian (James Daane, Gabriel Langfeldt, and John Middleton Murry), a "henotheism" of the community of the living (H. Reinhold Niebuhr), and insufficiently eschatological (Jürgen Moltmann, Barth, and Cullmann). As one might guess from their tone, such criticisms are based on assumed premises and involve prejudgment.

These extremes, indeed all previous work, share one thing in common: partiality of one kind or another. Surprising though it may sound, no previous study in the voluminous Schweitzer literature has examined Schweitzer's ethic in its completeness, or analyzed the theological, philosophical, ethical, and personal factors that led to his development of reverence for life. Previous scholarship has either confined itself to reiterating his terminology and ideas without sufficient critical analysis, or, most often, assessed reverence for life only on the basis of a small portion of his literary, and especially philosophical, writings. This approach has led to inevitable misinterpretation. Ignoring, for instance, the theological aspects of Schweitzer's thought, as many of his commentators and critics do, inevitably means misconstruing his ethic altogether. In short, previous studies of Schweitzer have left much to be discovered.

There are several obstacles in studying Schweitzer, not least the problem of how best to classify his enterprise. Is Schweitzer a theologian or a philosopher? He admits that it is characteristic of him not to make a "sufficiently sharp distinction between religious and philosophical thinking."[6] He views the two disciplines as inextricably bound and saw no merit in accepting (still less in presuming) that theology and philosophy are realms apart, with different (if not incompatible) vocabularies and modes of reasoning. Indeed, his intellectual career may be seen as a prolonged attempt to bring what are traditionally considered as two disciplines into mutual resonance. But it is worth noting that Schweitzer's attempt to combine the two disciplines has led him to be seen as not making a substantial contribution to either field. Not unexpectedly, when viewed as a philosopher, he is often charged with misusing philosophy for the purposes of propagating his religious views; when viewed as a theologian, he is accused of reducing Christianity into neutral, nontheological concepts. But if anyone can be blamed for this problem, it is Schweitzer himself as much as his interpreters.

Schweitzer's efforts to articulate his ethical thought in "neutral," philosophical language were well-meaning but shortsighted, and, in fact, a short-lived success. His nineteenth-century philosophical terminology coupled with his polemical and grandiose writing style have left him somewhat alien to modern readers. It is not surprising, then, that he has suffered misinterpretation and neglect. John Everett argued before the Schweitzer Convocation in 1966: "In all probability Albert Schweitzer could not get a job teaching philosophy in any one of the great American universities today. Schweitzer's work, according to many present day academic philosophers, belongs in the poetry division of the literature department, if indeed it belongs in a university at all."[7]

Philosophy has left Schweitzer high and dry. Theology, too, has not known how to deal with Schweitzer. Why is it that in some writings he focuses on Christ and the Holy Spirit and, at other times, even omits mention of God altogether? The lack of a readily apparent systematic, dogmatic, or confessional theology has made him a wanderer in the academic theological world.

There are other reasons that Schweitzer has not received careful consideration. His writings present the reader with many formidable ambiguities, if not apparent contradictions: his ethics are presented both as *rational* and yet *mystical*, and as *universal* and yet *subjective*. No matter how *elemental* he believes his ethical thought is, his moral reasoning is often disturbingly unsystematic. Also, many of his most significant writings have either only recently been translated into English or are to be found in obscure or even esoteric journals. Many of these obstacles surrounding serious engagement with Schweitzer's thought can be surmounted by detailed analysis of his writings.

It has been said that there is no ethics without metaethics; too true, Schweitzer would say. The philosophical ground plan against which Schweitzer operates—particularly Schopenhauer's and Nietzsche's metaphysics of the *will*—is explored in chapter 1, "The New Quest for Schweitzer," in order to understand Schweitzer's particular characterization of life as the *will-to-live*. Moreover, whereas previous commentators have focused on reverence for life as a philosophical ethic located in that tradition, this chapter demonstrates that Schweitzer's theology provides the hitherto undiscerned foundation for his *ethical mysticism*.

Engaging with reverence, far from being a peripheral subject, requires us to grapple with some frontline issues in theology and ethics. Few theologians have provided detailed analyses of Schweitzer's work. But of these, two major theologians of the twentieth century, Karl Barth and Emil Brunner, have both lauded and criticized reverence for life. Their comments and objections to Schweitzer's ethical mysticism are addressed in chapter 2, "Conversations across a Doorway." While critical, both support his concern for the lack of attention shown to nonhuman species in ethical discourse, and even adopt some of these insights. Especially telling is Barth's engagement with reverence: his discussion of the "command of life" presents in theological terms some of the key concepts that Schweitzer masked in philosophical terminology, and thereby brings Schweitzer out of the margins to the center of theology.

The tantalizing possibility that, while clothed in philosophical and theological garb, the original insight that Schweitzer appropriates is derived from Indian ethical thought, and specifically the Jain tradition, is exposed in chapter 3, "The Voyage to India." Contrary to the claim that he found the ethical concept that "had not been discovered in any philosophy,"[8] Schweitzer was clearly influenced by the Jain ethic of ahiṃsā (nonviolence, noninjury). Also highlighted is his analysis of ahiṃsā, and some of the close affinities between Schweitzerian and Jain ethics.

Schweitzer's preoccupation with Jesus' eschatology is his overarching concern with the triumph of reverence over both the loss of ethics in human society (what he normally calls the "decay of civilization") and the "ghastly drama" of life divided against itself encountered in the natural world.[9] Naturalism, particularly in the form of predation, is a dead moral trail. Ethics, therefore, requires a supranaturalistic, or, more precisely, eschatological, framework in order to flourish. Schweitzer's recently uncovered Lambaréné sermons, explored in chapter 4, "Seeking the Kingdom," demonstrate how vital he regarded the discovery of eschatology to the rediscovery of ethics itself. In other words, it is difficult to discern the ethical motivation in this world without hope for another, better world. But this is not simply empty hope; it is morally enabled by what Schweitzer calls *Christ-mysticism.*

Schweitzer's interest is not in mysticism per se, but in *ethical mysticism,* that is, mysticism directed outwards toward the service of other suffering life. Christ mysticism provides the entry into this new life of service and the heralding of a new creation. Chapter 5, "Knowing the 'One Unknown,'" exposes the organic link for Schweitzer between eschatology and mysticism, particularly in his notion of *practical eschatology,* which anticipates Barth's account of the moral life in terms of an eschatological activism, and, even more recently, Jürgen Moltmann's use of the very term in his theology of hope.

Contrary to the common view that reverence died in Lambaréné, modern theology, notably in its liberal Protestant and process forms, continues to be indebted to Schweitzer. In the telling confession of Paul Tillich, "[Schweitzer was with me] all my life since my student days." In developing their own "ethic of life," John Cobb and Charles Birch regard Schweitzer as "the one great Western twentieth-century thinker who took seriously the value of all living things" and acknowledge his reverence for life as having a "spreading influence of others."[10] Chapter 6, "Rediscovering Lambaréné," sets the stage for Schweitzer's contribution to the continuing debate on life-ethics.

In the last chapter, "The Quest Goes On," we confront directly the challenges that Schweitzer's ethic poses to contemporary theology and ethics. Chief among these are the mystical apprehension of the value of life itself; seeing one's attitude to life as a touchstone of ethics; and sensitivity to suffering life. What we learn from Schweitzer's concept is that the very notion of reverence cannot stand alone. Although it might have appeared as a moment of illumination in Schweitzer's own personal history, the reality is that the recognition of the value of life is almost wholly dependent on other philosophical and specifically religious presuppositions. Only by reference to something external to life itself can we establish, or indeed guarantee, its value. Schweitzer reinforces the sense that ethics is not and cannot be an autonomous discourse. The value of life is not another fact about the world that we can discover by the usual routes of reason; rather, it is a truth that may, and should, be properly apprehended through mystical intuition. It is this mystical apprehension of the value of life that lies at the core of Schweitzer's moment on the Ogowe River as well as his own life testimony.

Reverence for Life

I

The New Quest for Schweitzer

Schweitzer ought not to be regarded as a Christian. That, at least, was the view of Gabriel Langfeldt, the noted Norwegian psychiatrist who wrote his study after Schweitzer delivered his Nobel Prize address in Norway in 1954. Langfeldt concludes that "there is little point in calling Albert Schweitzer a Christian," as he "has been unable philosophically to subscribe to any religion." Sadly, Langfeldt is not a lone voice. D. E. Rölffs likewise concludes: "We are dealing here with a purely philosophical ethic.... Schweitzer's 'reverence for life' does not stand under the domination of religion at all." Oskar Kraus, a personal friend of Schweitzer's and professor of philosophy at the University of Prague, labeled Schweitzer an "agnostic." Jackson Lee Ice, ironically regarded at one time as the pre-eminent Schweitzer scholar, not only questions his theism but also denies his place in the community of theologians: "If Schweitzer is referred to as a 'theologian' at all, it is more or less used as an honorary epithet, a sort of complimentary pass to the inner sanctum of institutional Christianity for outstanding services rendered.... [For Schweitzer] it is man and life, not God or Christ that are important."[1] Such misunderstandings are still widespread, even, and especially, within the academic community.

These commentators have largely focused reverence for life as a philosophical ethic and as expounded in *The Philosophy of Civilization*. This narrowness of focus, confined to one academic discipline and to one book, has led such critics into serious errors of interpretation. For, in *The Philosophy of Civilization*, Schweitzer deliberately eschews (as a matter of policy) reference to his Christian faith, avoiding, for example, references to *God* and speaking instead of the *infinite Will-to-Live* or the *universal Will-to-Live*. That he should have done so has a significance that necessarily remains invisible to those unfamiliar with his other writings. To this significance we will return.

As seen, this choice of terminology is, in large part, responsible for leading many commentators to believe that Schweitzer was an atheist or agnostic. So powerful was this school of thought that it gave the impression that the matter was settled and did not remain open to new material, including different sets of Schweitzer's sermons preached from 1900 to 1913 and from 1918 to 1921 at St. Nicholas Church in Strasbourg.[2] But it is not difficult to find many passages in his sermons, letters, and other works that demonstrate otherwise.

The publication of Schweitzer's sermons further reveals the importance he placed on preaching his understanding of the Christian faith, perhaps the aspect of his public life most neglected by commentators. He viewed preaching as "a necessity" of his "being," and "felt it something wonderful" to use his sermons to address "the deepest questions of life."[3] Most important for the purposes of this study, these sermons elucidate some of the theological underpinnings of reverence for life, which are only implicit in his philosophy. Failure to take account of this evidence is understandable to some extent: some of the sermons have only recently been published and many other published theological writings are not easy to access, located in obscure journals and periodicals.

Understood strictly as a philosophical ethic, reverence for life is indeed open to misrepresentation and criticism. Among those whose criticism is based solely on *The Philosophy of Civilization*, we may mention Emil Brunner and Karl Barth. As theologians, they conclude, not surprisingly, that Schweitzer's ethic is "insufficiently theological."[4] The essence of the distinction drawn between understanding reverence for life from a philosophical standpoint as distinct from a theological perspective is obvious enough: in a theological ethic, one or more of the premises is based on religious faith or doctrine. This chapter demonstrates how Schweitzer's Christology provides the hitherto undiscerned foundation for his *ethical mysticism*, and that his reverence for life ethic should, on the contrary, be understood as theological.

Mysticism: Ethics' Friend or Foe

Schweitzer's term "ethical mysticism" ("*ethische Mystik*") encapsulates his belief that the moral and the spiritual are inextricably linked. "Mysticism must never be thought to exist for its own sake. . . . Such a mysticism is not the friend of ethics but a foe. Mysticism which exists for itself alone is the salt which has lost its savor."[5] He understands mysticism, as would many, to refer to an experience of inwardness without any correlation to the concerns of the external world. Mysticism puts one "on the road of inwardness, but not on that of a viable ethic."[6] By contrast, *ethical* mysticism is to be the (only) route to active engagement in the world and, hence, to mystical union with *infinite Being*. Schweitzer reinterprets the purpose of mysticism to its capacity to engender higher ethical awareness in realizing its own end of mystical union with the Divine.

This characterization of mysticism has, in turn, been the source of confusion. Although some of Schweitzer's writings have a mystical character, they do not primarily provide descriptive reports of individual experiences as do those of most other mystics. His writings offer reflections on the role of mysticism in ethics and society, which differs from the concerns of the individual mystical experience. Mysticism, as he understands it, refers not to the experiences of the individual achieved through prayer or meditation, but to those experiences achieved through integrating outer activities with inner life. Ethical mysticism implies an active relationship between the human person and other life; union with the Divine is afforded largely through interaction with life. He believes that this active, ethically grounded mysticism eliminates the problems of passivity and inwardness often associated with mystics.

Schweitzer rejects pantheistic or monistic identification between humans and God. Monism implies for him the loss of consciousness and involves a fusion of the individual, without distinction or qualification, with the Divine. The "great danger" is making such identification "an end in itself." This passivity is unsatisfactory inasmuch as "ethical existence," not passive harmony with the Divine, is deemed "the highest manifestation of spirituality."[7] Mysticism is thus seen as "valuable only in proportion as it is ethical";[8] he rejects all forms of spirituality that do not issue in action. The "ethical, living God cannot be found in the contemplation of the world";[9] rather, it is primarily through participation in the community of life, not strictly in thought, that one connects to the Divine. Schweitzer gives faith a theory not of intellectual realization but of praxis. Humans are to find a mysticism which both impels ethical action and is strengthened by it, as well as an ethic that is grounded in mystical experience and also enriched by it:

> It is only through the manifestations of Being, and only through those with which I enter into relations, that my being has any intercourse with infinite Being. The devotion of my being to infinite

Being means devotion of my being to all the manifestations of Being which need my devotion, and to which I am able to devote myself.

Only an infinitely small part of infinite Being comes within my range.... But by devoting myself to that which comes within my sphere of influence and needs me, I make spiritual, inward devotion to infinite Being a reality.[10]

The "manifestations of Being" are the various forms of life (in the fullest sense of the word) in the world. In short, Schweitzer's dogmatic view is that it is only through interaction with other life that one enters into union with the Divine.

This view entails two major differences from many other forms of mysticism. First, it retains an I-Thou relationship, combining unification and differentiation with the Divine. Such a view does not maintain an antithesis between the Creator and the life manifest in the world, rather, it proceeds from the notion that the Divine creates the world, is simultaneously manifest through its being ("all the manifestation of Being"), and wills human participation in it. Second, it introduces an interdependent relationship between humans, nonhuman life, and infinite Being—a mysticism not only to a spiritual end but also to a heightened ethical purpose.

Schopenhauer as Educator

Schweitzer's ethical mysticism, indeed nearly his entire metaphysics, emerges from reflection upon the key concept "will-to-live" ("*Wille zum Leben*"). "The essential thing to realize about ethics is that it is the very manifestation of our will-to-live."[11] This notion is central to reverence for life, as he believes mystical union occurs in the *will*. In addition to the will-to-live, there are three other key philosophical concepts:

1. infinite Will-to-Live
2. will-to-love
3. infinite Will-to-Love

As we shall see, these are theological concepts and not solely philosophical ones.

In Schweitzer's metaphysics, the greatest single philosophical influence to consider is that of Schopenhauer. Schweitzer would not have described himself as a Schopenhauerian (or any other discipline-implying name), and indeed was quite critical of many aspects of Schopenhauer's philosophy. But he was ready to acknowledge that Schopenhauer provided the basis of his own philosophical work. Indeed, as we will see, Schweitzer's debt to Schopenhauer is even greater than he admits. In seeking to place Schweitzer in his intellectual context, therefore, we shall turn to Schopenhauer for both the ground plan against which Schweitzer operates and the detailed points of controversy that give his system its life. Such an emphasis echoes elements in *The Philosophy of Civilization*, which gives an analysis of Schopenhauer's strengths and weaknesses and is a prerequisite for justifying Schweitzer's own ideas.

It is "generally accepted in the study of the history of philosophy," says Albrecht Dihle, "that the notion of will, as it is used as a tool of analysis and description in many philosophical doctrines from the early Scholastics to Schopenhauer and Nietzsche, was invented by St. Augustine."[12] Dihle claims that Augustine's purpose in developing the notion of the will (*voluntas*) was to forge a link between his theology and his anthropology, so that the force of the will becomes the personal reflection of the Divine Will. From Augustine's reflections emerged the concept of a human will, "prior to and independent of the act of intellectual cognition, yet fundamentally different from sensual and irrational emotion, by which man can give his reply to the inexplicable utterances of the Divine Will."[13]

Schopenhauer, and, following him, Schweitzer, extends this notion: the will is present not only in humans but also throughout the animate world (and perhaps beyond). Schopenhauer argues that the will is in all of nature and claims counterintuitively: "Spinoza says that if a stone projected through air had consciousness, it would imagine it was flying of its own will. I add merely that the stone would be right."[14] Schweitzer (and Nietzsche) follow suit.[15] But we will confine ourselves to a more narrow (and more generally acceptable) understanding of life as consisting of animate (e.g., not including inorganic) matter.

Schopenhauer's philosophy takes Kant's noumenal/phenomenal distinction as its point of departure. Tellingly, Schweitzer, too, started similarly, completing his 1898 doctoral dissertation in philosophy on Kant's philosophy of religion.[16] Kant criticized claims to knowledge, through reason, of that which is beyond sense experience. In *Critique of Pure Reason* (1781), he made distinctions between ultimate realities or *noumena*, things as they are in themselves (*Ding an sich*), and *phenomena*, or things as they are known for us by the senses and the human mind. Rationalistic claims to knowledge, through pure reason, of that which lies beyond sense experience are foundationless. For Kant, this differentiation, between noumenal and phenomenal worlds, delineates the absolute border of knowledge. But Schopenhauer sees otherwise.

It is of great importance for Schopenhauer to claim that we are aware of ourselves in two distinct ways: in the cognitive fashion through which we come to know external things, and *from within*, which may be described as *will*:

> The first step in the fundamental knowledge of my metaphysics is that the will we find within us does not, as philosophy previously assumed, proceed first of all from knowledge; that it is not, in fact, a mere modification of knowledge, and thus something secondary, derived, and like knowledge itself, conditioned by the brain; but that it is the *prius* of knowledge, the kernel of our true being. The will is that primary and original force . . . and expresses in itself in some way every thing in the world and is the kernel of all phenomena.[17]

After asserting the primacy of the will, Schopenhauer refines the concept, describing it as *will-to-live*:

> Every glance of the world . . . confirms and establishes that the *will-to-live*, far from being an arbitrary hypostasis or even an empty expression, is the only true description of the world's innermost nature. Everything presses and pushes towards *existence*, if possible towards *organic existence*, i.e., *life*, and then to the highest possible degree thereof.[18]

Schweitzer's specific use of the term *will-to-live* is derived (not without modification) from Schopenhauer. Schweitzer agrees that the will-to-live is not something secondary (i.e., a consequence of the knowledge of life), but rather is primary, immediate, and unconditioned.[19] He similarly posits that since the will-to-live does not arise in consequence of the world, but that the world arises in consequence of the will-to-live, the will-to-live should serve as the starting point for philosophical thought. Schweitzer lauds Schopenhauer's conviction that "the essence of things-in-themselves, which is to be accepted as underlying all phenomena," is the "will-to-live."[20]

Schweitzer is to be seen as inspired in part by the movement associated with Nietzsche and manifesting itself in such writers as Henri Bergson who sought to root their new philosophy in a strong affirmation of life. The notion of the will-to-live as an explanatory and evaluative concept rose to importance in the late nineteenth century in reaction to scientific materialism and Kantian transcendental idealism. The *vitalist* philosophy of Bergson, elucidated in his *L'évolution créatrice* (1907), contended that evolution was actuated by an *élan vital*, or creative life force.[21] For him, the élan vital was a mysterious life force, unknown to the natural sciences, which animated all life. To the vitalists, the will-to-live is known by intuition, as opposed to by concepts or through abstract reasoning. Agreeing with Bergson on this point, Schweitzer writes that "phi-losophizing means experiencing our consciousness as an emanation of the creative impulse which rules in the world."[22] For these thinkers, the élan vital, or will-to-live, is woven into the fabric of our existence and is the sine qua non of life.

Since the basis of one's self is experience as will-to-live, Schweitzer be-lieves the basis of all animate phenomena in the world, by "analogy" with himself, similarly to be will-to-live.[23] He is concerned, then, with the claim that an understanding of human nature is simultaneously an insight more gen-erally into the nature of reality. His metaphysics begin with the supposition that, despite the diversity and multiplicity of individual things in the world, all manifest the same inner essence, a will-to-live.

To this metaphysics of the will, Schweitzer brings a new (indeed subver-sive) element. He rejects Schopenhauer's conviction that "everything which helps to deaden the will-to-live is good,"[24] maintaining that, on the contrary, life is intrinsically good and is to be promoted. Schweitzer's yes to life stands against Schopenhauer's singular and final no. For Schopenhauer, the world and life is such "that we have not to be pleased but rather sorry about the existence of the world; that its non-existence would be preferable to its exis-tence; that is something which at bottom ought not be."[25] But as Schweitzer sees it, to turn the will-to-live into the will-*not-to-live*, as Schopenhauer does, would involve a "self-contradiction," since one is continually forced to make concessions to the will-to-live so as to maintain even basic bodily existence.[26]

Affirming the will-to-live ("life-affirmation") is "natural," Schweitzer says, because it corresponds with the instinctive will-to-live in each of us that "ur-ges" to maintain life. The human body instinctively affirms life by virtue of the fact that it wills to stay alive: an "instinctive will-to-live" or an "instinctive reverence" for one's own life.[27] It is apparent from the wording that this notion is more important to Schweitzer than he is capable of explaining. By striving to maintain life, the will-to-live is an affirmation of life. And by consciously affirming life, humans act in accord with the inner will-to-live, and "confirm an instinct" by repeating it in their "conscious thought."[28] *Life-affirmation* constitutes Schweitzer's declaration of independence from Schopenhauer. While he admires Schopenhauer for seeing reality as will-to-live, Schweitzer arrives at a position diametrically opposed to his: life is not to be denied but affirmed.

Schweitzer's argument largely rests on the question of whether knowledge from the inner experience of the will-to-live is more reliable than knowledge derived from empirical examination of the outer, physical world. His thought is that all reality must, like himself, have an inner nature (will-to-live), and he uses this notion to offer a new account of the relationship between the self, other life, and the Divine. The nonempirical quality of the will as the core self is a presupposition of his work, although often formulated as if it were a report of an established fact.

This brings us to some significant shortcomings of Schweitzer's metaphysics of the will. First, it can hardly be stated that he provides a coherent account of how there can be a way of knowing about oneself that is not a matter of representation. His view that there is no knowledge that is not some representation of the subject requires him to accept that to acquire knowledge of the thing-in-itself (as will-to-live) would mean denying a central part of his representation theory. Elsewhere, however, he claims that cognition (or intuition) of one's will makes one directly aware of the thing-in-itself; there is a contrast between experience of the world of material objects and the "immediate," "intuitive" awareness of one's will-to-live. He writes as if the latter constitutes knowledge of the thing-in-itself directly:

> The knowledge that I acquire from my will-to-live is richer than that which I win by observation of the world.... The right course is to let the ideas which are given in our will-to-live be accepted as the higher and decisive kind of knowledge. My knowledge of the world is knowledge from outside, and remains forever incomplete. The knowledge derived from my will-to-live is direct.... That is why it is so profoundly important... that [we] be determined solely by what is given within.[29]

This view appears to suggest direct cognitive contact with the thing-in-itself inside us. The tension between the representing subject and the willing subject remains. A second difficulty compounds this problem. By experiencing the will from the "inside," the knowing subject has the willing subject as its object. Following Schopenhauer, Schweitzer sees this as the basis on which the knowing subject understands itself as identical with the will as thing-in-itself. But it is only by abandoning the world as representation—"all that the knowing subject *ex hypothesi* has access to"—that Schweitzer is able to argue that the will constitutes our essence.[30] It appears that one needs to become a Schweitzerian metaphysician before the knowing subject can comprehend its identity as the will-to-live.

As an exercise in metaphysics, Schweitzer's doctrine of the will as thing-in-itself is flawed. It is perhaps not surprising that Schopenhauer's will theory did not have many other followers. Although Schweitzer's thought here collapses under analytical probing, it would be a loss if that were to blind us to its possible strengths. To these, and in particular to how his understanding of the self and the world provide the basis for other aspects of his ethical mysticism, we now turn.

Affirming Life

For Schweitzer, world- and life-affirmation consists in this: "Man regards existence as he experiences it in himself and as it has developed in the world as something of value *per se*." World- and life-negation, conversely, consists in "man regarding existence as he experiences it in himself and as it is developed in the world as something meaningless and sorrowful, and he resolves accordingly (a) to bring life to a standstill in himself by mortifying his will-to-live, and (b) to renounce all activity which aims at improvement of the conditions of this world."[31] His life-affirmation is an assertion of the intrinsic value of all the multifarious forms of life.

Ethical world- and life-affirmation has an added component that elevates it beyond an endorsement of mere existence; it entails active participation in helping all life forms in the world to thrive. The individual who accepts ethical life-affirmation "unceasingly urges" to serve "all that lives."[32] World- and life-affirmation, a theory born out of his prior conviction on the centrality and affirmative nature of the will-to-live, provides the framework for the development of his *world-view*.

For Schweitzer, *Lebensanschauung*, commonly translated as "life-view," pertains to the conception one gives to the meaning of human life as a whole. *Weltanschauung*, usually translated as "world-view," or even more broadly as "theory of the universe," refers to the aggregate of thoughts held by an individual about the nature and purpose of the universe as well as the role of humankind within it.

We need not agree with Schweitzer when he assumes that for most people world-view encompasses life-view, or that world-view is primary and life-view, secondary or derivative. But once that assumption is made (i.e., that one's understanding of the cosmos largely determines a conception of human life), he can go on to deny it. Western philosophy, as he sees it, has made a mistake in trying to arrive at a life-view through its understanding of the world:

> To understand the meaning of the whole—and that is what a world-view demands!—is for us an impossibility.
>
> I believe I am the first among Western thinkers ... to be absolutely skeptical about our knowledge of the world without simultaneously renouncing belief in world- and life-affirmation and ethics.[33]

Schweitzer rejects the possibility of sufficient knowledge of the workings of the world to draw out an ethic. Rather, one has to acquire a *docta ignorantia*, an "enlightened ignorance [that] admits how ultimately mysterious and unfathomable the world and life are."[34] The enlightened mind's first move is an act of resignation: it abandons its desire for complete comprehension about the universe or about God from knowledge revealed by external reality. An optimistic-ethical attitude to the will-to-live (life-affirmation) is not dependent on an optimistic-ethical interpretation of the world at large:

> Our relation to the world as it is given in the positive certainty of our will-to-live, when this seeks to comprehend itself in thought: that is our world-view. World-view is a product of life-view, not vice-versa.[35]

He holds that our conception of life and the world should be composed of those convictions given in our will-to-live, and accordingly is epistemologically skeptical about matters of knowledge that prevent him from locating a comprehension of the universe alongside a wholly affirmative attitude to life.

The predator-prey relations in the natural world prevent Schweitzer from locating a basis for ethics in the workings of the world. He is resolute that there is little discernible moral purpose in the natural world:

> Nature knows no reverence for life. It produces life in thousands of the most meaningful ways and destroys it in thousands of the most senseless ways. . . . Creatures live at the cost of the lives of other creatures. Nature allows them to commit the most terrible cruelties.
>
> Nature is beautiful and sublime, viewed from the outside. But to read in its book is horrible. And its cruelty is so senseless![36]

Schweitzer continues:

> The world is a ghastly drama of the will-to-live divided against itself. One existence makes its way at the cost of another. . . . The solution is not to try to get rid of dualism from the world, but to realize that it can no longer do us harm. This is possible, if we leave behind us all the artifices and unveracities of thought and bow to the fact that, as we cannot harmonies our life-view and our world-view, we must make up our minds to put the former above the latter. *The volition which is given in our will-to-live reaches beyond our knowledge of the world. What is decisive for our life-view is not our knowledge of the world but the certainty of the volition which is given in our will-to live.*[37]

Schweitzer views the world as parasitic, full of death and apparent cruelty. Outside ourselves, the will-to-live manifests itself as a creative-destructive force, leaving the physical world devoid of an overall morally affirmative telos. For this reason, Schweitzer maintains that in order to develop a system of thought upon which to found ethics, our world-view must not be wholly based on the workings of the natural world. Since an ethical principle cannot be discerned in the world processes, a *Lebensanschauung* cannot be based on a *Weltanschauung*. For him, it follows that ethics should stem from our life-view, which is born out of the affirmation of the will-to-live. The knowledge one acquires inwardly (will-to-live) transcends what one sees outwardly in the world: "I can understand the nature of the living being outside of myself only through the living being within me.... Knowledge of [external] reality must pass through a phase of thinking about the nature of [personal] being."[38]

Here again Schweitzer is in dialogue with Schopenhauer. His thought appears indebted to Schopenhauer's "revolutionary principle" which posits that "from yourself you are to understand nature, not yourself from nature."[39] Schopenhauer elaborates:

> The double knowledge which we have of the nature and action of our own body, and which is given in two completely different ways [as the subjective and objective aspects of our bodily knowing] has now been clearly brought out. Accordingly, we shall use it further as a key to the inner being of every phenomenon in nature. We shall judge all objects which are not our body ... according to the analogy of this body. We shall therefore assume that as, on the one hand, they are representation, just like our body, and are in this respect homogenous with it, so on the other hand, if we set aside their existence as the subject's representation, what remains over must be, according to its inner nature, the same as what in ourselves we call *will*.[40]

From a comprehension of oneself (the microcosm), one is able to acquire knowledge of the world (the macrocosm). The key to understanding the world is proper self-understanding, a proposition that would justify calling this work the world as "macranthropos."[41]

The assured tone with which Schweitzer speaks of the individual finding a life-view through the will-to-live suggests that he does not recognize the boldness of his conviction. He finds the will-to-live to be the most immediate and the highest knowledge available to the individual, and hence the soundest foundation for an ethical system. His theory of ethical optimism is of course not verifiable, but is a postulate or demand of the will-to-live that claims for itself knowledge independent of empirical sources. This view, like other aspects of his metaphysics, is not without difficulties.

Schweitzer seeks to prove this thesis by an argument from analogy—indeed, this would seem to be the only possible form of proof. The "truth" that the world is will is proved by "raising" it from the level of immediate consciousness to the level of abstract knowledge.[42] It follows that anyone in whom this will theory does not evoke a similar sense of recognition probably stands outside the whole affair. Although this may sound like radical subjectivity, Schweitzer believed (and needed to believe) everyone *would* recognize this feeling and provide an insight into an objective state of affairs. This enables him to affirm a public reality (as did the rationalists) and oppose solipsism or skepticism. But that is where his relationship with the rationalism ends. From his perspective, all we need to know is that reality is will-to-live.

Theological Premises

Ethical mysticism begins with a personal reflection on the self in the finite world that binds humans with nonhuman life and the *Creative Will*. Schweitzer claimed: "The most immediate and comprehensive fact of consciousness is that 'I am life which wills to live, in the midst of life which wills to live.' "[43] This experience is not an "ingenious dogmatic formula"; it constitutes nothing less than personal revelation:

> Day by day, hour by hour, I live and move in it. At every moment of reflection it stands fresh before me. There bursts from it again and again, as roots that can never dry up, a living world- and life-view—which can deal with all the facts of Being. A mysticism of ethical union with Being grows out of it.[44]

Still more explicitly: "In the universe, the will-to-live is a fact; in us, it is a revelation."[45] The direct, experiential identification of one's individual will-to-live (life) with other life, and through life with *Being*, is foundational to Schweitzer's ethical mysticism.

Schweitzer's mysticism thus starts from the individual subject ("I am life which wills-to-live") and extends to a generalization on the world ("in the midst of other wills-to-live"). He does not limit the will-to-live to humans; it is discernible in "the flowering tree, in strange forms of medusa, in the blade of grass, [and] in the crystal."[46] Concretely: "Everything, accordingly, which meets me in the world of phenomena, is a manifestation of the will-to-live."[47] This generalization is made cosmic by the completing mystical element of thought ("*all* is part of a universal Will-to-Live"[48]). Lastly and crucially, he returns to the finite manifestations of life to realize union with the Divine Will:

Ethics alone can put me in true relationship with the universe by my serving it, co-operating with it; not by trying to understand it. . . . Only by serving every kind of life do I enter the service of that Creative Will whence all life emanates. I do not understand it; but I do know, and it is sufficient to live by, that by serving life, I serve the Creative Will. *It is through the community of life, not community of thought,* that I abide in harmony with that Will. This is the mystical experience of ethics.[49]

Mystical unity with the Creative Will is achieved not primarily through contemplation but through service to other life. Human moral action is the locus of mystical relation to God and other life: "In loving self-devotion to other life we realize our spiritual union with infinite Being."[50]

The *infinite Will-to-Live,* the *universal Will-to-Live, infinite Being,* and the *Creative Will* are used by Schweitzer as philosophical terms for God. His use is deliberate. In a correspondence with Kraus he reveals:

Hitherto it has been my principle never to express in my philosophy more than I have experienced as a result of absolutely logical re-flection [i.e., as a matter of philosophical deduction]. That is why I never speak in philosophy of "God" but only of the "universal Will-to-Live" which meets me in a twofold way: as Creative Will outside me, and Ethical Will within me. But if I speak the traditional language of religion, I use the word "God" in its historical definiteness and in-definiteness.[51]

The expressions *infinite Will-to-Live* and *universal Will-to-Live,* employed throughout Schweitzer's work, are responsible for many misunderstandings and criticisms of his thought that presumably he did not anticipate. He was naïve about the dangers of self-deception that attend any such attempt.

Returning to Schweitzer's understanding of mysticism, it is possible to make some preliminary remarks on the theological framework of reverence for life and its notable departure from Schopenhauer's metaphysics. From Scho-penhauer's purely philosophical metaphysics of the will, an ethical mysticism with the Divine Will would be inconceivable. First, for Schopenhauer, the universal will-to-live has nothing to do with God. Schopenhauer was a staunch atheist. Theistic religions, he writes, "are exclusively for the great majority of people who are not capable of thinking but only of believing, and are sus-ceptible not to arguments, but only to authority." They have "only an indirect, not direct truth."[52] Furthermore, he rejects the notion that the "inner nature" of the world is created by a Creative Will and that the world is a "theophany."[53] On the contrary, for him the *world-will* is the source of all suffering. One cannot

help asking the question how Schweitzer could believe our union with Schopenhauer's "striving" and "suffering" *will* to be the source of pleasure and the
goal of mystical union.

In short, he does not.

Schweitzer is able to take Schopenhauer's same term—*will*—and arrive at
a diametrically opposed position by radically altering the sense of the term. The
point is, the use of the same term should not conceal the polar differences of
meaning attached to it by the two thinkers. Where and how Schweitzer departs
radically from a Schopenhauerian metaphysics of the will and inserts his own
theological premises will be discussed later.

Second, in Schopenhauer's philosophical thought, it is impossible for
mystical union (an I–Thou relationship) to occur between a human's individual will and the universal will-to-live. The human will is strictly identical
with the noumenal will-to-live that is the inner nature of all phenomena. For
Schopenhauer this is a *metaphysical* rather than a *mystical* relationship. It is
simply a matter of fact to him that the inner essence of all phenomena is will-
to-live; there is no possibility of the human will entering into it. In the light of
this, there would be no way of moving from a Schopenhauerian metaphysics of
the will to a Schweitzerian ethical mysticism except *via* theological premises
(which would radically alter the sense of that metaphysics). That is, unless the
infinite Will-to-Live is conceived of as the divine (i.e., God), and the divine Will
is personality, then a mystical relationship such as Schweitzer proposes could
not exist. Without underlying theological premises, it is difficult to see how in
any sense the infinite Will-to-Live is the Creator God (Creative Will), or the
infinite Will-to-Love is the Ethical Personality, except in mere name.

Reconciling Revelations

In Schweitzer's letter to Kraus, he asserts that God meets him twofold: "As
Creative Will outside me, and as Ethical Will within me." In *Christianity and the
Religions of the World*, he claims the "ultimate problem of religion [is that] in
Nature we recognize Him [God] as impersonal Creative Power, in ourselves we
recognize Him as Ethical Personality." For Schweitzer, these two "revelations
do not coincide." He continues: "They are one; but how they are one, I do not
understand."[54]

It is specifically in the light of predation in the natural world that
Schweitzer found it difficult to unite an understanding of God as *Creative Will*
and *Ethical Will*. He is capable of asserting the problem in the bluntest of
terms: "The God of love who meets us in love cannot be united with the God

who encounters us in nature. The ethical law cannot be made consonant with the laws of nature."[55] Apprehending God as *Ethical Personality* as well as *cosmic Will-to-Live*, Schweitzer now has the problem of reconciling the two. His resolution relies on knowledge of God as revealed "within" to our will as Ethical Will, and not on an understanding of the outer, physical world:

> Now, which is the more vital knowledge of God? . . . [It is] the knowledge derived from my experience of Him as Ethical Will. The knowledge concerning God which is derived from Nature is always imperfect and inadequate, because we perceive the things in the world from without only. . . . In myself, on the other hand, I know things from within. The Creative Will which produces and sustains all that is, reveals itself in me in a way in which I do not get to know it elsewhere, as Ethical Will. . . . All the mysteries of the world and of my existence in the world may ultimately be left on one side unsolved and insoluble. My life is completely and unmistakably determined by the mysterious experience of God revealing Himself within me as Ethical Will and desiring to take hold of my life.[56]

As we have seen, he remains convinced that knowledge of the physical world will always be incomplete (merely phenomenal). In contrast, knowledge of the *universal Will-to-Love* is the highest knowledge because it is derived from within: a connection of the will. Quite symptomatic, the obstacles to *absolute* knowledge of the external world are obvious to him; those of the inner world, not.

Notwithstanding Schweitzer's determination to refrain from mixing philosophical and theological strands (from which he might have derived support), it turns out that the "Will-to-Love" ("*Wille zum Lieben*") is his philosophical code word for the spiritually risen Christ within. The theological returns through the back door. We discover—not where he first and principally presents the term and idea in *The Philosophy of Civilization*, but in the last pages of his study of Paul—that the Will-to-Love *is* Jesus Christ: "In Jesus Christ, God is manifested as Will-to-Love."[57] As Schopenhauer had clearly seen, in these instances we are reminded of a conjuror who, to our great surprise, pulls out of the hat something which he had planted there all along. Schopenhauer is more perceptive: aware (as Schweitzer is not) that "in the centuries of Christianity, philosophical ethics has generally taken its form *unconsciously* from the theological."[58] Schweitzer's failure to justify this sharp move shows his unwitting allegiance to theology.

Through the Will-to-Love, humans experience the love of God, which seeks to fulfill itself in us: Christ pushes beyond "belief in the infinitely enigmatic Creator God, [to] a belief in the God of love."[59] It follows that Schweitzer's understanding of God cannot be resolved by simply affirming God as Will-to-Love instead of God as infinite Will-to-Live: "It suffices to know that in some mysterious way ... they are one."[60] His conception of God refuses to focus on this ambiguity; such intellectual conceptions of God are an abstraction. The Christian life, he preaches, "depends not on man being able to subscribe to a historically traditional conception of God, but on his being seized by the Will-to-Love."[61] The Will-to-Love is seen as action-eliciting divine activity. Ethical action, realized through the Will-to-Love, consistently holds priority.

Schweitzer's understanding of God appears (at least) twofold. First, God is the creative force working to bring about diverse manifestations of the will-to-live in the world. Second, God is the Will-to-Love and is the source of ethical affirmation in the human will that encourages reverence for these multiform wills-to-live. Through service to other life, our will can attain union with the infinite Will. Mystical union occurs in the human will where God, as the infinite Will-to-Live and the infinite Will-to-Love, is manifested.

But *complete* unity with other wills-to-live can never be realized. As Schweitzer repeatedly highlights, humans are subject "to the puzzling and horrible law of necessity" which forces them "to live at the cost of other life and to incur again and again the guilt of destroying and injuring life."[62] The division of the will-to-live against itself, namely, the necessity of damage to other life, does not, from Schweitzer's perspective, discredit his doctrine of continued reverence to all forms of life. Two responses to this problem are offered. The first is by now a familiar refrain—mystical union with the divine Will invigorates the human will and continually redirects it to further service to other life:

> Whenever my life devotes itself in any way to life, my finite will-to-live experiences union with the infinite Will in which all life is one, and I enjoy a feeling of refreshment which prevents me from pining away in the desert of life. . . . I choose for my activity the removal of this division of the will-to-live against itself, so far as the influence of my existence can reach.[63]

But this "active" response is not in and of itself sufficient. His second and complementary response to the division of the will-to-live introduces the term *resignation*:

> Resignation is the vestibule through which we enter ethics. Only he who in deepened devotion to his own will-to-live experiences

inward freedom from outward occurrences, is capable of devoting himself in profound and steady fashion to the life of others.[64]

Resignation is a "vestibule" not to ethics-as-mere-application but to ethics-as-battle. Schweitzer is reminding us of the tremendous pressures bearing down on our good intentions and of the corresponding effort needed to hold fast to the "nevertheless." Resignation, contrary to how it sounds to contemporary ears, is understood as the ethical act in which one affirms one's moral and spiritual self in spite of those elements of the world that conflict with it. It is a faith strong enough to endure the division of the will-to-live. This understanding of resignation is analogous to the Stoic ideal of *apatheia*, implying a certain inner liberty from the external happenings in the world over which one does not have control. Such a state may imply detachment, but never indifference; if a dispassionate person does not suffer on his own account, he suffers for fellow creatures. In a passage from his autobiography, Schweitzer admits:

> I feel the full weight of what we conceive to be the absence of
> purpose in the course of world events. Only at rare moments
> have I felt really glad to be alive. I cannot help but feel the suffer-
> ing all around me, not only of humanity but also of the whole of
> creation.[65]

Resignation consists not in ceasing to feel such sufferings, but in no longer yielding to them. It is not a negative condition of insensitivity, but a positive state of reintegration and spiritual freedom. One is not emotionally overpowered by the suffering in the world; rather, by resignation is one "enabled to work in the world as an instrument of God."[66] Some will see a barely disguised Christian metaphysics at play here. Serving in the world as "an instrument of God" and redemption through suffering are Christian motifs par excellence.

This inner freedom is an integral aspect of Schweitzer's theodicy as it empowers the individual who "regrets the pain," or the existence of natural evils, present in the world. He acknowledges: "It remains a painful enigma for me to live with reverence for life in a world which is dominated by creative will which is also destructive will, and destructive will which is also creative."[67] Indeed, the frustration of being unable to achieve union with other life would be unbearable and probably lead to an attitude of bitter despair if there were no mystical dimension in his ethics. But because the Ethical Will is mystically related to life as Will-to-Love, its suffering is redeemed:

> True resignation is not a becoming weary of the world, rather it is the
> quiet triumph ... which the will-to-live celebrates at the hour of its

greatest need over the circumstances of life. It flourishes only in the soil of deep world- and life-affirmation.[68]

The connection introduced here between resignation and life-affirmation appears to be taking issue with Schopenhauer and, this time, with his rather different notion of *resignation*.[69] Knowledge of the all-pervasive nature of suffering and its inextricable connection with the metaphysical will leads Schopenhauer to advocate denial of the will-to-live (life-negation). Schopenhauer's *resignation* holds a telic function; it offers hope for salvation and underscores his view that it is better for us not to exist. In this scheme, resignation is not related to Schweitzer's sense of ethical activity in that Schopenhauer's philosophy is one of abdication from the world; it means accepting the blows of fate not as a "stimulus" to struggle against difficulties but as an impetus to emancipation from the world. In Schopenhauer's *resignation*, there is no striving to change the world—only submission to fate: suffering is "inevitable," "insuperable."[70] Schweitzer takes the same term, but, not for the first or last time, turns it to quite different ends than Schopenhauer: resignation helps to affirm life, not deny it.

Resignation, for Schopenhauer, ends in quietist retreat. Schweitzer treats the same concept—or rather a concept to which he gives the same name—as bound up with his life-affirmation, and hence as culminating in a decidedly *un*Schopenhauerian emphasis on ethics: "The profoundest inner freedom from the world is that which man strives to attain in order to become an ethical personality and as such to serve the world."[71] Schweitzer employs Schopenhauer's very terms to undermine his thesis, adopting the surface of his terminology to subvert the core of his thought. In this sense, Schweitzer's resignation is to be understood as positive, not negative, and integrally related to ethical action. Our actions are to stand as a witness against the suffering of this world (but are also radically compromised by it). To help justify this important concept, Schweitzer enlists the support of theology. Apprehending "God as a Will [i.e., Will-to-Love] that is distinct from the world," he concludes that we are compelled "not to conform to the world" (blind will-to-live).[72]

Schweitzer takes this point even further and brings action, resignation, and mystical union with Christ together into a greater and even more anti-Schopenhauer concept: *peace*. Perhaps the clearest expression of his thought on their inter-relationship is found in the following passage:

> We must, no doubt, face all the enigmas of existence which present themselves to thought and harass it [i.e., the "law of necessity"]. But in the last resort it [human thought] must leave the incomprehensible uncomprehended, and take the path of seeking to be

united with God in the Will-to-Love, and finding in it both inner
peace and springs of action.[73]

His comments on peace and union with Christ are again not given in philosophical terminology.

> Where the active, suffering will seeks peace with God, there heart
> and mind are preserved in Christ Jesus.... There is one happiness in
> life: the peace of God, which passeth all understanding.[74]

It is not difficult to understand why Schweitzer should try to present his ideas
in terms derived (or apparently derived) from a purely philosophical tradition.
But it soon becomes apparent that appearance is deceptive and the foundation
of these ideas is merely a transposition of terminology. His *peace* refers to far
more than *resignation* or detachment; it implies *union* between the human will
and the Will-to-Love, Christ.

In *ethical action* and *resignation* alike, the goal is the same for Schweitzer:
union with Christ. It is now possible to see how for him ethical mysticism is
actually what he terms a *Christ-mysticism*, "that is to say, a 'belonging together'
with Christ, grasped in thought [i.e., resignation] and realized in experience
[i.e., ethical action]."[75] Schweitzer's direct equivalent to God is infinite Will-to-
Live, and similarly, Christ is infinite Will-to-Love. And it now becomes evident
that ethical mysticism is just Christ-mysticism. His philosophy (ethical mysticism), as we shall continue to see, *is* theology (Christ-mysticism).

In both *The Philosophy of Civilization* and *Out of My Life and Thought*,
Schweitzer attempts to present his ethical mysticism *independent* of religious
revelation or doctrine. As has been seen, his terminology is often disconcert-
ingly abstract—more indebted to the influence of the German tradition of
idealist metaphysics than to biblical understandings of God. Very different,
however, are his religiously motivated personal writings. In *Mitteilungen aus
Lambaréné* (*The Forest Hospital at Lambaréné*), Schweitzer describes in a style
strikingly more personal (and persuasive) his feelings after moving into the
new hospital building in confessional vein:

> For the first time since I have been working in Africa my patients
> are housed like human beings. How much I have suffered in those
> years because I had to herd them into airless, gloomy places! Full
> of gratitude I raise my eyes to God, who has allowed me to experi-
> ence such joy.[76]

Even more pious are his pre-dinner prayers. In Europe he prayed: "Mon âme
bénit le Seigneur et le remercie de tous ses bienfaits" ("My soul blesses the

Lord and is grateful to him for all his kindness"). In Gabon he affirmed: "Béni soit l'Eternel car sa miséricorde dure éternellement" ("Blessed be God, for his mercy endureth forever").[77]

It is apparent that Schweitzer's understanding of God is far more than a hypothesis advanced by the philosophy of religion or a strict Kantian postulate of reason. Rather, God (in the fullest sense of the word) is seen as an existent being with whom philosophy must come to terms.

It would be absurd to see this attempt to distinguish between philosophical and theological concepts and terminology as evidence that Schweitzer lacked religious convictions. It may be seen to stem from what could be loosely described as an "apologetic" task of expressing Christianity in a philosophical language able to be understood by a wider (or at least a different) audience. In contradistinction to dogmatics (the systematic presentation of Christianity to a specific faith-community), his apologetic task was geared toward reaching a wider readership which required ideas independent of claims to religious revelation and a language accessible to more than a particular faith-community. A metaphysics such as Schopenhauer's that claimed natural knowledge of matters apart from direct revelation—a prerequisite for any apologetics—was used. So, for example, in *The Philosophy of Civilization*, Christ becomes the Will-to-Love and Christ-mysticism is labeled ethical mysticism. But what appeared to be apologetics was perhaps a masked form of dogmatics or a transcription in philosophical terminology of his view of the Christian faith. And Schweitzer did hold reservations about this writing style. Even in *Christianity and the Religions of World*, his most apologetic piece of writing where he sought to demonstrate Christianity's "superiority" over other world religions, he used philosophical expression and had this to say in conclusion: "Forgive me. . . . I am almost afraid my presentation has been too one-sided, and I have spoken in a too exclusively philosophical way about Christianity."[78] But as Schweitzer makes clear regarding his choice of terminology: "In so doing I make no concessions to the philosophy of nature or the philosophy of religion. For I am anxious to impart to others my inwardly experienced thought in all its original vividness and in its relationship to traditional religion."[79]

It is sufficiently evident that Schweitzer took his lead from Christian theology. His key moral concept (Will-to-Love) makes sense only in a theological context where there is an Ethical Personality (Christ) who exists. Yet he (like Kant) proposes an ethics independent of theology—where that key concept would be meaningless. Of course, neither Schweitzer's attempt to found an ethics independent of theology nor the critique to which such attempts are exposed are without precedent; Kant had tried it, and Schopenhauer had already put his finger on the weak point: "Separated from the theological hypothesis from which they came, the [philosophical] concepts really lose all meaning."[80] Schopenhauer claimed that it was Kant's concealed theological yearnings and the logic of his moral language that compelled him to return to theology—the only possible basis for his view. By unmasking Kant's work as "an inversion and a disguise of theological morals,"[81] Schopenhauer helps to reveal how Schweitzer, too, betrayed his own claim, that his philosophy is separate from theology.

Philosophy held for Schweitzer both an instrumental and a foundational importance. His instrumental use is constructive: he employs philosophical patterns of argument to elucidate, reconstruct, and systematize the beliefs expressed in faith. This constructive use of philosophy in theology is implicitly combined with an apologetic use, which takes the justificatory form of support for Christian beliefs and shifts the apologetic utilization of philosophy in theology into its foundational application of theology. That is, in *The Philosophy of Civilization*, he conceives philosophy as providing the foundation of the theological superstructure. Philosophical or apologetic language, with its claims to universality, was an effective tool at that time for conveying his ethical convictions to a wider audience (but not necessarily by means that hold up). But it is evident that reverence for life is predicated upon a *prior* belief in Christ as spiritual authority of the will and has a distinct Christian foundation. Two passages from his correspondences reveal how reverence for life is his philosophical account of Jesus' ethic of love:

> The ethics of reverence for life is nothing but Jesus' great commandment to love—a commandment that is reached by thinking; religion and thinking meet in the mysticism of belonging to God through love.[82]

> Yes, indeed, the term "reverence for life" has a lot more substance than its mere wording seems to indicate. But that is as it should be— the thought greater than the verbal façade.
>   Reverence for life is the Christian love—universal and necessary to be thought about—that deals with reality.[83]

The form of ethical mysticism thus open is Christ-mysticism. This argument can be made analogically and inductively on the basis of the following remarks: if "Christianity alone is ethical mysticism,"[84] and "Christianity is a Christ-Mysticism,"[85] then ethical mysticism is thoroughly a Christ-mysticism. In fact, according to Schweitzer: "Christianity, as the most profound religion, is to me at the same time the most profound philosophy."[86]

Ethic of Love

For Schweitzer, Jesus incarnates love as compassionate self-devotion extended to others. Reverence for life is the way he expresses Jesus' "ethic of love" to all life. "The ethic of reverence for life is Jesus' ethic of love widened to universality."[87] He presents reverence for life as a "necessity of thought" or an "inward necessity" for the individual who conceives him,- or herself, as will-to-live.[88] Must then the individual *always* experience reverence for life? Schopenhauer proves this not to be so; he was fully conscious of himself as will-to-live but was far from drawing the conclusion that Schweitzer claims to be a necessary one.

Analysis of Schweitzer's understanding of the will-to-live uncovers the critical connection between it and the Will-to-Love in reverence for life:

> What shall be my attitude toward this other life which I see around me? It can only be a piece of my attitude toward my own life. If I am a thinking being, I must regard other life than my own with equal reverence.[89]

His ethic, as we shall see, is only sound in the light of the idea that a will intercedes between one's own will-to-live and the will-to-live in others. The will-to-live lacking an accompanying will-to-love is apt to become a *will-to-power* in its attempt to dominate other beings. Nietzsche's phrase "will to power" ("*Wille zur Macht*") described what he claimed was the innate drive in all living things toward life and domination. Following Schopenhauer, in his later works he even goes so far as to claim that stones and all inorganic matter have a will-to-power.[90] Nietzsche challenges the Schopenhauerian and Schweitzerian views that the will-to-live is the ground of all being by arguing that the will-to-*power* is the impulse behind life: "*This world is the will to power—and nothing besides! And you yourselves are also this will to power—and nothing besides!*"[91] Nietzsche does not soft-pedal this element: "Life itself is *essentially* appropriation, injury, conquest of the alien and weak, suppression, severity, obtrusion of peculiar forms, incorporation, and at the least, putting it mildest, exploitation.... Life is simply will to power."[92] He also claims: "All life strives after a maximal feeling of power."[93] For Nietzsche, the will-to-power, the will to a higher and stronger being, is the only instinct that exists. The will-to-love is nowhere to be found.

The influence of Jesus in Schweitzer's thought, and Schweitzer's belief in the activity of the Will-to-Love to transform the will-to-live to a will-to-reverence, is the unacknowledged yet integral *theological* presupposition throughout his philosophical work. Reverence for life is not a "necessity" of the will-to-live, but of the Will-to-Love. Once again, we discover not in *The Philosophy of Civilization* but in his New Testament work—this time on Jesus—the theology informing his metaphysics. Our relationship to Christ is one of human will to divine Will: "In reality He [Jesus] is an authority for us, not in the sphere of knowledge, but only in the realm of the will."[94] A passage from his autobiography is similarly revealing: "A true understanding of Jesus is the understanding of Will *acting on* [human] will."[95]

Christ helps to ensure that the human will-to-live does not act "unhindered" (will-to-power) but "always with special relations of solidarity with others" (will-to-love).[96] The Will-to-Love is a charity or love that directs our human will toward reverence for life, not domination of it. It awakens the human will to a new form of existence that discovers itself by offering itself to others in love. In "love," man longs "to go beyond himself," to be "concerned with all the human destinies and all the other life-destinies which are going through their life-course around him."[97] Life is no longer experienced "individually." Schweitzer extends the traditional concept of Christ as Mediator: Christ not only mediates between God and humans but also among humans and all life.

The core of reverence for life is found in the influence of Christ as Will-to-Love acting upon human will. It is only when this massive presupposition is taken into consideration that reverence for life becomes a "necessity of thought." But even with this clarification, the problem encountered by this position is serious. Schweitzer's claim is that in the Will-to-Love, humans experience a "transformation" in which nature (i.e., our mere will-to-live) is, to a certain extent, redeemed from itself.[98] But it is unclear how a change of the natural self (defined by him as will-to-live) is possible. Although he posits that the Will-to-Love causes a transformation, the notion of a transformation of nature cannot easily escape the criticism of being a euphemism for contradictory metaphysical assumptions. That is, if the will-to-live can *change* itself and become will-to-*love*, then it was not accurately defined as will-to-*live* at the outset. The will-to-live that can change under the influence of the Will-to-Love cannot be the same as the postulated ground of all being.

Schweitzer's theological convictions are the crucial link in his exposition of reverence for life. Not only is this a biographical claim on how Christianity influenced his thinking, but it is also a conceptual claim on how the ethic of reverence for life should be understood. The Christological component, only transparently masked in his philosophical writings, is the theological foundation of ethical mysticism.

Examining Schweitzer's writings directed to the Christian community of his time (in which he is far less reticent about using theological language) shows even more clearly how the theological stands behind the philosophical and how the Spirit acts in like fashion to his quasi-philosophical Will-to-Love.

For Schweitzer, the Will-to-Love is manifested in Jesus to the highest intensity and continues to reveal itself to us through his Spirit. In a letter to a school group, he speaks of the Spirit as "God's voice of love speaking to . . . our hearts."[99] His sermon "The Tornado and the Spirit" offers a deeper account of his understanding of the Spirit:

> It is difficult to open our hearts to the Holy Spirit. The Holy Spirit is strange to us. It wishes to control our lives.
>
> The Holy Spirit is not the spirit of ordinary men [i.e., those who have not found reverence for life]. In it we become another kind of being. Indeed we must be born again through the Holy Spirit.[100]

Though the Spirit is understood here as something external and not possessed by "ordinary men," only under its power can one become "another kind of being."[101] The self becomes reconfigured in the Spirit. In Schweitzerian theological anthropology, the human will finds its true ethical self through the action of the Spirit. In the Spirit, the will of God is no longer external; it confers the will-to-love inwardly: "Through the Spirit they [believers] feel in their hearts love."[102]

It is clear in the above that the Spirit helps to move the will-to-live to a higher life-affirmation. But Schweitzer presents a different position in some of his philosophical works. Certain passages in *The Philosophy of Civilization* even omit reference to the mediation of the Will-to-Love; on the contrary, they stress how such ethical characteristics are "given with our existence," and that the will-to-live is "endowed with" them.[103] Change is almost exhaustively collapsed into a human process. His interpretation of Goethe's work similarly presents a doctrine of immanence: "Let man fulfill the good that is in his personality and thereby become truly himself. . . . The greatest measure of love will be attained when each one realizes the love, the special love, that is within him."[104]

This inconsistency may be explained by two factors. First is Schweitzer's reticence to express his religious convictions in philosophical texts. In a letter to Rölffs (who, as we saw, claimed reverence for life was "purely philosophical"), he hints: "The holy music of religion sounds softly but clearly. I am very reticent (too much so, no doubt) about [expressing] my religious feeling, but everything is summed up in the concluding words of *The Quest of the Historical Jesus*: Jesus the Lord! Peace in Christ!"[105] Second is Schweitzer's interest in emphasizing the importance of the individual's role in the process of ethical and spiritual development. To a less charitable reader, this view is not entirely convincing. There is a wider anomaly here. On the one hand, he wants privacy for his personal faith, but, on the other, he wishes to be most publicly known by the religious concept of reverence.

Schweitzer believes that by serving other life, our human will remains in accord with the Will-to-Love, making the divine Will no longer external to us. In this sense, the Spirit can appropriately be seen to disclose the will of God to humans as the will-to-love: "The Holy Spirit would prevent us from killing."[106] Schweitzer has changed. It is now the Spirit (ci-devant Will-to-Love) that is the motive force of ethical existence that exalts our ethical willing to a point that would otherwise be unattainable.

Holophrastic Reverence

Devotion to other life is incomplete (i.e., is unable to attain mystical union) until it acquires a cosmic dimension:

> Only a complete ethic has mystical significance. An ethical system which is only concerned with the attitude of man to his fellow-man and to society cannot really be in harmony with a world-view. It has no relationship with the Universe.... Only when ethics embrace the whole Universe is an ethical world-view really possible.[107]

Two significant aspects of his ethic are illuminated here. First, reverence for life is an *absolute* or *complete* ethic. Schweitzer's quest for an underlying principle—an absolute ethic—universally applicable has strong Kantian undertones. It is possible to see this aspect of reverence as a kind of outworking of Kant's categorical imperative. Regardless of the circumstances, injury of any sort to a will-to-live cannot be deemed wholly ethical. Although Schweitzer acknowledges that reverence for life can never be fully realized ("law of necessity"), an unqualified claim is nonetheless demanded. He develops neither a *relative* ethic nor a strict set of rules that the individual must obey.

Reverence for life cannot be described in detail once and for all. Neither can it be expressed in convenient formulas nor reduced to a list of imperatives. His basic definition of the moral proclaims: "It is good to maintain and to encourage life, it is bad to destroy life or obstruct it."[108] Beyond this statement, he offers only examples, not rules, of the type of action expected from one who upholds reverence for life. The ethical person is one who

> tears no leaf from a tree, plucks no flower, and takes care to crush no insect. If in the summer he is working by lamplight, he prefers to keep the window shut and breathe a stuffy atmosphere rather than see one insect after another fall with singed wings upon his table.

If he walks on the road after a shower and sees an earthworm
which has strayed on to it, he bethinks himself that it must get
dried up in the sun, if it does not return soon enough to ground into
which it can burrow, so he lifts it from the deadly stone surface,
and puts it on grass. If he comes across an insect which has fallen
into a puddle, he stops a moment in order to hold out a leaf or a stalk
on which it can save itself.[109]

Schweitzer's ethic enjoins responsibility for all the various life forms with
which one comes into contact. This absolute aspect of reverence is closely
related to its second quality, *universality*. Reverence for life is universal in that it
does not limit itself strictly to human relations: "Ethics are responsibility
without limit towards all that lives."[110] The presence of the will-to-live establishes value but not distinctions in it; no difference of species or degree of
sentience should qualify this universality. Schweitzer repeatedly stresses this
important point:

A man is truly ethical only when he obeys the compulsion to help all
life which he is able to assist, and shrinks from injuring anything that
lives. He does not ask how far this or that life deserves one's sympathy as being valuable, nor beyond that, whether and to what degree
it is capable of feeling. Life as such is sacred to him.[111]

I'll be damned if I recognize any *objectively valid* distinctions in life.
Every life is sacred! ... Value judgments are made out of subjective
necessity, but they have no validity beyond that. The proposition that
every life is sacred is absolute. In this respect I will always remain a
heretic. It is a question of principle, one that reaches deep into the
foundation of my outlook on life.[112]

He expressly rejects the idea of a hierarchy of beings in nature, with humans at
the top, reflecting varying degrees of value in creation.[113] Our relation to the
nonhuman world, he tells us, should not be one of moral hierarchies or in-
strumentality. His life-affirmation is a recognition of the intrinsic value of *all*
life. Though in practical matters humans must make decisions about the
relative priority of diverse life forms, our judgment in this matter is irreducibly
subjective (anthropocentric) and not to be taken as an objective measure of the
value of other life forms:

The ethics of reverence for life makes no distinction between
higher and lower, more precious and less precious lives. It has

good reasons for this omission. For what are we doing, when we establish hard and fast gradations in value between living organisms, but judging them in relation to ourselves, by whether they seem to stand closer to us or farther from us. This is a wholly subjective standard. How can we know the importance other living organisms have in themselves and in terms of the universe?[114]

The presence of the will-to-live affords a being its inherent worth. But the will-to-live itself is not seen as the direct *source* of its value; the origin of value lies in the infinite Will-to-Live. Schweitzer explains:

> my existence joins in pursuing the aims of the mysterious universal Will of which I am a manifestation.... With consciousness and with volition I devote myself to Being.... I become like that [Creative Will] which works mysteriously in nature, and thus I give my existence a meaning from within outwards.[115]

Value comes not from human estimation, but from the view that the human will-to-live (and *all* wills-to-live) are of a shared source in the infinite Will-to-Live. Both human and nonhuman beings have the same ontological basis in God. The common origin of all wills-to-live is a doctrine that carries with it epistemological and ethical implications. Schweitzer affirms that "life" is "something possessing value *in itself*"[116] and believes "the mystery of life is always too profound for us, and its value is beyond our capacity to estimate."[117] The experience, or apprehension, of moral value is primary for him.

As Schweitzer sees it, one can arrive only at a "subjective criterion" for making ethical decisions. In the conflict between the preservation of one's own existence and the injury or destruction of that of another, the ethical and the necessary cannot be united to form a "relative ethic." Any time that life is sacrificed or injured, either "for the sake of maintaining [one's] own existence or welfare" or "for the sake of maintaining a greater number of other existences or their welfare," one is no longer wholly "within the sphere of the ethical."[118] A decision must be made between the *ethical* and the *necessary*, and, if the latter is chosen, one must bear the responsibility and guilt of having injured life. Guilt becomes an inescapable feature of existence.

"Whenever I injure life of any sort, I must be quite clear whether it is necessary," Schweitzer explains. "Beyond the unavoidable, I must never go, not even with what seems insignificant."[119] Although Schweitzer proclaims here the boundless demands of reverence for life, he is not—as many other commentators have assumed—advocating the inviolability of life. He acknowledges that in order to maintain life, humans are forced to harm or sacrifice other wills-to-live. In German, the very word for "reverence" makes this clear: *Ehrfurcht*, from *Ehre* (honor and praise) and *Furcht* (fear); the English "reverence" fails to capture fully the sense of awe present in the German.

Ehrfurcht, then, indicates that Schweitzer's reverence for life is not concerned with obedience to moral law, but with "a mental attitude"[120] and "a new temper of mind,"[121] which includes the development of emotions, dispositions, and attitudes that influence action. *Ehrfurcht* is an ideal of character toward other life which "penetrates unceasingly and in all directions a man's observation, reflection, and resolutions."[122] Schweitzer is hesitant to codify ethical options in advance and can often be seen to provide less an *ethic* of principle than an *ethos*, in the sense of a preparation of attitudes prior to the decision of moral action.

Reverence is holophrastic. It holds wider connotations than does an ethic or a philosophy of life. Inescapably, Schweitzer's reverence for life "therefore has a religious character" and contains "the surmising and the longings of all deep religiousness."[123]

2

Conversations across
a Doorway

In a moment of puzzled reflection, Schweitzer offered this cri de coeur: "Christian theologians are reluctant to come in through the door I have tried to open."[1] Why they have not come in through Schweitzer's door is worth exploring. Indeed, few theologians have even looked through the door, let alone peered in inquiringly. According to Schweitzer, they would find a Christianity released from "confinement to the human form of life" and see a "vital" connection to the "sacredness of life."[2] For him, what is deeply objectionable in Christian theology is the exclusive moral preoccupation with the human species which he regards as a betrayal of the Christian message. To expand his own metaphor, Schweitzer offers this thought:

> Just as the housekeeper who has scrubbed out the parlor
> takes care that the door is kept shut so that the dog may
> not get in and spoil the work by the marks of his paws, so
> do European thinkers watch carefully that no animals run
> about in the fields of their ethics.... Either they leave
> out altogether all sympathy for animals, or they take care
> that it shrinks to a mere afterthought which means
> nothing.[3]

Exceptionally, however, Brunner and Barth have at least—to extend the metaphor—stepped foot into the room and given its content a serious viewing.

Moral Hierarchies

One of the primary criticisms leveled against Schweitzer's absolute and universal ethic of reverence for life is that it dissolves value hierarchies (i.e., gradations of higher and lower life) and, practically speaking, is not instructive. Brunner's critique in *The Divine Imperative* is representative of this position, even though he begins by commending reverence for life for its concern for "lower" forms of life and agreeing with Schweitzer that "we should have reverence for every creature."[4] Brunner agrees further with Schweitzer's concern for all life: "Since it is the will of God to 'conserve' life, we should do so as well. We, too, are bound to 'preserve'—in our own appointed place—'what our God has created' in all the world around us: in the animate or inanimate creation, in human or animal life."[5] Brunner also accepts Schweitzer's rejection of an instrumentalist understanding of creation as well as an ethic restricted in scope to human-to-human relations:

> It [the non-human creature] is indeed related to man, but it is
> not simply there for the sake of man. This non-human creature,
> like humanity, possesses, in a relative way, a certain "end" of its
> own.... We feel it is displeasing to God deliberately to spoil a
> tree or a flower. The dumb creatures have a share in the inviola-
> ble character of human life. Hence Albert Schweitzer's protest
> against the current ethic, "in which no animals are allowed to run
> about," is certainly justified.[6]

Brunner not only espouses Schweitzer's concern for nonhuman life (both animal and vegetable) but also appears to make the stronger claim that animal life is, at least to some degree, as *inviolable* as human life. In his own footnote to the passage, Brunner makes an especially strong claim: "Inevitably, we cannot do otherwise than look at all creatures as we look at man."[7] Indeed, Brunner stresses that the "primary duty of man is to adopt a positive attitude towards life—an attitude of affirmation, acceptance, and adjustment to its claim."[8]

But this is not the whole picture. Brunner then backpedals and does not unreservedly endorse reverence for life. He finds the universality of Schweitzer's ethic problematic and opposes it at several points:

> This direct reverence for life as the divine does not perceive the
> distinction between the Creator and creature; it is pantheistic and its
> ethical influence is disintegrating. Life claims our reverence not in
> itself but as the Divine Creation; therefore we are not to reverence life

in a mechanically uniform manner, but in the various "grades" or "degrees" ordered by the Creator. It is His will that we should distinguish and retain degrees as well as differences. We ought to deal more freely with lifeless material than with living beings, with lower forms of existence than with the higher forms....

Every kind of ethics is sentimental and finally inhuman whose principle is "reverence for life," that is, an undifferentiated conception of life itself. *The Philosophy of Civilization,* whose main conception is that of "reverence for life," is a curious and remarkable hybrid, composed of the pantheistic mystical attitude towards life,...[and of] humanistic personalism. Schweitzer's own lifework is the most convincing proof of the inadequacy of this concept for the basis of an ethical system, since he, as a doctor, is obliged to kill a million forms of life in order to preserve *human* life, and knows that in so doing he is acting *ethically.*[9]

Brunner makes two key interrelated criticisms. His first criticism asserts that Schweitzer's ethic blurs the distinction between creation and Creator; the emphasis on life lapses into *pantheism,* that is, the loss of adequate distinction between the God and life ("reverence for life as the divine"). He is not alone in this view. Kraus also argues that Schweitzer's ethic "is a peculiar mixture of agnosticism and animistic pantheism."[10] And Ice similarly claims that Schweitzer's "whole ethical philosophy strongly reflects a *monistic* attitude, particularly when it assumes the form of an ethical pantheism."[11]

Two responses are appropriate to this initial charge. First, Schweitzer was himself aware of this "danger": he repeatedly returns to the problem of distinguishing his understanding of ethical mysticism from strict *pantheism* or *monism,* which he sees as related: "A religion is monistic if it considers God to be the sum-total of all the forces at work in the universe....Thus, in its very nature, monism is pantheistic."[12] Contrary to Brunner, therefore, he purposely avoids *ethical pantheism* and argues that "all ethical piety is superior to any pantheistic mysticism, in that it does not find the God of love in nature, but knows him only from the fact that He announces Himself in us as the will-to-love."[13]

Further evidence of Schweitzer's thought on the tragedy of life in conflict with itself makes Brunner's pantheistic critique impossible. Schweitzer is not a pantheist, that is, someone who thinks that the world is God or coterminous with God. He is sharply critical of those who seek to deify rather than recognize the natural world's essentially tragic and incomplete nature: "He [God] is a dynamic Power for good, a mysterious Will, *distinct* from the world and *superior* to the world."[14] It would be difficult to find a stronger rejection of the idea of the sameness of God and the world than in Schweitzer's repeated description of the world as a "ghastly drama of the will-to-live divided against itself." Because of this present state of affairs, "we apprehend God as a Will that is distinct from the world."[15] He also distinguishes between the present world of predation and suffering and its original, "perfect" state:

> We are convinced that from the world we cannot gain our knowledge
> of God, who is an ethical Personality.... We dare to admit that
> the forces at work in Nature are in so many ways different from what
> we should expect them to be in a world which owes its origin to
> a perfect Creative Will.[16]

Also, Schweitzer makes a sharp distinction between the present tragic nature of the world and an eschatological future where "the creatures [who] sigh with us . . . will be freed from anxiety and perishability."[17] Interestingly, Brunner's critique of pantheism adopts a similar position to that taken by Schweitzer. Brunner rejects pantheism on the grounds that creation is presently distorted: "God does not will it [the world] in so far as in it the form of creation has been distorted and spoilt by sin.... To identify the will of God with things as they are [i.e., the present world] would be to turn the Image of God into a devilish caricature."[18] He proceeds to present an understanding of cosmic redemption which is also in accord with Schweitzerian eschatological insights: "For God has planned His creation for an end which is still unrealized.... We are to be faithful to 'the earth' as those who through faith belong to the world to come, to the new aeon, in which all creaturely bondage will be done away."[19]

Brunner's second criticism maintains that reverence for life, due to its lack of moral hierarchies, is actually *unethical*. The concept of reverence for "life itself" is "inhuman" because of its indiscriminate view of life. He claims that life is to be differentiated into different "degrees" and even offers an Aristotelian *scala naturae* which moves from "dead matter to plants to lower animals to higher animals to man."[20] Hans Leisegang's critique takes a similar, if more general line: the notion of civilization involves gradations of "higher" and "lower" life forms.[21] Because Schweitzer defines *reverence* as an absolute ethic that enjoins "responsibility without limit towards all that lives,"[22] it is perhaps not surprising that Brunner judges Schweitzer's ethic (with particular regard to his medical work where "he is obliged to kill a million forms of life") as entailing inconsistency in practice. Indeed, Schweitzer is not immune from such charges, since, for example, he notoriously had fish caught to feed his sick pelicans:

Someone brought me four pelicans whose wings had been so badly
slashed by insensitive people that they cannot fly. It will take two
or three months before their wings heal and they can fly freely. I have
hired a fisherman to catch the necessary fish to feed them. I always pity the poor fish to the depths of my soul, but I have to choose
between killing the fish or the four pelicans who would surely
starve to death. I do not know whether I am doing the right thing
in deciding one way instead of the other.[23]

These inconsistencies are made more glaring in the light of Schweitzer's
rejection of any moral hierarchy which some commentators, notably Brunner,
have understood as suggesting that no form of life should ever be destroyed
and that all creatures, humans to microbes, should have the same moral worth.
It is doubtful whether this was Schweitzer's intention. He readily and regret-
tably admitted that it is sometimes necessary to make choices between various
forms of life, but he wanted to underscore the essentially *subjective* and arbitrary nature of such decisions. What Schweitzer objects to is any fixed conception of a moral hierarchy.

Perhaps the biggest problem with Brunner's reading of Schweitzer's ethic
is his failure to appreciate reverence for life as *mystical*. Reverence for life is
neither a moral principle that upholds the absolute inviolability of life nor a
strict set of obligations to be construed as moral law. *Ehrfurcht* holds a vaster
connotation: it is attitude, experience, and mysticism. Brunner's criticism that
Schweitzer's "own life work is the most convincing proof of the inadequacy of
this concept for the basis of an ethical system" *reduces* reverence for life to a
rule or list of moral prescriptions, the application of which, Schweitzer would
agree, is untenable. Indeed, shorn of its mystical aspect, his thought *does* look
absolutist and impracticable. But that is precisely how he wished *not* to be read.
Schweitzer never explicitly propounds a scale of values; reverence is primarily a
mystical experience of the intrinsic value of all life, which in turn guides action.
Of course, every time one comes to a question of inconsistency or some relation that does not seem immediately obvious, it is easy to see how Schweitzer
can cry "mysticism" (which conveniently enough "passes all understanding")
and does not need to give any further explanation.

Brunner's remarks help to emphasize Schweitzer's refusal to systematize
ethics. Schweitzer does not propound a set of absolute principles and there is
no obligation construed only as a rule: ethics cannot be systematized because
"reverence for all being, love for all creatures, and . . . compassion and sympathy" must attend to each specific situation.[24] In some circumstances, one may
decide, like Schweitzer, to sacrifice fish in order to save a sick pelican, but

"every day the responsibility to sacrifice one life for another caused me pain."[25]
Brunner's disposition to read Schweitzer in a legalistic sense is all the more
surprising in the light of his own view "that true ethics cannot be conceived in a
legalistic general manner, by means of a principle." Schweitzer would have
certainly endorsed Brunner's statement that an "ethic of love," or "sacrifice," is
"impossible to define in legalistic terms."[26]

Schweitzer further suggests that there are other values of deeper import
than the strict preservation of life. For instance, "prolonged" and "intense"
suffering is "a more terrible lord of mankind than even death."[27] This important point is made with particular emphasis and deserves to be read in full:

> However seriously man undertakes to abstain from killing and
> damaging, he cannot entirely avoid it. He is under the law of ne-
> cessity, which compels him to kill and to damage both with and
> without his knowledge. In many ways it may happen that by slavish
> adherence to the commandment not to kill *compassion is less served*
> than by breaking it. When the suffering of a living creature cannot
> be alleviated, it is *more ethical* to end its life by killing it merci-
> fully than it is to stand aloof. It is more cruel to let domestic animals
> which one can no longer feed die a painful death by starvation than
> to give them a quick and painless end. . . . Again and again we see
> ourselves placed under the necessity of saving one living creature
> by destroying or damaging another.
>
> The principle of not-killing and not-harming *must not aim at*
> *being independent, but must be the servant of, and subordinate itself to,*
> *compassion.* It must therefore enter into a practical discussion with
> reality.[28]

Active compassion supersedes even strict observance to the principle of
nonviolence. Since reverence for life is rooted in life-affirmation, Schweitzer
maintains it is in accord with Jesus' ethic of "active, enthusiastic love of one's
neighbor."[29] As Jesus' emphasis on love suggests, the ethical implications of
reverence for life are greater than a promotion of noninjury or nonviolence to
other wills-to-live; it involves an active concern toward all life. Such compassion
may include the killing of an animal in pain rather than standing "aloof" and
watching it suffer. It is clear that although no killing can be seen as a moral
good, it may be considered "justifiable" in situations of crisis where competing
claims conflict.

Inconsistently, however, although Schweitzer believes it to be an ethical
responsibility for humans to euthanize an animal whose pain cannot be alle-
viated, he apparently stands against euthanasia for humans:

Reverence for life orders us not to take even the . . . agonizing life of man. If I see an animal that suffers, I may be his redeemer in that I put an end to his existence. With a suffering person, however, I may not do so. I ought not to shorten his life by even an hour. . . . Several years ago an old physician told me of a temptation he had experienced. He was called to a feebleminded child who was sick with diphtheria. A few hours' delay in the administration of the appropriate treatment and the child would be freed from his suffering existence. "I fought with myself," he said, "and in the end, reverence for life triumphed. The child was saved, and I bear the responsibility that his miserable existence goes on from year to year."[30]

Despite Schweitzer's best efforts not to judge according to a hierarchy, he implicitly accepts one.

Schweitzer always saw a moral tension in killing; it could never be considered the norm. Even and especially in his medical work was he cognizant of this moral ambiguity: "I rejoice over the new remedies for sleeping sickness, which enable me to preserve life, where once I could only witness the progress of a painful disease. But every time I put the germs that cause the disease under the microscope I cannot but reflect that I have to sacrifice this life in order to save another."[31] While killing may sometimes be viewed as "necessary" it can never be considered "ethical."

Necessary versus Ethical Decisions

The distinction between *the necessary* and *the ethical* results from Schweitzer's sense of the tragic ("the division of the will-to-live") and his understanding of the ethical as disassociated from the relative, instrumental, or utilitarian. In *The Philosophy of Civilization*, he proclaims that "all destruction of and injury to life, under whatever circumstances they take place, they [the ethics of reverence for life] condemn as evil." Each individual has "to decide for himself how far he can remain ethical and how far he must submit himself to the necessity for destruction of and injury to life, and therewith incur guilt."[32] Even in the realm of necessity, all killing and injury, regardless of the circumstances, is considered incompatible with ethics and brings guilt upon the individual.

In *Indian Thought and Its Development*, Schweitzer appears less adamant and asserts that under some conditions (for example, when an animal is suffering) it is more ethical to kill a creature "mercifully" than to allow it to continue to suffer. Similarly, in his autobiography, *Out of My Life and Thought*, he speaks of a feeling of "responsibility" when it is necessary to take other forms of life:

To the person who is truly ethical all life is sacred, including that
which from the human point of view seems lower. He makes distinctions only as each case comes before him, and under the
pressure of necessity, as for example, when it falls to him to decide
which of two lives he must sacrifice in order to preserve the other.
But all through this series of decisions he is conscious of acting
on subjective grounds and arbitrarily, and knows that he bears *responsibility* for the life that is sacrificed.[33]

Here, as well as in *Indian Thought and Its Development*, it is the individual
who is to bear the "responsibility" for the sacrificed life, rather than be deemed
"evil." In these two texts, published ten and twelve years after *The Philosophy of
Civilization* respectively, Schweitzer acknowledges that reverence for life allows
for some *ethical activity* that entails killing nonhuman life. Nevertheless, the
individual who assumes such ethical activity still bears the responsibility for
causing a death.

The deep tension between the universality of reverence for life and the
necessity of sacrificing some wills-to-live to help others recurs frequently in
Schweitzer's writings. He repeatedly underlines the importance of the choice
between the necessary and the ethical, as well as the sense of responsibility one
is to feel each time one is forced to sacrifice life:

I have just killed a mosquito that was buzzing around me in the
lamplight. In Europe I wouldn't kill it even if it were bothering me,
but here in Lambaréné, where mosquitoes spread the most danger-
ous form of malaria, I take the liberty of killing them, although
I don't like doing it. The important thing is for all of us to properly mull over the question of when damaging and killing are per-
missible. Much will be achieved once people become reflective
and wisely realize that they should damage and kill only when necessary. That is the essence. The rationalization of individual cases
is a different matter.[34]

The injury or destruction of any creature requires moral justification,
though even such justification does not make killing ethical. To keep "adjust-
ments between ethics and necessity all ready for use" in order to ease one's
conscience is unethical. Responsible action means the abandonment of any
claim to ethical righteousness: "The good conscience," Schweitzer never ceases
to remind us, "is an invention of the devil."[35]

The principal means by which one can alleviate the guilt or responsibility
incurred by the injury or destruction of life is to increase service to other wills-

to-live. In heavy sermonic language, Schweitzer tells us that "some atonement for that guilt can be found by the man who pledges himself to neglect no opportunity to succor creatures in distress. . . . Whoever does not know the heights we then experience, when the wonderful light of being able to help falls into the gruesome night of having to destroy, does not know how rich life can be."[36] The necessity of harming or killing does not discredit the claims of reverence for life; rather, it only seems to strengthen and renew his determination to its practice.

Schweitzer is cognizant that the absolute ethic of reverence for life cannot be "completely achieved" in practice, though hastens to add that "that fact does not really matter." The import of an ethic is not to be judged on the basis of whether it is *"practicable"* as distinct from *"absolute."*[37] Reverence for life is absolute in that it "cannot be completely achieved" and "demands of one what is actually beyond" practical realization. It does not appoint a maximum limit as to how one should act; it cannot, as an ethical mysticism, fit into tabulated rules and regulations. The problem with this position is that Schweitzer is left with the notion of an absolute that "does not really matter."

For Schweitzer, making choices between life forms (as in his examples of the pelican and mosquitoes) is "subjective" and "arbitrary." His claim that ethics cannot be systematized because reverence for life, including "love" and "compassion," must attend to the particular situation in which it finds itself attempts to strike a balance between antinomianism and legalism. But his resultant position is fraught with logical difficulties.

First, Schweitzer's position is self-contradictory. He contends that there are no rules *except* the "absolute ethic of love."[38] Second, his notion of *necessity* is as subjective as any species-based ethic. Who decides what necessity is in any given context? He fails to explain *the necessary*, to assist us in discriminating different kinds of necessity, and in establishing limitations on various kinds of necessity. Necessary for what? To whom? It may be necessary to kill fish to feed a sick pelican, but it would be considered necessary by some to force-feed a goose if one is to enjoy foie gras.

With necessity left to itself, it can turn into a license for permissiveness. Additionally, as is clear from Schweitzer's examples, out of necessity even the most cherished principle of nonviolence may be put aside if it conflicts in any concrete case with compassion such as euthanasia for a suffering animal. Compassion and love apparently become intrinsic goods; other values are not so important. But *love*, or even *necessity*, is too general to inform us just what we ought to do. And, as Schweitzer readily concedes, what we think is right may very well be wrong. In the light of the undirective nature of necessity and the difficulty (due to his departure from moral hierarchies) in determining appropriate action in a given situation, precise moral guidance and specific values need serious consideration and not just to be set aside.

More positively, Schweitzer's notion of *the necessary and the ethical* serves as a corrective to legalism. It moves away from a moral absolutism that allows no exceptions. It also helps to draw attention to the complexity of moral decisions when a value hierarchy is abandoned. The "law of necessity" and the interdependence of life in the world make no line of absolute consistency possible, but for Schweitzer it is still morally correct to strive for that ideal. Reverence for life, far from Brunner's more literal interpretation of the phrase, is not meant to establish specific rules for each possible circumstance, but to create an attitude of universal reverence that motivates action.

Hearing the Word

Schweitzer and Barth met on at least one occasion. Barth invited him to lecture in Münster. Barth's recollection was faintly patronizing:

> I told him in a friendly way that his views were a "fine specimen of
> righteousness by works" and that he was a man of the eighteenth
> century. After that, we talked and on the whole got on very well.
> There is no point in wanting to quarrel with him. He sees himself,
> like everything and everyone else, in relative terms, and it is cer-
> tainly true that one should be compassionate. He gives us a great
> deal to think about.[39]

One senses a certain one-upmanship in the following exchange recorded by biographer George Seaver. During their meeting, Schweitzer apparently remarked to Barth: "You and I started from the same problem, the disintegration of modern thought, but whereas you went back to the Reformation, I went back to the Enlightenment."[40]

More than any other theologian, Barth offers a detailed examination of Schweitzer's ethic. Unlike Brunner, who deems reverence for life "sentimental" and impractical, Barth maintains:

> It was easy of course to criticize this teaching [reverence for life]
> by raising all kinds of questions about the practicability of such
> rules, and even to poke a little fun at it as Alsatian sentimentality.
> I regard that as cheap.[41]

Likewise, in *Church Dogmatics*:

We certainly cannot dismiss it [reverence for life] as "sentimental." Nor may we take the easy course of questioning the practicability of the instructions given, let alone the wider consequences and applications. The directness of the insight and feeling revealed (not unlike those of Francis of Assisi), and the constraint expressed, are stronger than all such criticism.[42]

Barth claims that one of the most common representations of humanity's sinful egotism is the assumption that as "lord" of creation, one has the right to kill animals indiscriminately or find amusement in cruel sports.[43] He questions whether

man has really heard God's command of reverence for life, if he knows nothing about the *synodinein* and *systenazein* of the *ktisis* that is shut up in corruptibility, if it does not matter to him that we continually contribute to it in the most outrageous fashion, if for him the slaughterhouse and vivisection, the chase, and the pitiless locking up of all kinds of forest animals and birds behind the bars of zoological gardens present *no* questions, or no questions applicable to him, since directly or indirectly we all of us have a share in these things?[44]

Within the sphere of life, the freedom to which humans are summoned is "the freedom to treat life . . . as a loan from God."[45] To recognize and treat life as a loan from God is to "reverence" it. It is important to note that Barth's translators have translated his use of *Ehrfurcht* as "respect," instead of the stronger "reverence." *Reverence* conveys more precisely Barth's concern with ethics and also suggests the proximity-*cum*-remoteness in which he stands with Schweitzer's thought. For Barth, the attitude of reverence is "man's astonishment, humility and awe before a fact in which he meets something superior—grandeur, dignity, holiness, a mystery which compels him to withdraw and keep his distance, to deal with it modestly, circumspectly and carefully."[46] Under God's command, reverence for life assumes a practical direction; it entails humanity's "determination and readiness of *action* in the direction of its confirmation."[47]

Barth is at times fulsome in his praise of Schweitzer's ethics. For him, it is the whole of life that is to be reverenced and affirmed and he credits Schweitzer with "render[ing] a great and significant service to theological ethics when he discovered this principle [reverence for life] and stressed it so emphatically."[48] He is in accord with Schweitzer's account "of the 'narrowness of heart' with which previous ethics had limited its attention to self-giving to men and human society."[49] Like Brunner, he cites approvingly Schweitzer's statement that the place of animals in European ethics is like a kitchen floor scrubbed clean by a housekeeper who is "careful to see that the door is shut lest the dog should come in and ruin the finished job with its [dirty] paws."[50] Barth further commends Schweitzer's appeal against humans' "indifferent and thoughtless" treatment of animals and states that "one must be grateful for Schweitzer's achievement...in view of the greater relevance of the weak point [i.e., neglect of nonhuman species] in all previous ethics which he has underlined....It is surely to Schweitzer's credit that he has warned us so warmly and earnestly to consider this [i.e., the moral worth of "life outside the human sphere"]."[51]

Barth recounts with respect Schweitzer's examples regarding the care and regard to be displayed to the worm on the dry road, the insect in the puddle, and the wayside flower, claiming that "those who can only laugh at this point are themselves a little deserving of our tears."[52] Like Schweitzer, Barth notes the abusive activity of humans towards plants when one behaves "like a boy and beheads thistles" while walking along. Concretely: "Indifference, wantonness, arbitrariness or anything else opposed to reverence cannot even be considered as a commanded or even permitted attitude."[53]

Despite this initial enthusiasm, Barth develops several criticisms of Schweitzer's position. Notwithstanding the wayside flower and the thistles, Barth is unwilling to extend equal moral consideration to plants and vegetables. In *Ethics*, he includes plant life alongside animals in the "test whether we really hear this claim [reverence for life]...when it can address us only in silence, when we must detect it in the 'groaning of creation' (cf. Rom. 8:22), when it is enigmatically concealed behind the apparent objectivity of animal and plant life."[54] But, in *Church Dogmatics*, he deems an animal, unlike plant life, "a single being, a unique creature existing in an individuality which we cannot fathom but also cannot deny." Whereas the use of vegetable life does not constitute its "destruction," but instead entails the "sensible use of its superfluity," the "nearness of the animal to man irrevocably means that when man kills a beast he does something which is at least very similar to homicide."[55] Actually, Barth's reflection here overlooks how harvesting vegetables often requires their destruction rather than a "sensible use of [their] superfluity," which could be argued as the case with regard to the harvesting of fruits where the mother-organism remains intact.

Reverence for life, claims Barth, pertains "analogically" to human-to-animal relations, and, though animal welfare is considered important, it is "a serious secondary responsibility."[56] Like Brunner, he is troubled by the universality with which Schweitzer characterizes reverence for life: although reverence may apply analogically to animals, it cannot apply to plant life.

Along with Brunner, Barth points to Schweitzer's work as a physician as evidence that he values human life over other forms of life and as evidence that Schweitzer's practice of reverence is inconsistent: "It is a further help to our understanding that Schweitzer himself did not finally take up service as a veterinary surgeon but set a fine example of medical work among the natives of the Ogowe."[57] Unfortunately for Barth's arguments, Schweitzer cared for all wounded animal life at the Lambaréné hospital. His medical notes recorded the arrival of both sick humans and sick animals at the hospital. Charles Joy wrote how Schweitzer "once showed me a page [of his diary] where he had noted two significant arrivals at the hospital on the same day—the Dutch nurse, Maria Lagendijk, and the little, frightened antelope, Leonie." Joy continues, "It was no disparagement of the work of one of Lambaréné's most competent and devoted nurses that the doctor seemed to think one arrival as worthy of notation as the other." In at least one case, Joy notes that Schweitzer risked his life to save a wounded and stranded dog.[58] In practice, Schweitzer attempted to display the "ethic of love" to all life forms around him. Prior to lowering a stone into a foundation for a new building, he states: "I always look back to see whether any ants or toads or other creatures have fallen into it. And if so, I take them out with my hands, that they may not be crushed by the pile or later by the pounding down of earth and stones." And similarly: "We burden ourselves with some extra work out of compassion for the palm trees with which the site of our future home is crowded. The simplest plan would be to cut them all down. . . . [Practically speaking], an oil palm is useless, there are so many of them. But we cannot find it in our heart to deliver them over to the axe. . . . So we devote some of our leisure hours to digging up carefully those which are transplantable and setting them elsewhere."[59] Like many commentators, Barth was unaware of how Schweitzer's work at Lambaréné, however practically challenging at times, embodied his own conscience.

Barth's criticisms of reverence for life are grounded in his theological critique: Schweitzer fails to understand the moral distinction between plants, animals, and humans because of his misunderstanding of the doctrine of the incarnation. According to Barth:

> Man is the creature to whom God reveals, trusts, and binds Himself
> with the rest of creation; with whom He makes common cause
> of a particular history which is neither that of an animal nor that of a
> plant, and in whose life-activity He expects a conscious and delib-
> erate recognition of His honor, mercy and power.[60]

Human life, because of its privileged position in creation, has the right to "lordship and control." Barth defines lordship as having "the primary meaning of requisitioning, disciplining, taming, harnessing, exploiting, and making profitable use of the surplus forces of nature in the animal world.... For what is human lordship over the beast if it cannot take this form of 'domesticating' animals?"[61] His definition of lordship here is predicated on the use of the natural world for human wants and appears to contradict much of that for which he praised Schweitzer's reverence. "[Although] we may entertain beautiful and pious thoughts ... concerning the independent reality of animal and vegetable existence, man is not addressed [by God] concerning animal and vegetable life, nor life in general, *but concerning his own human life*."[62] More strongly, Barth argues that "God's eternal Son and Logos did not will to be an angel or an animal but man ... this and *this alone* was the content of the eternal divine election of grace."[63] Likewise, Brunner observes: "God became man and not an animal. It is not an arbitrary fact that God reveals Himself to us as man and not as an animal."[64] Barth sharpens this criticism: reverence for life is unsatisfactory because Schweitzer places "life" where we should see "the Word of God," or "the command of God."[65]

No doubt Barth's observation, in response to the articulation of reverence for life as presented in *The Philosophy of Civilization*, is correct insofar as Schweitzer does not give—for reasons previously examined—attention to the Word or to theological concepts. However, a reading of Schweitzer's sermons makes Barth's criticisms problematic and affords a different perspective of reverence for life from that commonly offered by his interpreters. It may first be instructive to examine the anthropocentric thrust of Barthian theology.

Barth's Christology involves a narrowing of focus; it is associated almost exclusively with human beings.[66] Nonhuman creation is at best a backdrop to the important revelation that happens to humans. At the center is a concern for humanity and God: "The Word of God does not contain any account of the cosmos ... The Word of God is concerned with God and man."[67] More strongly still: "He who in the biblical message is called God is obviously not interested in the totality of things and beings created by Him, not in specific beings within this totality, but in man."[68] Likewise, Brunner puts it bluntly: the world of nature is theologically "never anything more than the 'scenery' in which the history of mankind takes place."[69] God's Word incarnate is almost completely disconnected from the Creator-Word, or Logos. Barth's Christology is thus reduced to anthropology: the doctrine of creation means "in practice anthropology, the study of *man*."[70] Barth concludes: "God is the God of man and man the man of God. This is the epitome of the whole order of creation."[71]

Creation and Creator

Far from necessarily excluding an ethic of reverence for all life, several Christological insights overlooked by Barth can be seen as central to Schweitzer's
exposition. Drawing from the doctrine of the Logos, there appear to be at least
two Christological components omitted from Barth's discussion of Schweitzer's work. An examination of these may illuminate the anthropocentricity of
Barth's Christology and defend some of Schweitzer's insights.

The second person of the Trinity is the Son of God, God's *Word* or *Logos*.
As St. John makes clear (14:6), in and through the Son, God is revealed to us.
But it is the person of the incarnate Word who is also at the core of all creation:
in the Johannine Prologue, the Word that became flesh is also involved in
God's creative activity. All things come to being from the Logos: "All that came
to be was alive with his life," St. John affirms (1:4). The Logos is found in life,
and all creaturely life—to some extent—participates in it. From this perspective, the Word can be seen to underscore the unity of all created life.

In summary, Barth asserts that Schweitzer's reverence for life is insufficiently theological because the concept of *life* usurps the position that rightfully
belongs to *the Word of God*. However, the same Christ incarnate is also God's
co-eternal, the Creator Logos, who constitutes both the source and destiny of
each logos in creation. In this sense, the Logos acts as a unifying cosmic presence drawing all things towards God. By contrast, in Barthian theology, God
becomes one with humanity in the person of Jesus Christ. He reduces the biblical proclamation of covenant to an anthropocentric head. But Barth's appeal
to Christology does not necessarily preclude Schweitzer's reverence.

If Christ is the co-creator through whom all life comes into being, then
Barth's view that there is a human nature, utterly different from all other na-
tures, seems unfounded. Schweitzer's understanding of the incarnation helps
to underscore this notion. Although he did not appear to have explored the
doctrine of the incarnation in a systematic fashion, his Lambaréné sermons
afford some insight on this point. He preached that Christianity "is the religion
of the Infinite become flesh," and again of Jesus as "the Divine made flesh."[72]
The key word is *flesh*: this terminology suggests the possibility of seeing creation from a more inclusive perspective. As Brunner himself observes: "In his
personal being, man's organic and animal existence connects him with the
whole of the rest of the created world, gives him a share in its existence."[73]

Schweitzer's description of Jesus' incarnation can be seen to signify the
incarnate solidarity of his fleshly existence with all creation. This Christological
point is perhaps given fullest expression in Philip Sherrard's exegesis. In

Human Image: World Image, Sherrard highlights how "'flesh' (*sarx*) can be taken to signify not only the flesh of the human body, but all matter, all physical nature."[74] Sherrard maintains:

> Everything, not only man, but every living form of plant, bird or animal, the sun, moon and stars, the waters and the mountains, [is] seen as signs of things sacred (*signa rei sacrae*), expressions of the Logos.[75]

Likewise, John Muddiman comments on the prologue to John's Gospel: "The Word did not merely become human: he became flesh, the term which defines the solidarity of humanity with the rest of creation in its bodiliness: 'All flesh is grass and its beauty like the flowers of the field; the grass withers and the flower fades, but the Word of the Lord remains for ever' (Isa. 40:6–8)."[76] For Jürgen Moltmann "'all flesh' is of course human life first and foremost but it also embraces all the living generally—plants, trees and animals."[77] John B. Cobb, Jr., also develops this theme in Schweitzerian language: "The Word takes on unique form, is 'made flesh,' in Jesus. But it is present in every creature. It is the life of all that lives. To reverence Christ is to reverence life in all its forms."[78] The Christological considerations presented by these theologians extend Schweitzer's insight into the connection between "Divine made flesh" and the flesh of all life, as well as express the notion that all life shares a common nature and Source.

More directly, Schweitzer's Lambaréné sermons depict the Holy Spirit as actively participating in creation. His sermon on 1 Corinthians 6:19 relates the Spirit in the human body with the Creator-Spirit:

> But what then is the Spirit? When we say, "God is a Spirit, the eternal Spirit of the world," ... this means that God is invisible, eternal, and everywhere. It is the Spirit of God that has created the earth. It is he that has given light to the sun and stars. It is he that gives life to the grass and trees. *The Spirit of God is the power of all that lives.*[79]

From this pneumatological standpoint, God is (through the Spirit) the life in the world. God's Spirit fills everything created in such a way that all things live from God.

In Schweitzer's account, the interpenetration of the spiritual and material given at creation ("the Spirit of God . . . created the earth"), and through the incarnation ("the Divine made flesh"), can be seen to give humans access to the Divine (infinite Will-to-Live) *via* the physical world (wills-to-live). From these Christological and pneumatological positions, it is difficult to understand on what grounds Barth bases the following criticism:

Schweitzer himself robbed his argument of its true and final force when he failed to base the command of reverence on the concept of God, but retreated into his mystical experience and thus gave his whole presentation an element of biographical contingency.[80]

Two responses need to be made to this critique. First, it is not so much that Barth is dissatisfied with Schweitzer's ethical insights; rather, that he is radically antipathetic to even the slightest suggestion of mysticism which he holds to be incompatible with Christianity. Barth states: "Reverence for life cannot be accepted in the broad sense . . . [because] Schweitzer's ethics, as he himself describes it, is mystical."[81] As Harvey Egan writes in his *Anthology of Christian Mysticism*, both Barth and Brunner "sharply distinguish biblical, prophetic religions from Oriental mystical religions, claiming that the two are mutually exclusive."[82] In Evelyn Underhill's *Essentials of Mysticism*, this revealing (if perhaps debatable) sentence is found: "We cannot honestly say that there is any wide difference between the Brahman, Sufi, or Christian mystic at their best."[83] Barth and Brunner could not wish to have their point put more exactly. For them, the Christian mystic, qua mystic, is virtually indistinguishable (or so they thought) from a Brahman counterpart, which is tantamount to saying that one is not distinctly Christian at all. Moreover, Barth and Brunner reject the longstanding Christian mystical tradition as "a pagan, neo-Platonic infection and deformation of Christianity."[84] Barth typifies this view in *The Epistle to the Romans*, when he accuses mysticism of being even worse than self-righteous Pharisaism "because it [claims to] lie so near to the righteousness of God."[85] It is apparent that Barth, and likewise Brunner, was predisposed to rejecting Schweitzer's reverence for life inasmuch as it represented an ethical *mysticism*.

Notwithstanding the above, it is striking that certain aspects of Barth's theology appear to develop the very elements he felt were absent from Schweitzer's thesis. In the following passage, Barth seems to do no more than present in *theological* terms what Schweitzer presented in masked philosophical terminology in *The Philosophy of Civilization*:

> What is meant by the "form of this world"? What is the characteristic feature of the world that we know? I should like to ask whether it might not be this: We see in all that which we call world the sway of an impulse, a vital impulse [élan vital] which we can well take *to have been imparted by God to all life at the creation*. But in the form in which we see this vital impulse, it is a movement—this *will-to-live*, this urgent desire of the creature for life. And secondly (and in consequence of that): movement, an impulse that has got to come to an end somewhere, victim to death, to the transitoriness of all things

earthly. All things living have their day. And if I have just spoken of a curse, which burdens the world, that is simply the curse of death, to which all earthly life is subjected.[86]

Here, Barth renders explicit three of the most fundamental aspects of Schweitzer's thesis and brings his thought out from the margins into mainstream theology.

First, the life in the world, Barth points out, is from God the Creator. From this, he affirms that the *command* of God the Creator is the command of life, that is, an affirmation of the will-to-live. This command "always contains, even if imperceptibly, incidentally or anonymously, the imperative: Thou shalt will-to-live."[87] Barth's understanding here of the command of God the Creator follows closely Schweitzer's thought on the will of God the Creator: "For in world- and life-affirmation . . . I carry out the will of the universal Will-to-Live [God] which reveals itself in me."[88] The epistemological correlate to this life-affirmation that Schweitzer draws is that "the mystery of life is always too profound for us, and its value is beyond our [i.e., human] capacity to estimate."[89] Schweitzer asks, "How can we know the importance other living organisms have in themselves and in terms of the universe?"[90] Barth, too, is epistemologically skeptical about human's capacity to apprehend the command of God the Creator in "reality" and likewise rejects the concept of a definitive order (or orders) of creation:

We do not know what particular attitude God may have to them [nonhuman creatures], and therefore what might be their decisive particularity within the cosmos. . . . We can and must accept them as our fellow-creatures with all due respect for the mystery in which God has veiled them.[91]

Second, Barth maintains that the "characteristic feature of the world" is the "will-to-live," the drive of all creaturely life to maintain existence. The correspondence with Schweitzer's foundational notion that "everything which exists is will-to-live" is evident. Barth also appears to accept Bergson's notion of the élan vital that Schweitzer develops in his thought. Further, for both Schweitzer and Barth, the affirmation of life is an affirmation of the "community of life."[92] For Barth, we come to know other life "only as we know the fact of our own life. My knowledge of the life of my fellows, . . . the life of animals and plants, not to speak of a real or supposed knowledge of the reality of life in general, is an analogous knowledge going back to my knowledge of my own life."[93] Barth appears to follow Schweitzer's principle that "I can understand the nature of the living being outside of myself only through the living being within me. . . . Knowledge of [external] reality must pass through a phase of thinking about the nature of [personal] being."[94] This is tantamount to providing a basis for the created relational structure of all life. Indeed, both Schweitzer and Barth use this principle as the basis for their presentation of reverence:

> Schweitzer: What shall be my attitude toward this other life which I see around me? It can only be a piece of my attitude toward my own life. If I am a thinking being, I must regard other life than my own with equal reverence. [95]

> Barth: The will-to-live which is the form of reverence for life will always be distinguishable from an inhuman and irreverent will-to-live contrary to the command [of God], by the fact that it considers the existence and life of others together with its own, and its own together with that of others.[96]

Third, following Schweitzer, Barth highlights that the world is incomplete and that the will-to-live stands, at present, "divided against itself." Barth explains, "In this *conflict of life with life* I would see the real characteristic form of life in this world."[97] Elsewhere, he reflects on "the incalculable contingencies of life and the never-to-be-forgotten conflicts between life and life."[98] As such, our perception of creation "is always of life *and* death, becoming and decaying; in virtue of which the big fish does not greet the little fish but eats it."[99]

These very Schweitzer-like thoughts take on a similarly Schweitzerian ethical significance for Barth. The protection of life lies in the will of its Creator: God's command gives us the rule that we should reverence life. Barth concludes that "the protection of life . . . is simply the protection which God wills to demand of man as the Creator of this life and the Giver of the future eternal life."[100] With an eye to this future life, Christians must now regard themselves as responsible,

> to be perhaps a little bit of new world within the present world. Have a care! . . . bear witness on the one hand against the form of this world, and on the other, in favor of the form of the coming world! That is the double meaning of action of ours.[101]

Or again, those who pray for the coming of the kingdom of God, "the sabbath day of the light of God *which abolishes all the division of the present*,"[102]

> are claimed for action in the effort and struggle for righteousness. . . . On no pretext can they escape responsibility for it: not on

that of the gratitude and hope with which they look to God and wait for his action; not on that of their prayer for the coming of his kingdom. For if they are really grateful and really hope, if their prayer is a brave prayer, then they are also claimed for a corresponding inner and outer action which is also brave.[103]

The reconciliation of the "conflict of life with life" cannot be seen as *only* an eschatological act, but requires humans to "have a care" and anticipate the peace of the "new world within the present world." For, wherever humans exercise "lordship" over creation,

there should be written in letters of fire the words of St. Paul in Rom. 8:18f. concerning the "earnest expectation" of the creature—for what?—for the "manifestation of the children of God," and therefore for the liberation of those who now keep them imprisoned and even dispatch them from life to death. And it [nonhuman creation], too, is determined for liberation . . . together with the liberation of the children of God, so that for the moment it groans and cries with us in the birth-pangs of a new aeon.[104]

Here Barth brings us to the edge of endorsing an ethic of reverence for life, fashioned on an eschatological vision of liberation for all creation. In so doing, he offers us a portrait of the moral space in which human action stands, always rooted in the broader context of God the Creator, Reconciler, and Redeemer's goal for peace in creation.

For Barth, there may be good reasons for viewing the election of humanity in Christ as the focal point of divine action and hence the unique place of humans in the cosmos. Indeed, Schweitzer's ethic also places humans in the special role of moral agents in creation participating with the Will-to-Love in cosmic reconciliation. But since the *flesh* assumed in the incarnation is the flesh of all creation, it is reasonable to conclude that what is realized in the incarnation for humans holds similar consequences for the nonhuman creation. Barth's anthropocentric Christology severs this link between humans and nonhuman creation that is integral to Schweitzer's vision of cosmic unity:

Ethics alone can put me in true relationship with the universe by my serving it, co-operating with it; . . . by serving every kind of life do I enter the service of that Creative Will whence all life emanates. . . . This is the mystical experience of ethics.[105]

Schweitzer sees service to other life as service to and union with the Creative Will, God. This model of service, a consistent theme in his Strasbourg sermons, is most clearly presented in "Ethics of Compassion": "What is the sort of love toward God which compels us to be kind to others? What does love for our neighbor mean? . . . The presupposition of morality is to share everything that goes on around us, not only in human life but [also] in the life of all creatures. This awareness forces us to do all within our power for the preservation and advancement of life."[106] This "awareness" inspires a response to God, knowing that humans are responsible for serving God who seeks to bring all life into harmony.

The Cosmic Christ

If Christ as the Logos binds both intelligible and sensible beings to himself and to one another, then Barth's conception that Christ is of import to human beings and of little significance to the rest of creation appears untenable. By Christ's incarnation as flesh, he affirms that all creation, all *sarx*, can be redeemed.

Barth's Christology generally fails to take into consideration this notion of the *cosmic Christ*. In response to a question at an ecumenical seminar, he stated that the cosmic Christ "is not another Christ but Christ crucified or risen; the cosmic Christ is Christ's real presence and activity as the living Savior, Lord, Creator in every element in nature and history." Another notable exception can be found in *Church Dogmatics*: "Jesus Christ . . . has given the cosmos its hope and our life its promise. . . . [Christ] accomplished the salvation of the world and our own."[107] Outside these observations, Barth seems to neglect the importance of Jesus to "every element of nature," and the cosmic Christ was not part of his common theological terminology.

By contrast, Schweitzer develops this *cosmic* theme on two levels. First, as has been examined, through the influence of the Will-to-Love on human wills and, in turn, their role as will-to-love in creation, Christ can be seen to have an indirect relationship with the sum totality of the created order. The universality that Schweitzer sees as characteristic of reverence for life makes his ethic cosmic, not anthropocentric, in scope.

Second, and more clearly, Schweitzer sees Christ as pertaining *directly* to his relationship to the cosmos. For him, the redemptive death and resurrection of Jesus Christ is a "cosmologically conceived," eschatological event.[108] The event, universal in scope, ushers in the beginning of the kingdom. Human salvation is not out of and apart from the rest of the world. Rather, the redemption of the individual person is inextricably bound up with a cosmic eschatology: "The redemption which the believer experiences is therefore not a mere transaction arranged between himself, God, and Christ, but a *world-event* in which he has a share."[109] In *The Christian Life*, Barth arrives at a similar position and speaks of the eschatological reconciling work of God where "the lordship of Jesus Christ over *all creation* is manifested, and with it the reconciliation of the world to God."[110] This position is highly reminiscent of Schweitzer's readings of Paul's "marvelous passage" in Romans on the liberation of creatures "from perishability" and of "the prophet Isaiah" who proclaims that "the Lord will save the world."[111]

Barth's appeal to Christology does not necessarily exclude (as he believed it did) an ethic of reverence for life as advanced by Schweitzer. Although reverence for life may not constitute doctrine, it can be reasonably viewed as deducible from, if not integral to, a Christological understanding of creation and redemption. What we may accept is Barth's cautionary reminder that reverence for life "is *only* one *component* or modification of God's command." It is the all-pervasiveness of Schweitzer's ethical stance that worries Barth:

> We shall not follow Schweitzer to the extent that we cannot set up and
> accept the necessity of life as *the* standpoint of ethics. Ethics, preci-
> sely as theological ethics, does not have to speak an ultimate
> word but only a series of penultimate words.... The necessity of
> life is one such penultimate word, one unavoidable and gener-
> ally valid standpoint from the command, because it is given to man,
> has to be understood.[112]

He insists that "theological ethics should not in any way try to say directly what God's command is."[113] Barth also advises that we remain open to the Word to reveal new ethical and theological insights. Nothing human-derived should restrict the freedom of the Word of God or attempt to dissolve the "Command of the Creator," as the "commandment of life," into *an* ethic. Indeed, *no* ethic can make a claim to a conclusive declaration: "It can only be a challenge, a suggestion, a consilium, not an ultimately and absolutely binding command."[114] Barth wants to emphasize that reverence for life should not be considered the sole criterion of moral life. He longs to protect the freedom of the Word to continue to reveal God's command. In no circumstances may the Word:

> be limited through a sovereignty which we already impose on its
> testimony: it must be allowed its own sovereignty.... Of course
> we will always have some kind of ontology or world-view in our heads.
> And that is not prohibited.... What we have to do, rather, is quite
> simple: we must see that we keep the doors and windows open.

We must not keep to a shut room ... "Open the window!" "Open the door!" so the wind can come in.[115]

Presumably, the wind could have carried to Barth's room the connection between Christianity and the "sacredness of life" that Schweitzer was at pains to present through his own door.

Although reverence for life is not the final word in theological ethics, the moral principle "that life should be accepted, treated and preserved with reverence" is valid even if not seen as the supreme law.[116] On this, at least, Schweitzer and Barth agree.

3

The Voyage to India

In 1952, Jackson Lee Ice (then a doctoral student at Harvard University) wrote to Schweitzer in Lambaréné, asking him to comment on what had been the major influences on his work. Schweitzer's response is vague (if not evasive): "I have never taken into account just what philosophy has had special influence upon me." But later on in the letter, he reveals: "I felt, even at the age of eighteen, that Schopenhauer's work under the influence of Indian thought . . . was an event for me." Schweitzer concludes apologetically but nonetheless dismissively: "Forgive me for not complying with your wishes. . . . You will have to find the answer to your question in the works I have written."[1] Schweitzer, therefore, presents us with a conundrum. But it can be unraveled.

Others who have tried have plainly ventured into culs-de-sac, never journeying beyond the European continent. In an attempt to discover the roots of Schweitzer's notion of *reverence*, Charles Joy speculates that the term *reverence for life* stems from Goethe's *Wilhelm Meister*. "Somehow what Goethe had written and taught must have become so integral a part of Schweitzer's subliminal self that he failed to recognize in the words [reverence for life] that came to him on the mount the accents of Goethe's voice."[2] At one point in *Wilhelm Meister*, three older men are in conversation with young Wilhelm. This is the relevant passage: "One thing there is which no child brings into the world with him; and yet it is on this one thing that all depends for making man in every point a man. If you can discover it yourself, speak it out." After much reflection, Wilhelm shakes his head and asks what it is. The three men exclaim: "Reverence!" Wilhelm pauses. "Reverence!" the three men declare again. "All want it, perhaps you yourself."[3] The men continue to explicate this threefold reverence: reverence for that which is above us, around us, and below us. The last type of reverence is not isolated; it calls one to stand forth and reverence that which is beneath the earth and nourishes us.

It is true that Schweitzer was well versed with Goethe's thought. He even delivered an address on Goethe in Frankfort, Germany, on his receiving from the city the Goethe Prize, awarded in 1928 in recognition of "Service to Humanity." Soon after, on 22 March 1932, Schweitzer delivered the Goethe Memorial Oration at Frankfort at the hour of the day of the poet's death a century before. He also gave a series of speeches on Goethe in Aspen, Colorado, in 1949, which were translated and published in 1961 as *Goethe: Five Studies*. Despite this attention and reverence for Goethe, Schweitzer denies categorically that Goethe's *Wilhelm Meister* played any part in "the genesis of the idea or of the words."[4] As he claims in his moment of illumination on the Ogowe River: "The idea of reverence for life came to me as an unexpected discovery, like a revelation coming upon me in the midst of intense thought."[5] Indeed, he recalls being disturbed by Goethe's "superficial" treatment of *reverence*. Schweitzer calls on one to reverence not only that which sustains us from below, but also all beings in the universe. The fundamental feature of his reverence is its boundlessness, including all of life as it does. The main point of difference (as even Joy agrees) is Goethe's limitation of reverence, among creatures lower than man, only to those who serve and nourish us, where Schweitzer understands it to include "the mosquito that stings us, the snake that bites us, and the bacterium that kills us."[6] Schweitzer understands the problems that such a boundless ethic presents, but still maintains a limitless reverence.

Joy concludes with the statement that to "say that Schweitzer's idea of reverence for life came originally from *Wilhelm Meister*, although Schweitzer himself has forgotten the spring from which he drank, is not, however, to depreciate his originality."[7] Though Schweitzer and Goethe share philosophical views, Schweitzer's vision is broader. He develops the notion of reverence into an ethic, for which there is no evidence in Goethe's work.

From the sidelines, the partial similarity seems as evident as the difference. But there is no acknowledgement that Goethe took at least the first step in expanding the range of reverence. The modern reader will grant Goethe his due, while seeking further afield for possible sources of that part of Schweitzer's thought that goes beyond Goethe. Among these, the Indian sources are perhaps the most revealing.

The Allure of Ahimsā

In 1900, at the age of twenty-five, Schweitzer set himself the grandiose task of analyzing the major religions and great philosophies of the world, as well as the writings of various mystics. The majority of this work was published in 1923 in *The Decay and Restoration of Civilization* and *Civilization and Ethics*, parts I and II of *The Philosophy of Civilization*. In these two volumes, Schweitzer rejects past efforts in Western philosophy to posit ethical foundations in civilization and advances reverence for life.

Schweitzer intended to follow the two parts of *The Philosophy of Civilization* with two more, *The World-view of Reverence for Life* and *Civilized State*. In the third volume, he initially wanted to devote a chapter to his studies of Eastern religions, philosophies, and mystics. But the resulting manuscripts of his study exceeded the confines of a single chapter and were therefore laid aside until 1935, when they were published as *Indian Thought and Its Development*. Although Schweitzer does not explain how existing ethical or mystical doctrines directly influenced the development of reverence for life, it is clear that he undertook major studies of Indian ethics and mysticism at least two decades before (and while) he was engaged in writing *The Philosophy of Civilization*. His Indian researches provide a key to understanding one influence on his articulation of reverence for life.

How did Schweitzer's awareness of Indian religions develop? In the preface to *Indian Thought and Its Development*, he writes, "Indian thought has greatly attracted me since in my youth I first became acquainted with it through reading the works of Arthur Schopenhauer."[8] Similarly, in *Memoirs of Childhood and Youth* and *Out of My Life and Thought*, Schweitzer recounts the significance of his early exposure to Schopenhauer and how, since childhood, Indian thought interested him. Three months before he died at the age of ninety, Schweitzer wrote to the Asiatic Society in Calcutta, India (who was awarding him the Rabindranath Tagore medal), and offered this account of the influence of Indian thought from his youth onward:

> I studied Indian philosophy early on, when I was attending the
> University of Strasbourg, Alsace, even though no course was being
> given on that subject. But then, around 1900, Europe started get-
> ting acquainted with Indian thought. Rabindranath Tagore be-
> came known as the great living Indian thinker. When I grew conver-
> sant with his teachings, they made a deep impact on me. In Germany
> it was the philosopher Arthur Schopenhauer who first recognized

the significance of Indian thinking. A pupil of Schopenhauer's was director of the Mülhouse Secondary School in Alsace, which prepared students for the university. His name was Deecke. In this way I got to know Indian thinking at an early date. And by the time I completed my doctoral examination in philosophy, I was familiar with Indian thought. By then I was teaching at the University of Strasbourg. Focusing as I did on the problem of ethics, I reached the conclusion that Indian ethics is correct in demanding kindness and mercy not only toward human beings but also toward all living creatures. Now the world is gradually realizing that compassion for living creatures is part of true ethics.[9]

This letter is quite puzzling for several reasons. First, Schweitzer's assertion that "around 1900 Europe *started* getting acquainted with Indian thought" is evidently quite erroneous.[10] The establishment of the Asiatic Society in Calcutta (to which Schweitzer was writing) in 1784 by Sir William Jones was a watershed, as was the Society's publication *Asiatic Researches*, which attracted wide European readership and which was translated and re-issued into German and French. Still more directly, one early commentary was Schleiermacher's *Über die Religion* (1799). Schleiermacher is in principle open to complementary insights from India though his knowledge, understandably enough, of Indian and Asian religions was too shallow to allow any fruitful encounter. Hegel's 1821 *Lectures on the Philosophy of Religion* revealed that he too was scanning the Indian horizon with much interest. He gave formulation to the idea (central to the Upanishads) of the divine as Absolute Spirit that realizes itself in the forms of time. But Hegel did not give Indian thought much serious attention either, regarding Hinduism as an inferior form of religious life.[11]

Perhaps no other Western philosopher so signals the turn to India as Schopenhauer, whose interest dates from 1813. For him, the religious tradition of the Buddha (and apparently of "the Jains, who differ from Buddhists only in name"[12]) "is the most excellent upon the earth."[13] He showed an unprecedented readiness to integrate Indian ideas into his own thinking and acknowledged this: "I admit that I do not believe that my doctrine could have ever been formulated before the Upanishads, Plato, and Kant were able to all cast their light simultaneously onto a human mind."[14] It is clear that Indian religious and philosophical concepts were used in the development of early nineteenth century European thought.

Second, Schweitzer is remarkably vague on the nature and extent of his debt. He says that his own ethical conclusions follow along the same path as "Indian ethics" in its incorporation of all living beings within the realm of moral concern. In correspondence with Prime Minister Lal Bahadur Shastri, he acknowledges again that his ideas "are consistent with Indian ideas."[15] Was his relation to Indian thought one merely of confirmation, of ideas he reached independently, or something more? Schweitzer does nothing to discourage the former interpretation. He tells us that as early as the age of six he was ambitiously praying for the peace of all creatures. Puzzled by the absence of animals in his traditional nightly prayers, he prayed, "Dear God, protect and bless all beings that breathe, keep all evil from them, and let them sleep in peace."[16] By his early teens, he reached the conclusion "that we may inflict death and suffering on another living being only when there is an inescapable necessity for it."[17] But these accounts of childhood do not appear to be plain narrative; the reader is presented with selected history. As an aside, while traveling across Switzerland, Schweitzer used a two-hour train stopover to visit his friend and prominent psychologist and pastor Dr. Oscar Pfister. He recounts, "[Pfister] urged me to tell him some incidents of my childhood just as they would come into my mind," as the psychologist wanted to publish the tales in a young people's magazine. Later, Pfister sent him the shorthand notes he had taken during those two hours. Unfortunately, these notes do not survive; Schweitzer requested that the notes be sent to him to edit before the text was published. Inasmuch as Schweitzer was aware of Pfister's plans to publish the memoirs, it is possible that he (intentionally or unintentionally) recounted those memories that were most in accord with his mature self. At the very least, it is evident that he edited the text in such a way that many of his reflections take on a heavy didactic form. It is doubtful, then, that these are Schweitzer's genuine reflections. More likely, they reflect a later understanding of reverence for life.

Many of Schweitzer's remarks on Indian thought are oddly ambivalent, supporting either a theory of confirmation or development. For example: "*What I like* about Indian ethics is that they are concerned with the behavior of man to all living beings and not merely with his attitude to his fellow-man and to human society."[18] Yet Schweitzer recognizes (as indeed he could hardly fail to do) that he is coming to many of the same conclusions that had been previously reached by some Indian religions long before he articulated reverence for life: ethical concern for "all living beings existed in Indian thought for more than two thousand years."[19] This "boundless" ethic was *first clearly expressed by Jainism*" in the "ethic of ahimsā."[20] Whether or not Schweitzer had reached the same conclusion independently, he cannot but acknowledge their precedence.

This ambivalence is sufficiently sustained to raise queries: can this be an attempt, consciously or not, to evade an issue, to cover tracks, to remove certain matters from the possibility of scrutiny? A close comparison with Schweitzer's sources might throw light on the problem, but, remarkably enough, he gives not a single reference to an Indian text, only passing mention of a few thinkers (Moritz Winternitz, Romain Rolland, and C. F. Andrews). So it appears almost impossible—or Schweitzer has *made* it nearly impossible—to say how much he had read, and how much he had understood, about the subject and, hence, to evaluate his debt (if any).

Given this reticence, the following statements on ahimsā are deeply significant. Schweitzer heralds the Jain articulation of "the commandment not to kill and not to injure as one of *the greatest events in the spiritual history of mankind.*"[21] The adulation given to ahimsā is unparalleled in any of his other writings. It is difficult to find a passage even on Jesus where Schweitzer's praise is so unstinting. And his acclamation continues: "What is new in Jainism is the importance attained by ethics [in a religion]."[22] He lauds the Jains' departure from the traditional ethics and ceremonial sacrifices of the Brahmins where the principle "not to kill and not to harm living creatures (ahimsā) first becomes a great commandment."[23] Through ahimsā, human thought "reaches the tremendous discovery that ethics know no bounds!"[24] By placing "all life" in the realm of ethical consideration, he credits Jainism with having "pushed forward to a stage of knowledge which is quite outside the purview of European thinking"[25] and for "preserving safely through the centuries the great ethical thought which is connected with ahimsā."[26]

Schweitzer's enthusiasm could hardly be greater when he discovers (in "later" expositions) the union of ahimsā with affirmation philosophy: when ahimsā "is united to the idea of activity directed on the world [it] has the importance not merely of an event in the thought of India but in that of humanity."[27] On balance, these quotations should not be taken as offhand praise or as isolated remarks, but rather as the signaling of an (inconsistently acknowledged) intellectual influence.

Third, in Schweitzer's phrase *Indian thought,* it is not only the noun that puzzles the reader. As also with *"Indian ethics," "Indian religions,"* and the *"philosophy of the Indians,"* the terminology suggests a monolithic conception of the highly diverse religious and ethical beliefs and practices of the subcontinent; though he is not the only Western scholar of which this might be said. A similar latitude of meaning is at play in the major attempts to write a history of *Indian literature* during the second half of the nineteenth century and the first half of the twentieth. This is certainly true of classic studies such as Albrecht Weber's *Vorlesungen Über indische Literaturgeschichte* (1852), Friedrich Max Müller's *History of Ancient Sanskrit Literature* (1859), and Moritz Winternitz's *History of Indian Literature* (1907). Winternitz (whom Schweitzer mentions as a source of information on Indian religions) made the all-encompassing meaning of *In-*

dian literature explicit when he remarked that, as far as the contents of his project were concerned, "'Indian literature' embraces everything which the word 'literature' comprises in its widest sense."[28] Of course, there were many translations of Jain *Sutras* and numerous studies specifically of Jainism available in Europe in Schweitzer's time.[29] But thanks to him, we cannot say with certainty which, if any, he read.

As far as is known, Schweitzer never saw Indian religious life in practice. Neither did he acquire a personal knowledge of Indian religions nor study them from within each tradition by their own adherents. In a letter to Prime Minister Lal Bahadur Shastri in the year before he died, Schweitzer acknowledges several Indian friends, including Prime Minister Jawaharlal Nehru, C. F. Andrews, and Gandhi, whom he contacted through Andrews. He writes, "So those were my Indian friends. Little by little they were joined by others because I was seriously studying Indian thought, to which I felt drawn."[30] In the absence of his correspondences, it is impossible to say how much discussion of Indian religious ideas was involved. What is known is that he did not read Sanskrit (or Prakrit, the original language of the Jain canon), and often the critical research available on such subjects was not written from within the Jain community and reflected many of the same European prejudices to Indian religions that Schweitzer held. These issues raise questions about what historical, philosophical, or theological knowledge of Indian religions Schweitzer held when comparing them with his own beliefs. His criticisms and characterizations are those of an outsider and are not always wholly factual.

At first reading, Schweitzer's general terminology allows for little in-depth analysis on the influence of a specific Indian religion. But the solution to these puzzles is evident. The reader soon learns that by his terms *Indian thought*, *Indian religions*, and *Indian ethics*, he often means no more than some feature of a particular religion in which he is himself particularly interested. Thus when Schweitzer writes "I reached the conclusion that *Indian ethics* is correct in demanding kindness and mercy not only toward human beings but toward all living creatures," he is evidently referring specifically to the doctrine of ahimsā within the Jain tradition, and not for example to the Brahman "ethic of ritual sacrifice" where "the great commandment not to kill and not to injure living creatures plays no part" and which is "unethical."[31] Although the concept of ahimsā is present in various forms in several Indian religions, it is clear that he understood this nonviolent, universal ethic to be most closely associated with Jainism: "The Indian religion of Jainism praises nonviolence, which they call ahimsā, and regard it as the highest form of ethics."[32] His lack of attention to detail appears intentional, and not to stem entirely from lack of knowledge:

The deliberate brevity of my treatise may give occasion to all kinds of misunderstanding. I had no intention of describing Indian philosophy in detail, but only wanted to show how it regards the great problems of life and how it undertakes to solve them. To bring this as clearly as possible into the light of day I drew my sketch with broad, firm lines. This is why anybody who is at home in Indian thought will miss so many details which in his eyes belong to the ideas and thoughts concerned and specially characterize and color them.[33]

Despite acknowledging that this lack of detail may result in "all kinds of misunderstanding," Schweitzer nonetheless proceeds in this careless fashion. To even the mild skeptic, the passage smacks of disingenuousness; it lends further support to the view that he is attempting to hide his intellectual indebtedness in a veil.

Affirmation and Negation

Following Schopenhauer's view that the *"fundamental difference* in all religions is to be found in the question whether they are optimistic or pessimistic," Schweitzer distinguishes Indian and European thought on the basis of *affirmation* and *negation* philosophies.[34] Schweitzer's understanding of affirmation and negation philosophy is based on what can only be called a crude polarization between Western and Indian religious worldviews. Such notions represent ideal types. In his scheme world- and life-affirmation consists in this: "That man regards existence as he experiences it in himself and as it has developed in the world as something of value *per se*."[35] World- and life-negation, conversely, consist in "man regarding existence as he experiences it in himself and as it is developed in the world as something meaningless and sorrowful, and he resolves accordingly (a) to bring life to a standstill in himself by mortifying his will-to-live, and (b) to renounce all activity which aims at improvement of the conditions of this world."[36]

As Schweitzer grasps it, world- and life-negation philosophies largely developed through the rise of Jainism and Buddhism and their emphasis on a doctrine of reincarnation and *karma*. "It was only when the idea of reincarnation began to interest the masses, and when fear of constantly returning to existence began to rule men's minds, that there arose the great movement towards renunciation of the world which then continued for centuries."[37] The historical accuracy of this comment is certainly open to debate. But as he presents it, liberation from the cycle of rebirths (i.e., *moksa* or *nirvana*) is accomplished through and equated with freedom from the physical world (a negation of the will-to-live).

Negation philosophy is illogical to Schweitzer. To turn the will-to-live into will-*not-to-live* would involve a self-contradiction; one is forced to make constant concessions to the will-to-live in order to maintain basic physical sustenance:

> To remain alive, even in the most miserable fashion, presupposes some activity conducive to the maintenance of life. Even the ascetic, who is most strict of all men in his world- and life-negation, cannot escape from that. He picks berries, goes to the spring, fills his drinking-cup, perhaps even washes himself now and then.
>
> Passing from concessions to concessions, which have to be made if men who live the world-view of world- and life-negation are to remain alive, the decision is reached that what really matters is not so much actual abstention from action as that men should act in a spirit of non-activity and in inner freedom from the world so that action may lose all significance. In order not to be obliged to confess to themselves how much of world- and life-negation is abandoned, they have recourse to a method of regarding things which savors of relativity.[38]

Any "concession" to maintaining life (even eating or drinking) is deemed incompatible with life-negation. Schweitzer shows no knowledge of how for Jains, *sallekhana* (sacred death), or voluntary fast unto death, is considered the most auspicious way to die for those who are spiritually prepared. Often misunderstood as suicide, Jains view this "holy death" not as suicide but as a ritualized leaving of the body, the purpose of which is spiritual advancement. Schweitzer likewise dismisses the idea that individuals follow life-negation in a spirit of nonattachment, and not in a literal manner of total nonmovement. The choice is clear but hardly fair: to avoid *relativity*, we have to decide either on suicide through starvation and dehydration or on life-affirmation. It comes as little surprise that life-affirmation was the only *logical* response to him.

Schweitzer does not discuss Jain soteriology and how it embraces an entirely different understanding of activity and karma. To this soteriological relation between *action* and *intention* and the relevance of his critique we will shortly turn. For now, it is worth noting that similar charges of relativism and inconsistency are often brought against Schweitzer. Although he endorses an absolute, life-affirming ethic, he acknowledges that in some cases it is "more ethical" to kill the animal than to keep it alive. But Schweitzer fails to see the relativism inherent in his own position or in his use of arguments against Jainism which he rejects when used against him. He is considerably less flexible in his interpretation of Jain life-negation than with his own views.

Schweitzer uses this skewed interpretation of Jain negation philosophy as a means to mark the difference with his own "ethical life-affirmation" that "takes an active interest in the welfare of beings that belong to this world."[39] Since, in his opinion, ethics involves activity, life-negation (i.e., a withdrawal from worldly affairs) and ethics are "incongruous." In order to "escape this fate" of inconsistency, Jainism "limits itself" to a "*non*-active ethic." Such an ethic can only demand "that in a spirit of kindliness completely free from hatred [one]...refrain from destroying or damaging any living thing." But, crucially, "*active love* it cannot demand of him."[40] His critique, as we shall see, misses the mark. In short, he is unable to discern that for Jains, ahimsā is not inextricably bound to negation philosophy. On the contrary, it embraces active service.

Schweitzer's presentation of life-affirmation promotes social service and meaningfulness of life, while life-negation takes little interest in the world and exalts immobility. It is a caricature to focus on an Indian mystic lost in contemplation and with little interest in the world, while his or her Western counterpart is actively engaged in the world and in fruitful union with the Divine. This portrayal of Jain negation philosophy provides a rhetorical instrument for him. Jainism functions as a model of a life-denying way of thought, useful as a counterpole to his own ideas, as a device for saying succinctly (if not always accurately) what it is he disapproves of and wants to change. As with his treatment of Schopenhauer and Nietzsche, Schweitzer takes a key idea from Jainism whose general case is repugnant to him, indeed his antimodel. The persistence of these binary oppositions is a blinker of his thought.

In general, the approach to other religions is less factually descriptive than typological and evaluative, in particular regard to ethical inquiry. The primary interest of his text on Indian thought is an examination of the extent to which their various ethical doctrines are in accord with his ethic of reverence for life. He uses *his* own ethic and *his* own world- and life-view as the basis from which to evaluate other religious and ethical thought whilst presenting it as objective. If Schweitzer highlights everything severe and intransigent about Jain negation thought, it is perhaps because he needs it as a foil to his own exposition of affirmation philosophy. He is partial to those notions that are in accord with his own views, and too readily dismissive of alternative ideas. Schweitzer's eye was more European than trans-European; or, his trans-European vision saw Jainism through a powerful Schweitzerian lens.[41]

The Jain Vision

Closer examination of the precepts and practices of Jainism may help our understanding at this point. Among political, social, economic, and artistic achievements, sixth to fifth century B.C. E. India is distinguished by the propagation of Jainism, Buddhism, and other heterodox religious sects. In opposition to the Brahmans, many ascetics and spiritual aspirants (*Sramanas*) rejected the Vedic tradition. In their origin, both Jainism and Buddhism were *Sramana* movements. Whereas the Vedic tradition was believed to be founded on inequality, Jainism and Buddhism were established on ideas of greater equality (*karma*). Brahman inequality was held to be manifested in three ways: through social class, namely, the caste system; with reference to the aim and view of prosperity here and in heaven; and with regard to the ethical consideration of living beings and the Vedic ritual sacrifices. Each of these three inequalities, and particularly the last one, were addressed by the development of ahimsā. The principle and practice of ahimsā is most closely identified with the Jain tradition.

The name Jainism, derived from the word *jina*, means "conqueror." Jains are followers of the path established by the Jinas who were said to have "conquered" the suffering (*dukkha*) of this world. Ahimsā, a practice of non-injury that respects all life, constitutes the primary religious and moral precept for all Jains. In the presence of a holy person, a Jain aspirant repeats the ancient formula:

> I will desist from the knowing or intentional destruction of all great
> lives. As long as I live, I will neither kill nor cause others to kill.
> I shall strive to refrain from all such activities, whether of body,
> speech or mind.[42]

The first written documents in Jainism offer a doctrine of rebirth that advances strict adherence to ethical principle of ahimsā.[43] Jainism claims immemorial antiquity. Its last leader, Lord Mahavira, restored an ancient faith; he is not held to have originated it. He is believed to be the last of twenty-four *Tirthamkara* (or Fordmaker, the person who shows the crossing to the other shore of existence). According to Jain tradition, Mahavira (Great Hero) was born in 599 B.C.E., though some scholars put his date fifty or more years later. Like the Buddha, at the age of thirty he renounced the world to lead the life of a wandering holy man to search for happiness. After twelve years of penances and austerities, he gained release from this world to a state of omniscience. Aged seventy-two, Mahavira is held to have attained final moksa. Mahavira's message was that one's karma was of the utmost significance, while birth and caste were of no importance. One's future happiness depended on the elimination of karma that was directly related to avoiding the injury or destruction of any *jiva* (soul, or life-monad).

Broadly speaking, Jain practice is conditioned by three separate but interrelated beliefs. First, nearly all matter in the natural world is alive; that is, matter contains souls (*jiva*). Second, injury to any living being is unethical. Third, actions inevitably have results that will affect future states and future rebirths of the agent. This third belief, the doctrine of karma, entails a strict observance of ethical tenets based on ahimsā. For Jains, ahimsā is not simply the first among virtues but constitutes the supreme moral virtue (*ahimsā paramo dharma*). Of the five *Anuvratas*, the fundamental tenets of Jainism whereby karmic influx can be contained, ahimsā is the first.

Though *himsā* is often understood as harm done to others, for Jains, it includes injury to oneself—to that behavior which hinders the soul's capacity to attain liberation. The killing of animals, for example, is reprehensible not only for the suffering produced in the victims, but "even more so because it involves intense passions on the part of the killer, passions which bind him more firmly in the grip of *samsāra* [the cycle of rebirths]."[44] Harmful action (*himsā*) results in karmic bondage which ensures that, upon death, the jiva will be reborn either in this world or another world, as opposed to achieving a state of liberation and bliss at the top of the universe.

To avoid bondage, it is necessary to observe a vow of non-violence toward all creatures. Additionally, in order to liberate oneself from the negative influences of karma, Jains take a series of vows (*vratas*) that are believed to aid them in a purging of karmic residue previously accumulated through bad activity. But since jivas are held to embody everything in the natural world (including things often considered as inanimate), it is evident that to perform almost any physical action without harming them is extremely difficult. Indeed, in early Jain doctrine there is no mention of meritorious activity; physical activity of any sort was harmful to other jivas and binding. Only by restraint from action could one decrease the amount of bad karma "stuck" on the jiva and attain a better rebirth. The intention behind one's actions is important in the early texts only insofar as it could lead to or away from himsā; what is significant for salvation is the physical harm done, its cause being secondary.

Jain thought later shifted away from a strict emphasis on one's *actions* to a focus on the *intentions* of the individual committing himsā. But Schweitzer's critique of Jain life-negation, as might be expected, fails to appreciate these complexities (or it was not in his nature to be alert for them). "Jainism" is not monolithic, any more than "Indian religions."

Path to Liberation

The impact of this doctrine of internalization is apparent in the writing of Umāsvāti. The first textual synthesis of Jain doctrine is his *Tattvārtha Sutra* (Manual for Understanding the Reals), written sometime between 150 C. E. and 350 C.E. The *Tattvārtha* was an attempt to systematize the various components (epistemological, metaphysical, cosmological, ethical, and practical) of the Jain path to liberation and also to reconcile monastic and lay (or active) concerns. The key to this synthesis and reconciliation was a new doctrine of the mechanism of bondage (*bandha*).

The new synthesis advanced a *kasāya* doctrine, positing that greater or lesser degrees of bondage were the result of the degree of intention that motivated the act. Umāsvāti provided what has become the standard definition of himsā: "The destruction of life out of passion."[45] Nearly the whole emphasis—at least doctrinally—is changed to the internal state of the agent.

In addition to Umāsvāti's doctrine of internalization, it is important to note that ahimsā (far from Schweitzer's understanding of it) represents not only nonviolence as a negative duty, but is also seen to evoke compassion for all life. The Jain commitment to ahimsā is reflected in *active* concern with the prevention and alleviation of suffering. For instance, an attempt by an eighteenth-century monk called Bhikhanji to found a sect based on the doctrine of total nonassistance to any living being (except monks) was met with protest by nearly the entire Jain community. Bhikhanji's view was that the saving of the life of an animal makes one responsible for all the violence the animal commits in the future and, therefore, should be avoided.

Bhikhanji brings to light the difficulties inherent in the Jain espousal of total nonviolence leading to moksa, and the importance afforded to compassionate and charitable behavior leading to rebirth in the realm of heaven. His view typifies Schweitzer's rigid understanding of negation philosophy. To Bhikhanji's and Schweitzer's defense, some of the canonical teachings may well be seen to justify this interpretation. But Bhikhanji's theory was rejected. Schweitzer's "broad brush strokes" glide past these details, complexities for which most likely he lacks the necessary antennae.

In addition to nonviolence, ahimsā has another role, that of *karuna* (compassion), and calls forth action to alleviate suffering. This notion captures the positive spirit that is to accompany the negative injunctions. The following two quotations highlight the centrality of reverence in Jainism. In one passage from the *Agamas* (scriptures), Mahavira spoke of ahimsā in this way: "Unless we live with non-violence and reverence for all living beings in our hearts, all our humaneness and acts of good[ness] . . . are fruitless."[46] Jain Yogasastra also gives a definition of nonviolence in Schweitzer-like language: "Reverence for life is the supreme religious teaching. Non-injury to life is the supreme moral guidance. . . . There is no quality of soul more subtle than non-violence and no virtue of spirit greater than reverence for life."[47] Sadhvi Shilapiji comments:

> Ahimsā in its truest sense does not only mean not to injure others but also embraces the universal law of love and compassion for all beings. . . . Abstention from all kinds of injury to anyone is the negative approach of ahimsā. The development of strong fellow feeling and compassion can be achieved by adopting ahimsā in its positive sense.[48]

This life-affirmation aspect of ahimsā is absent in Schweitzer's critique of Jainism. As he presents it (or needed to present it to proclaim novelty), reverence for life departs from the Jain application of ahimsā. Reverence prescribes not only noninjury to other life, but also enjoins active love: "The characteristic attitude [of ahimsā] is less a positive reverence for life, than a negative duty to refrain from destroying."[49]

Schweitzer neglects Umāsvāti"s emphasis on intention (kasāya) and the "positive virtues," such as compassion (karuna), inherent in Jain ethics. His negligence cannot be attributed to the inadequacy of extant information; in 1906, Hermann Jacobi brought forth a translation and commentary on this doctrine in *Eine Jaina-Dogmatik: Umāsvāti's Tattvārthādhigama-Sutra*. Far from Schweitzer's narrow presentation, it is clear that ahimsā shares considerably more in common with reverence for life than he realized or wished to make clear.

Treasures of Thought

Having considered some of the main elements and deficiencies of Schweitzer's analysis of ahimsā, we are now in a position to examine some of the other lines of correspondence between Schweitzerian and Jain thought. Both are concerned with establishing a spiritual and ethical ground that will serve all life. For Schweitzer, the physical and spiritual dynamic of life is located in the will-to-live, in Jainism the jiva is the life-force and soul of each being. Each arrives at a focus on the will-to-live or the jiva through meditation on life and existence itself.

If we ask, "What is the immediate fact of my consciousness? What do I self-consciously know of myself, making abstraction of all else?" according to

Schweitzer, "the simple fact of consciousness is this, *I will to live.*"[50] He criticizes Descartes' dictum "I think, therefore I am" (*Cogito, ergo sum*), and locates apprehension of the will-to-live as the starting point of philosophy:

> Descartes built an artificial structure by presuming that man knows
> nothing, and doubts all, whether outside himself or within. And
> in order to end doubt, he fell back on the fact of consciousness:
> *I think.* . . . Who can establish this fact that he thinks, except in rela-
> tion to thinking *something*? And what that something is, is the im-
> portant matter.[51]

Although by no means the first thinker to criticize Descartes on this point, what is significant is Schweitzer's conception of personhood. For him, underlying Cartesian method is the assertion that the self is autonomous (i.e., the "I" that "thinks") and stands above and apart from nature. In contrast, Schweitzer conceptualizes personhood as a matter of living in the presence of other life: "True philosophy must start from the most immediate and comprehensive fact of consciousness, which says: 'I am life which wills to live in the midst of life which wills to live.'"[52] This proposition originates from the physiological make-up and the ontological unity of all life: "This, then, is the nature and origin of ethics; it is born of physical life, out of the linking of life with life."[53]

Schweitzer's view that all living things are of the same will serves as the basis of his ethics. His (ethical) anthropology is predicated on the human as person-in-community rather than individual being: "No human being is ever totally and permanently a stranger to another being."[54] In commentary, Schweitzer takes a swipe at Cartesianism: "It seems as if Descartes with his dictum that animals are mere machines had bewitched the whole of European philosophy."[55]

In *Sacred Books of the East* (a seminal translation of various Indian religious texts available to Schweitzer), Hermann Jacobi writes that Jainism arrived at the concept of the soul "not through the search after the Self, the self-existing unchangeable principle in the ever-changing world of phenomena, but through the perception of life."[56] For the most general Jain term for soul is "life" (*jiva*), which is identical with "self" (*āyā, ātman*). As Padmanabh S. Jaini affirms, "external demonstrations for this reality" are considered "superfluous; the simple experience of self-awareness (*ahampratyaya*) is proof enough."[57] He explains:

> Even doubt—for example, "is there really a self here?"—supports this
> view when one asks the further question, "who is it that has the
> doubt?" The answer given, of course, is *jiva*, the basic "I" that stands
> behind all human actions.[58]

The likeness of Schweitzer's conception of existence (life) and consciousness (self) with the Jain position is evident. But, unlike Schopenhauer, who acknowledges that his theory of the self "could not have been formulated" without the Upanishads, Schweitzer is silent on these matters.

A key parallel between Schweitzerian and Jain thought is found in their conceptions of the tragic nature of life. For both, the world is the source of much suffering. As Schweitzer repeatedly discusses, life and suffering are interconnected: "Life means feeling, sensitivity, suffering."[59] In Jainism the existence of a karma-bound self is readily evident. This underscores the view that suffering (dukkha) is inherent in the very fabric of life. For both, sensitivity to the suffering in the world requires humans not only to renounce violence against life as far as is possible, but also to alleviate it.

In Jainism, as one comes to understand the extent of suffering in one's own life, there is a development in concern for others' sufferings. The importance of "comparing oneself with others" is stressed repeatedly: "All living beings love their life. For them happiness is desirable; unhappiness is not desirable. No living being likes to be killed. Every living being is desirous of life. Every living being loves its own life." Likewise, the Kritānga Sutra advises that one should go about "treating all creatures in the world as he himself would be treated." Similarly, at Ayāramga 1.4.2.6, the suffering of others is proved by inference from personal suffering: "Is pain pleasant to you or unpleasant? ... For all sorts of living beings pain is unpleasant, disagreeable and greatly feared."[60] Echoing the moral sensitivity to other life present in the Jain Sutras, Schweitzer encourages the extension of moral concern to other species:

> The poor fly which we would kill with our hands has come into existence like ourselves. It knows anxiety, it knows hope for happiness, it knows fear of not existing any more.... The beetle that lies dead in your path—it was something that lived, that struggled for its existence like you, that rejoiced in the sun like you, that knew anxiety and pain like you.[61]
>
> The friend of nature is the man who feels himself inwardly united with everything that lives in nature, who shares in the fate of all creatures, helps them when he can in their pain and need, and as far as possible avoids injuring or taking life.[62]

Schweitzer and Jainism both take the view that it is unethical to inflict on other beings what you yourself find unpleasant. Other beings are just like oneself in desiring pleasure and disliking pain. Schweitzer and Jainism appeal to one's own experience, extended to other beings through empathy and compassion, as a reason for practicing reverence for life and ahimsā. Of course, based on Schweitzer's writings, it is impossible to say how knowledgeable he was of Jain conceptions of the tragic. But his position corresponds too closely to deem it pure coincidence.

It is worth pointing out that the empathy and compassion called for by both Jainism and Schweitzer is not without its own problems. It applies to all creatures without exception. But if the degree of "inward unification" with other creatures is carried to extreme, it is open to Max Scheler's criticism that if the moral agent identifies with the sufferer to the extent that he or she loses his or her identity and is no longer distinguished from the sufferer, then compassion becomes impossible. If identification with the sufferer is to such an extent that the sufferer's pain becomes one's own pain, then compassion will not arise. Rather, the motivation to relieve suffering will be "egotistical," since one would be trying to relieve one's own pain. Compassion, Scheler argues, presupposes a *distinction* between beings and is always directed toward others. Awareness that one is different from the sufferer is necessary for an action to have moral worth.[63]

Is the distinction between beings abolished in Schweitzer's theory of the will and his conception of compassion? Does he have the same kind of identification in mind as Scheler does? It is true that Schweitzer sometimes writes in such a way as to invite this criticism. His sermon on Romans 14:7 ("None of us lives to himself, and none of us dies to himself") gravitates in this direction:

> Wherever you see life—that is you! In everything you recognize yourself again, . . . a compassionate sharing of experiences with all of life. I can do no other than to have compassion for all that is called life.
>
> We are ethical if we abandon our selfishness, if we surrender our estrangement toward other creatures, and share in and empathies with that from their experience which surrounds us.[64]

Schweitzer's understanding of compassion is literal; that is, agents actually experience another's suffering through compassion. But he fails to explain the possibility of this extraordinary experience in his sermon. The tables are turned; for once his philosophy may help elucidate his theology. Returning to his metaphysics, Schweitzer claims that the individual who sees only the diversity and plurality of beings in the world (i.e., phenomenal objects devoid of any inner nature) misses the crux of the matter: although all beings are separate, they share the same underlying reality (will-to-live). Following Kant's transcendental aesthetic, Schweitzer maintains that space and time, which make plurality possible, are subjective (i.e., simply a function of human cognition) and apply only to appearances and do not belong to things-in-themselves.[65]

Consequently, for Schweitzer, separateness is an illusion. So long as one perceives the world in this phenomenal fashion, one is precluded from the Schweitzerian truth about the inner nature of reality: the will-to-live and its source, the infinite Will-to-Live. According to his identification theory, the compassionate person recognizes other beings as inhabited by the same nature as him- or herself—experiencing a similar kind of suffering—and pursuing the other's well-being as if it were his/her own. Schweitzer presents the idea that we need not accept our individuality as the only perspective from which to regard other life. But grounding compassion in his metaphysics of the will, as Scheler might point out, certainly involves him in groundless assumptions.

The next affinity pertains to another aspect of the tragic in nature, or what Schweitzer calls the *law of necessity*, which forces humans to live at the cost of injuring and destroying life. But he wrongly suggests that Jainism does not grasp this idea and actually criticizes the tradition on this point.

> Ethics without limits cannot be completely complied with, but Jain thinking did not discuss this fact. It did not admit it at all. In incomprehensible fashion it clung fast to its illusion, as if not-killing and not-harming were completely possible of fulfillment by anyone who takes the matter seriously. Thus the Jains pass by the great problem as if it did not exist. However seriously man undertakes to abstain from killing and damaging, he cannot entirely avoid it. He is under the law of necessity, which compels him to kill and to damage both with and without his knowledge.[66]

As we have seen, Schweitzer is oblivious to Umāsvāti's *kaṣāya* doctrine which (acknowledging the impossibility of an injury-free life) focuses on the internal state of the agent and distinguishes between intentional and unintentional killing. Far from Jainism passing by this "great problem as if it did not exist," it is Schweitzer who in "incomprehensible fashion clung fast" to his own illusions. For, he falls even further into error when he claim that Jainism "did not discuss" and "did not admit at all" the complexities intrinsic to a boundless ethic. As one Jain thinker noted:

> Life thrives on life. The ideal practice of non-injury is not possible. Do whatever we will, some life must be transformed into our life in order to sustain it. Therefore what is meant and enjoined is simply this: "Do not destroy life, unless it is absolutely necessary

for the maintenance of a higher kind of life." The purer souls will, of course, not like to sanction even this. But, as formulated above, the rule does not sanction hurting or injury: it limits it to the lowest possible minimum.[67]

Acknowledging the impossibility of total non-violence, the Jain tradition anticipates two key elements of Schweitzerian thought. First is the recognition that "life thrives on life," or, as Schweitzer put it: "Creatures live at the cost of the lives of other creatures."[68] This appears to be one of the rare occasions of close correspondence between presumed source and Schweitzer's thought. And the similarity continues: "Man cannot take his nourishment from the air and the earth as the plants do. The higher form of life destroys the lower in order to live from it. . . . But only when necessity leads us, can we [kill]. . . . We must perceive every act of destruction as something terrible and ask ourselves whether it is necessary or not."[69] Second, and in the light of this, Jainism makes a distinction between *necessary* and *ethical* killing. As seen, Schweitzer also affirms that humans "should damage and kill only when necessary." For both, although some killing is necessary, it is neither sanctioned nor ethical. It seems inconceivable that Schweitzer could have developed such insights independently.

Schweitzer believed that Indian and Western forms of thought could benefit from one another: "Both are the guardians of valuable treasures of thought." Through comparative study, Indian and European ethical thought could become aware of their "inadequacies" and be "stimulated to turn in the direction of what is more complete."[70] Since he regarded European thought which restricted moral concern to humans as spiritually and ethically impoverished, it is of little surprise that his praise for ahimsā is so profound. But Schweitzer is good at smokescreens; it seems all too likely that the question whether "the knowledge [i.e., ahimsā] imparted to Jainism by a marvelous dispensation of providence"[71] was a substantial influence, or no more than a confirmation of conclusions already reached independently, will always remain less than clear.

Schweitzer tells us that the phrase reverence for life "flashed" into his mind whilst traveling on the Ogowe River. But the ethical concepts present in the phrase were cultivated long before. Schweitzer reacts to a great range of intellectual stimuli, assimilating, modifying, picking and choosing, and then gradually constructing his ethic of reverence for life. Among the significant influences of Jesus, Paul and others, Schweitzer's rapport with Jainism and ahimsā helped him to articulate and discern the meaning of *reverence*.

4

Seeking the Kingdom

Schweitzer is sometimes only too aware of the caricature of himself as a former scholar now hidden away in the primeval forest. At dinner one evening at Schweitzer's home in Gunsbach, a guest was amazed by his knowledge of current theological works. Schweitzer exploded: "Yes, you are surprised that I know about this, aren't you! The learned theologians here in Europe are thinking, 'The jungle doctor sits in his hospital down there in Africa and doesn't know what we are thinking and writing up here.' Well, let me tell you something—I read it all!"[1]

The important thing to grasp is that the quest for reverence was not a separate path from his quest of the historical Jesus. It is a mistake to see Schweitzer as someone simply pulled in multifarious directions—philosophy, world religions, biblical studies. Rather, these were all fertile avenues of the overarching quest for the "basic principle of the moral" that he found in reverence.

Indeed, there is some evidence that Schweitzer conceived of a schema, beginning with Jesus, moving on to Paul, and culminating in reverence for life (with Bach as a musical interlude). Taken together, *Paul and His Interpreters* and *The Mysticism of the Apostle Paul* were to form the second volume of a comprehensive collection, *History of the Early Church*, with *The Quest of the Historical Jesus* as the first volume. The third volume was to trace the development of the Hellenisation of Christian thought through the Johannine literature and the sub–apostolic age to the Fathers of the Church. Schweitzer intended to follow the two parts of *The Philosophy of Civilization* with two more, *The World-view of Reverence for Life* and *Civilized State*, although time forbade the completion of this grandiose task. Also, a three-volume edition on Bach's Chorale Preludes never came to fruition.[2]

Central to the enterprise is Schweitzer's fascination with the figure of Jesus. Unsurprisingly, his research on the historical Jesus was far from neutral. Against those like Schopenhauer and Renan who "stripped off Jesus' halo and reduced him to a sentimental figure," Schweitzer's "aim" is "to depict the figure of Jesus in its overwhelming heroic greatness and to impress it upon the modern age and upon the modern theology."[3] There is a deep autobiographical significance to his observation that "there is no historical task which so reveals a man's true self as the writing of a life of Jesus."[4]

Between 1950 and 1951, he composed *The Kingdom of God and Primitive Christianity*, although, quite strangely, this work was not published until released by his daughter in 1969, three years after his death. This text shows how Schweitzer's *academic* convictions on Jesus had changed significantly from his first publication. In a footnote he acknowledges:

> I still believed that in the pre-Messianic tribulation a load of guilt that encumbered the world and was delaying the coming of the Kingdom could be expiated by believers, and that Jesus, therefore, in accordance with the Servant passages, regarded his vicarious sacrifice as an atonement. *As the result of further study of late Jewish eschatology and the thought of Jesus on his passion, I find that I can no longer endorse this view.*[5]

This footnote, perhaps the most important passage in the text, marks a critical shift in Schweitzer's historical research on Jesus. But, as we shall see, his *personal* (spiritual) convictions about Jesus remained almost the same throughout his life: fellowship with Jesus is not defined strictly by our historical knowledge, but primarily by union with his Spirit.

Painting the Portrait

The eschatological element of the "historical Jesus," previously disregarded, underemphasized, or "spiritualized" by the liberal Protestant life-of-Jesus research of the nineteenth century, was placed at the center of research primarily by Johannes Weiss and Schweitzer. In *Jesus' Proclamation of the Kingdom of God* (1892), Weiss maintained that Jesus expected the imminent establishment of the kingdom, a cataclysmic event in which humans had little or no role.

Schweitzer applied Weiss's thesis not only to the preaching of Jesus but also to his ministry and passion: "Weiss had gone only halfway. He realized that Jesus thought eschatologically but did not conclude from this that His actions were also determined by eschatology."[6] Schweitzer held that when Jesus sent out the Twelve, he did not expect them to return before the coming of the kingdom.[7] When they did return, Schweitzer postulates that Jesus realized it was necessary for him to assume the suffering that would precede the arrival of the kingdom and act as its necessary prelude. According to the eschatological hopes of ancient Judaism, this entailed his journey to Jerusalem to die. Jesus, thus, went to Jerusalem, so as to "at last compel the Coming of the Kingdom." Entering as the Messiah, Jesus "violently cleanses the Temple, and attacks the Pharisees, in the presence of people, with passionate invective," resulting in "the deliberate bringing down of death upon Himself."[8]

Although Jesus died in anticipation that his death would secure the establishment of the kingdom on earth, the kingdom was not fully consummated. In the oft-quoted passage from the *Quest*:

> Jesus...in the knowledge that He is the coming Son of Man lays
> hold the wheel of the world to set it moving on that last revolu-
> tion which is to bring all ordinary history to a close. It refuses to turn,
> and He throws Himself upon it. Then it does turn, and crushes Him.
> Instead of bringing in the eschatological conditions, He has de-
> stroyed them. The wheel rolls onward, and the mangled body
> of the one immeasurably great Man, who was strong enough to think
> of Himself as the spiritual ruler of mankind and to bend history
> to His purpose, is hanging upon it still. That is His victory and His
> reign.[9]

Schweitzer found it relatively unimportant that Jesus' eschatological expectations were not completely realized at that moment. What is of the utmost importance to him was Jesus' *attitude* toward the kingdom. Working in this determined and sacrificial spirit for the kingdom, as we shall see, becomes a dominant motif in Schweitzer's theology and ethics.

In order to understand better the historical Jesus, Schweitzer stresses the need to examine the setting of Jesus' own time. The world-view of Jesus' day was one in which apocalyptic thought, the idea of the imminent catastrophic end of the world-process, was prevalent. Schweitzer challenged the view held by much of the liberal Protestant school, which saw Jesus as primarily an ethical teacher; this historically inaccurate "modernization" of Jesus could be defended only by disregarding the eschatological dimension in the accounts of Jesus' ministry. Jesus was not a modern liberal expecting the progressive moral consummation of the kingdom, but, rather, a person of his own time expecting the imminent entering of the kingdom. Jesus' ethics could not be separated from his eschatology; they were *interim ethics*. Liberal theology could not justifiably dismiss the eschatological dimension to Jesus' ministry and restrict its focus to the "timeless" elements of his ethical teaching.

As evidenced by subsequent New Testament research, many of the details of Schweitzer's eschatological hypothesis are problematic, especially his emphasis on certain isolated texts in Matthew, such as 10:23. Though his reconstruction was perhaps less of a modernization than those of his predecessors, he belongs with the biographers of Jesus whom he criticized in that he placed weight on the Gospel as a historical record that could afford an accurate picture of Jesus. This is made plain by his remark that "the historical problem of the life of Jesus cannot be recognized, much less solved, from the fragmentary record of Mark. The differing narratives of the two oldest Gospels are equally valuable, but Matthew's fullness gives it greater importance."[10]

Characteristically, he does not subject his own picture of Jesus to the criticism he practices on other scholars.

Inward Revelation

That Jesus died and that history did not end does not, from Schweitzer's perspective, detract from his "superhuman greatness," or from the "abiding" power of his life, or from the "eternal" value of his words.[11] As we have seen, Schweitzer altered his academic conclusions on the historical Jesus. But he remained committed to the view that "spiritual truth...lies on a different plane from the knowledge of affairs of this world, and it is quite independent of it."[12] Spiritual knowledge of Jesus supersedes historical information about him. Thus, Schweitzer begins to construct with his own theological convictions a *spiritualized* version of the historical Jesus.

Without reservation or modification, Schweitzer states, "The Jesus of history is for our time a stranger and an enigma."[13] Christians entrenched in the modern outlook of world- and life-affirmation could not relate to Jesus' eschatological thought (which contained elements of negation philosophy) and brushed it aside. For Schweitzer, our historical and spiritual knowledge of Jesus remains shallow so long as the eschatological basis of Jesus' thought is disregarded. Understanding the historical Jesus' eschatology is not strictly an intellectual matter. As J. C. O'Neill points out, Schweitzer maintains that New Testament scholarship alone will not inform the historian:

Schweitzer's contemporaries failed to understand Jesus not because they could make nothing of the bizarre eschatology, but because their willing and hoping was not strongly determined towards achieving [the kingdom]. They had no equivalent to the thought of Jesus.[14]

Understanding the historical Jesus is related to a personal commitment to the kingdom. The more our "willing and hoping" resembles that of Jesus, the greater our understanding of him: "We possess just so much of an understanding of the historical Jesus as we possess a strong, passionate faith in the Kingdom of God."[15] Despite Schweitzer's emphasis on keeping the historical lineaments of Jesus as a first-century Jew, he believes that no matter how detailed our historical knowledge of Jesus may be, it will not reveal to us what we "want to know," since "historical knowledge cannot call spiritual life into existence." The primacy of the spiritual over the historical is apparent:

> Jesus means something to our world because a mighty spiritual force streams forth from Him and flows through our time also. This fact can neither be shaken nor confirmed by any historical discovery. It is the solid foundation of Christianity.[16]

On the one hand, Schweitzer emphasizes the necessary limits to all historical research. Historical knowledge, no matter how detailed and abundant, cannot call spiritual life into existence; we need to find a way to transcend historical analysis in order to receive spiritual knowledge of Jesus. On the other hand, Schweitzer stresses that the *abiding and eternal* in Jesus must not be disengaged from the historical forms from which it was derived. Historical knowledge can help to kindle spiritual apprehension of Jesus. But it cannot be the sole basis of faith: "History will force it [theology] to find a way to transcend history, and to fight for the lordship and rule of Jesus over this world with weapons tempered in a different forge."[17] Schweitzer's weapon of choice, as we shall see, is the Spirit.

In spite of Schweitzer's lengthy historical investigation on Jesus, historical findings are deemed secondary to inward spiritual revelation:

> But the truth is it is not Jesus as historically known, but Jesus as spiritually arisen within men, who is significant for our time and can help it. Not the historical Jesus, but the Spirit which goes forth from Him and in the spirits of men strives for new influence and rule, is that which overcomes the world....
>
> ...The abiding and eternal in Jesus is absolutely independent of historical knowledge and can only be understood by

contact with His Spirit which is still at work in the world. In proportion as we have the Spirit of Jesus, we have the true knowledge of Jesus.[18]

Attempts to know Jesus must move beyond the quest for knowledge of the historical Jesus ("Christ after the flesh"), and seek to know him through his Spirit. Schweitzer's remarks about the apostle pertain equally well to himself: "Paul abides by the principle that the truth about Christ ... is not received from the traditional narratives and doctrines, but from revelations given by the Spirit of Jesus Christ."[19] The "quest" leads to fellowship with Christ through the Spirit which for Schweitzer is nothing short of an "inner revelation."[20]

An integral characteristic of Schweitzer's Christology is the activity of the Spirit beyond the history of Jesus; the Spirit serves as the trans-historical mode of Jesus' relationship with humanity. Schweitzer points to Jesus' Spirit as a new hermeneutic to transcend positivistic historicism: the historical Jesus is present wherever the Spirit is attendant because "the Spirit was in Him."[21] The Spirit within is, for Schweitzer, continuous with the Spirit of Jesus.

In *The Mystical Element of Religion*, Friedrich von Hügel draws attention to the "apparent interior antinomy" that exists between "the particular concrete experience that alone moves us and helps us to determine our will but which, seemingly, is untransferable, indeed unrepeatable; and the general abstract reasoning which is repeatable, indeed transferable, but which does not move us or help directly to determine the will."[22] This "apparent interior antinomy" is analogous to the two tendencies Schweitzer understands in relation to the historical Jesus. In the historical and the spiritual, there is an antinomy between what is communicable but inadequate, and what is less easily communicated but which he feels to be the core. A good deal of historical research is communicable. But the core of the matter (i.e., inward revelation of the Spirit) is something that one must apprehend for oneself.

Schweitzer's account appears still under the influence of the liberalism he thought he rejected. He attaches his *own* doctrine of the Spirit to Jesus and the Gospel and, in so doing, makes the same "mistake" that he accuses his liberal predecessors of making. Following one of the central tenets of liberal Protestant theology, the foundation of the Christian faith is more spiritual than historical and, therefore, timeless. He cannot escape the criticism of interpreting Jesus according to the Spirit and the moral problems of his own time. Schweitzer, too, looking deep into the well for Jesus found the reflection of his own face. His New Testament scholarship, as we shall continue to see, merges with his ethical convictions.

Historical Puzzles

For Schweitzer, an (historical) appreciation of Jesus' eschatology is important because it can spur on our own ardor to realize the kingdom. An eschatological world-view is appropriate for any time, "for in every world they raise the man who dares to meet their challenge . . . above his world and his time."[23] Christians are called upon to uphold an eschatological world-view that encourages them to live, like Jesus, *as if* the kingdom was imminent.

"That which is eternal in the words of Jesus," argues Schweitzer, "is due to the very fact that they are based on an eschatological worldview."[24] This last line helps to elucidate the unstated hermeneutic: eschatology is important because it serves moral purposes for all times. The central features of Jesus' eschatology, as Schweitzer presents them, are its transtemporality and moral import. Jesus' eschatological discourse addresses the future in such a way so as also to speak about and to every time. The transtemporal nature of eschatological discourse goes together with its ethical character in that, as a discourse about the future of time, eschatology makes moral judgments on all times. Eschatology serves not only as the principal lens by which Schweitzer performs his academic investigation into the historical Jesus, but it is also the primary means by which believers can capture the importance of Jesus' ethical teaching in the present.

Although eschatological thought can be seen to exhort people away from working to improve the present conditions of the world which could soon pass away, this is not, Schweitzer believes, applicable to Jesus. Jesus' affirmation of a more perfect world to come did not spur him toward asceticism or withdrawal: "Instead of denying the material world because its gaze is directed to pure Being, Jesus only denies the evil, imperfect world in expectation of a good and perfect world which is to come."[25] The dialectic of Schweitzer's eschatology rests upon the belief that this world continues to exist, and we must work in it and improve it ("active in the world"), and yet we must not be absorbed into it ("free from the world"), since the kingdom is coming. The eschatological foundation of Jesus' sayings is seen neither to abolish their significance nor to impart passivity, but rather to afford them immediacy and retain something like the original urgency:

> What matters is this: that the significance of the concept of the
> Kingdom of God for our world-view is the same as it was for Him,
> and that we experience in the same way that He did the urgency and
> the power of that concept.[26]

The continuity between Jesus and the present lies in eschatology. But Schweitzer does not question whether it is hermeneutically possible that the concept of the kingdom could be "the same" for our world-view as it was for Jesus.

Schweitzer's interpretation, here, of the kingdom again appears consistent with those of his Protestant liberal counterparts. Although he vehemently rejected liberalism's historical account, he accepts many of its ethical insights. The liberal Protestants' account of Jesus went historically astray, but their account of eschatology as inspiring ethical engagement in this world held merit to him.

The question arises as to what extent Schweitzer consciously or unconsciously used his New Testament scholarship as a means for conveying his ethical convictions. Although he does not reduce the religious to the ethical, at every point, the religious is interpreted in relation to the ethical.

Preaching the Kingdom

The association of eschatology and ethical action in Schweitzer's work dates back to his earliest publications. In 1900 (at the age of twenty-five), he presented the theme of the "decay of civilization" in his essay "Philosophy and General Education in the Nineteenth Century," where he anticipates many of the concerns later refined in The Philosophy of Civilization. At the same time, he was also engaged in writing The Mystery of the Kingdom of God. It appears that while writing these two works—one on the decay of civilization and the other on Jesus' eschatology—Schweitzer saw an association between civilization, ethics, and eschatology. His sermons "Creative Suffering" and "Compelling Hope" (also written during that time period) illustrate this same connection. As he presents it, the more nineteenth-century European thought became detached from an eschatological worldview, the further civilization moved away from making spiritual and ethical progress. For this situation, Schweitzer preached the following solution: "Modest work for the kingdom of God is the order of the day."[27] A connection is made between one's work toward the realization of the kingdom and the ethico-spiritual advancement of civilization. This idea comes to full expression in Schweitzer's 1934 essay "Religion in Modern Civilization," where he states that it is "through the idea of the Kingdom of God that religion enters into relationship with civilization."[28]

In The Decay and Restoration of Civilization (part I of The Philosophy of Civilization), Schweitzer states that the decay of civilization stems primarily from the lack of an "ethical world-view," and omits any discussion of eschatology in acquiring such an ethical basis for civilization's restoration. He hoped his philosophy would stand independently, but, in fact, it lacks a theological leg. As such, his philosophical writings conceal his personal convictions on the kingdom of God and human moral action. Once again, an examination of Schweitzer's Strasbourg and Lambaréné sermons gives us an insight into his theology.

Before turning to Schweitzer's understanding of the kingdom as presented in his sermons, some discussion of the advantages and disadvantages surrounding the sermons' use is needed. His sermons pose some potential problems for academic analysis. They are neither theological nor philosophical treatises. A sermon is often a simplified expression which is designed to convince by inspiration as much as by reason. Schweitzer often does not present argumentation so much as rhetoric; his missionary impulse, presented at emotional and devotional levels, is different from his academic thought.

But consideration of his sermons is helpful in gaining a wider perspective. Although it is unclear whether or not he planned to publish his Lambaréné sermons, Schweitzer did request that they be translated from French into the local Gabonese languages (Pahouin and Bendjabis) and transcribed, word for word, while he preached.[29] These sermons (preached to the Gabonese patients and gatherers to whom he had introduced the Christian faith), especially those on the Lord's Prayer, offer insight into what he considered the fundamentals of Christianity: "The important thing out there [in Lambaréné] is to preach the essentials of the Gospel."[30] Also revealing is this remark from Schweitzer: "Whatever I make my starting-point, I always lead on to the innermost facts involved in becoming a Christian ... so that even the man who is only present at one Service can get an inkling of what it really is to be a Christian."[31] Recalling a previous theme, this is hardly the talk of an atheist or agnostic.

While working as a physician, Schweitzer largely discontinued writing theological and philosophical works and often used his sermons to address theological and socio-political issues of the period. In the light of this, Erich Grässer suggests that Schweitzer's preaching affords insight into some of his primary concerns and reveals his innermost thoughts.[32] Although Schweitzer's sermons are not academic theology, viewed alongside his other writings, they contribute to a more holistic picture of his theology.

Spiritual Kingdom

Broadly speaking, three general positions have emerged in the interpretation of Jesus' eschatology. First, the *futurist* view propounds that the kingdom of

God is something that remains in the future, and will intervene disruptively in the midst of human history. Second, the *inaugurated* position claims that the kingdom has already begun to exercise an influence within human history, but its full realization still lies in the future. Third, the *realized* perspective holds that the kingdom of God has already been realized in Jesus' coming.

New Testament scholars have associated Schweitzer's academic conclusions in the *Quest* with a futurist view of the kingdom. It is easy to see why: Jesus is depicted as expecting the cataclysmic end to the world when he throws himself on the wheel of the world in anticipation of the kingdom. But this is not the whole picture, at least as far as Schweitzer is concerned. His *own* theological position is readily identifiable with and, as we will later see, predicated on an inaugurated view. "We must grasp the appearance and dying of Jesus as the *beginning* of the realization of the Kingdom of God." Again, the "death of Jesus has its significance for believers, not in itself, but as the event in which the Kingdom of God begins."[33]

Many of Schweitzer's most considered statements on the kingdom are found in a series of seven sermons preached on the Lord's Prayer in Lambaréné in 1930. In "Thy Kingdom Come!" and "Send Thy Kingdom!" he expostulates:

> When Jesus came into the world, there were already many people who prayed and said, "Oh, that the kingdom of God would come into the world!"... Then on the day when Jesus was raised before men, and when men saw him as the King of men whom God had sent, *then the kingdom of God began.* So we know that the kingdom of God began with the Lord Jesus Christ. *But it has only begun.* That is why when Jesus Christ taught men to pray, he taught them to pray, "Thy kingdom come." Since Jesus came, men have prayed this prayer for many, many years though ... there has only been a little beginning to the kingdom of God. Nevertheless, we who see that the kingdom of God is so small and poor, believe that the kingdom of God will one day be great.[34]

> We pray for two things. We pray to God, "Send Thy kingdom!" into the world, and we pray again, "O God, send thy kingdom into our heart![35]

For Schweitzer, the inauguration of the kingdom is associated with the influence of Jesus in our *hearts.* But the kingdom is not fully realized. Before examining Schweitzer's theology of the heart and its relationship to his understanding of the kingdom of God, his outdated kingship language needs some commentary.

If one pictures the image of political despotism, it is certainly the case that Schweitzer's notion of Jesus' kingship does not offer a sound association. It denotes hierarchical, and specifically patriarchal, oppression and a submissive relationship. Schweitzer obviously did not anticipate these later negative connotations or see how such a model stands in stark contrast to his ethical mysticism which speaks of union and avoids dominance. But a closer examination of ways in which he characterizes Jesus' kingship may help to clear up some of these problems. Understood in eschatological terms, his use of kingship language functions as a critical concept by affirming Christ's ultimate reign over the world. Jesus' kingship is seen to offer a corrective to human abuse of earthly power. To this end, Schweitzer contrasts the injustices of "the kingdom of men" with the reconciliation of the "kingdom of God": "Throughout the whole world, where the kingdom of men is, [there are those] who are wicked, unjust, and who wage war.... But there were men who knew the Word of God. They said, 'No, it does not have to stay like that—war, injustice, and cruelty—someday the Kingdom of God will come.'"[36] Schweitzer portrays Jesus' righteous rule as an alternative to oppressive, earthly rule. He can see without any apparent contradiction Jesus' kingship as liberating and far from authoritarian. For some of the rest of us there is a potential contradiction at least in terminology.

In Schweitzer's sermons, the heart represents the spiritual center of the human person; it is the point from which the spiritual life proceeds, the place where humans encounter the Spirit. The heart refers to that part of the human person that is capable of a feeling that is deeper than discursive thought—a spirituality that penetrates to the depths of the human person.

Schweitzer's theology of the *heart* is analogous to his metaphysics of the human *will*. His philosophical exposition of the Will-to-Love animating the human will-to-live toward a higher will-to-love finds its theological equivalent in the Spirit "bestowing on man a new mind and a new heart."[37] Their connection is evident: "Love is a gift of the Spirit.... Love is the highest of the 'fruits of the Spirit.'"[38] Love is not something purely metaphysical, it is directly ethical. The Spirit moves the individual to a full personhood which is manifested in self-giving love. His theology of the heart, like his metaphysics of the will, ends up in ethics: "In the traditional language of religion...I speak of 'Love' in place of 'Reverence for Life.'"[39]

Schweitzer describes the Spirit's impact on the heart in pastoral terms by referring to the "tinder" within everyone that "catches fire successfully only when it meets some flame or spark from outside, i.e., from some other person."[40] The "other person" is Jesus, who is "Lord" of our heart. This elucidates the distinction in Schweitzer's thought between the potentiality that is a part of the empirical self (will-to-live) and the ethical enlightening (will-to-love) that is in Jesus Christ. Before this potential can be realized, humans must have the help of the Will-to-Love: "Let the Lord Jesus Christ put love into our hearts; and may this fire of love burn always in our hearts."[41] Though the Spirit is external to us, through its force we are able to achieve the potential that is inside us and enable the "tinder" to catch light.

Working for the Kingdom

Throughout the nineteenth century, it was widely held by the liberals that Jesus founded the kingdom of God as an inward and spiritual reality. God reigned within the believer's heart and filled the individual with the Spirit, inspiring him or her to realize, in social life, the values of Christ. The goal of social progress was to be realized through human Endeavour; the community of believers would lead humankind toward the establishment of the kingdom on earth. Christian morality was brought into harmony with the widespread belief in social development.

Albrecht Ritschl is perhaps most closely associated with this view. The religious (redemption through Christ) and the ethical (the kingdom of God), which Ritschl likened to two foci of an ellipse, were united in the whole, which formed the Protestant religion: Christian perfection was not attained in an other-worldly realm, but, rather, in obedience to a "worldly-vocation" as "the place for the practice of love" that was the "fundamental principle of Protestantism."[42] Christians did not find perfection in some higher realm but precisely "through continual intercourse with the world and their distinctive vocations in worldly society."[43] The redemption actualized by Christ had the result of inspiring activity motivated by love which led to a new organization of humanity, the kingdom of God. Christianity was "an impulse to activity from the motive of love [that] aims at moral organization of mankind."[44] Ritschl credited Kant as being "the first to perceive the supreme importance for ethics of the 'Kingdom of God' as an association of men bound together by laws of virtue."[45] Ritschl's understanding of the kingdom was a realm of ethical values supporting the development of German society. Civilization was seen to be in the process of being divinely guided toward perfection.

One of the most serious defects in Ritschl's theology lay in his untenable historical premises to establish his vocational ethic in the life and teachings of Jesus. It was Jesus himself, he maintained, who founded a community on earth directed to the realization of the highest ethical good. As briefly mentioned, it was Weiss (Ritschl's son-in-law) and Schweitzer who recognized the impossibility of this conception of the historical Jesus. For Weiss, the idea of the kingdom that dominated Ritschl's dogmatic concept was contrary to Jesus' eschatology.

> In the school of Albrecht Ritschl I convinced myself of the incompa-
> rable importance of the systematic concept of the Kingdom
> of God which was the central organizing theme of this theology.
> I am today still of the opinion that his system and just this cen-
> tral concept represent that form of Christian doctrine which
> is most likely to bring our race closer to the Christian religion and
> which, when it is correctly understood and correctly evaluated, is most
> likely to inspire and encourage the wholesome and robust life which
> we stand in need of today. But from the outset I was disturbed by the
> clear discovery that Ritschl's concept... has a completely different
> form and resonance from the concept in the faith of the early Church.
> Further studies have convinced me that the actual roots of Ritschl's
> idea were in Kant and in the theology of the Enlightenment.[46]

The fact that Ritschlian theology produced an inadequate account of a this-worldly kingdom need not obscure his achievement in correctly identifying the kingdom of God as a central concern of Jesus' teaching. Although Ritschl's portrait was unhistorical, Weiss believed it was still useful to theology: "How-ever modernizing and dogmatizing Ritschl's biblical-theological basis might be, the concept of the Kingdom of God as he formulated it is still not without its uses."[47] Weiss tried to remain a Ritschlian in theology without compromising his integrity as a historian. His solution was to remove the historical sphere and concentrate on the future perfection of humanity on earth which (con-sistent with *his* historical findings) was ultimately achieved by God alone. The meaning of history is understood in relation to the future.

> The final results of history are as follows: God surrounds himself
> with a highly diverse horde of perfected spirits, who represent
> the human ideal in the most different forms, and who are all simi-
> larly perfected because they have become the most perfect they
> could be to the best of their capacities and strengths. It appears to us to
> be a fitting conclusion to history and also for God, whose highest
> and most beautiful creation is the human personality, because it is not
> merely the last generation of humanity which has climbed onto the
> shoulders of the previous generation which finds its joy, but all
> achieve the goal of their development, each in their own way, from the
> rich abundance of individuals from all times. It is within this context
> that the biblical idea of the perfected Kingdom of God has its place.[48]

Weiss clearly appreciated Ritschl's focus on faith and ethics. But when Weiss disengaged the kingdom from its rootedness in history and focused on the future it lost connection with the present: "The actualization of the Kingdom of God is *not* a matter for human initiative, but entirely a matter of God's initiative."[49] In this process, he stripped Christian eschatology of the world-transforming power that belongs to it.

As we have seen, Schweitzer likes to define the (self-proclaimed) originality of his ideas in relation to some predecessor, or predecessors, whose ideas in part (never wholly) resemble and in part are antithetical to his own. How, then, does Schweitzer stand (or how does he think he stands) in relation to these two theologians? Like Weiss, Schweitzer accuses Ritschl and the liberal Protestants for placing "on the stage a Jesus who is dominated by modern ideas of development."[50] But this accusation is puzzling, since Schweitzer's conception of reverence for life as "Jesus' ethic of love widened to universality"[51] can hardly be seen to stray from "modern ideas of development." Given this similarity, it is not too surprising that Schweitzer considered himself, to some extent, to "subscribe" to liberal Protestantism.[52] But his understanding of the kingdom differs from the liberal view on three key points.

First, whereas Ritschl and liberalism were inspired by the belief that humanity was ascending upward into new realms of moral and spiritual progress, Schweitzer thought civilization was in "decay": "The last decades [i.e., late nineteenth century] have produced a standstill in our culture which is noticeable in every sphere. Signs which imply an actual *retrogression* are even evident, and to no small degree."[53] Historical crises in the twentieth century, such as the two world wars, the Holocaust, and nuclear proliferation, made historical progressivism untenable to Schweitzer. Liberals saw their ethics (i.e., working for the kingdom as a human moral community) as divinely guided toward perfection. But their ethics could never make the true kingdom come; Schweitzer considered ethics in need of divine inspiration from the Spirit:

> The usual conclusion drawn . . . is that the Kingdom of God can be
> established on earth by an understanding between the nations.
> That is *not* the right way to picture the Kingdom of God and its
> coming. In reality, it can only happen thus, that first through the
> Spirit of Jesus the Kingdom of God enters into the hearts of men, and
> then through them into the world.[54]

Like the liberal Protestants, Schweitzer sees the Spirit directing humans toward realizing the kingdom in the world. But against liberal tendencies, he explicitly rejects the view of the kingdom as peace "between the nations" or as a Kantian-Ritschlian idealist notion of a human moral community. The liberals, he contends, confused the values of human society with the kingdom of God and stripped it of the eschatological transcendence that belongs to it:

> What they [the liberals] think is that the Kingdom is something
> ethical and religious, to be conceived as developing in this world, and
> requiring ethical effort on the part of believers. This is so obvious to
> them that they can conceive of no other way of looking at the subject;
> they understand the Gospels to say that Jesus came into this world to
> found the Kingdom, to call men into it as fellow-workers.... Modern
> Protestantism substitutes its view of the Kingdom of God and its
> coming for the eschatological view which Jesus presented as if it
> really represented the original.[55]

Ritschl was on the right *religious* track (ethics). But he had the wrong basis (ahistorical) and put too much weight on cultural achievements. As Schweitzer sees it, no matter how far those achievements go, they cannot go nearly far enough for the realization of the transcendent kingdom. The kingdom is not some objective entity to be expounded and applied by human beings. Indeed, such a scenario is unthinkable for Schweitzer, since it places the human agent in ultimate control of *God's* kingdom. In this sense, eschatology also provides Schweitzer with a source of critique for the type of society humans have created. The kingdom, precisely because it is eschatological, helps to draw individuals beyond their present state of being and prohibits claims to authority by temporal governments or institutions: "[When living] our lives, in genuine nonconformity to the world, reveal[s] something of what it means to be apprehended by the living, ethical God, then something of the truth of Jesus goes out from us."[56]

Schweitzer appears to draw on the Pauline motif of nonconformity to this world (notably, Romans 12:2) when he writes that Jesus "compels us not to conform to the world."[57] The continued relevance of Jesus, Schweitzer tells us, rests—among other ways—in the espousal of eschatological hope that affords a distance from present institutions. Indeed, contrary to the popular image as simply a dogged paternalist, even during his early years at Lambaréné, when he was most accused, sometimes justifiably, of siding with colonialism, he produced the "Book of African Reminiscences," which reads like a bill of rights, critiquing the negative influences of colonialism and capitalism in West Africa. He addresses such issues as profit, world trade and exploitation of natural resources, and the rights of women.[58]

Second, whereas Ritschl's theology was disconnected from the historical Jesus and Weiss' notion of the kingdom, Schweitzer, focused on the final consummation, sought a connection of present and future, ethics and eschatological transcendence:

The Messianic consciousness of the uniquely great Man of Nazareth sets up a struggle between the *present* and *beyond*, and introduces that resolute absorption of the beyond by the present, . . . of which we are conscious in ourselves as the essence of religious progress and experience—a process of which the end is not yet in sight.[59]

The pressure of the end of history impacts the normal course of history; the temporal expectation of the kingdom is preserved within the tension of "*present* and *beyond*" even when an imminent end is dropped. Schweitzer sought to reveal the consequences of the historical Jesus' eschatology for the present and to recapture the sense of urgency, not delay, of eschatological faith. To the liberal theological community of his time he commented:

Modern Kingdom-of-God religion has today lost its power and influence, and has had to find itself looked down upon as "Protestantism with a tincture of sociology" [*Kultur-protestantismus*]. An epigonic theology, which has adapted itself to the ideas of the time, . . . allow[s] the belief in the Kingdom of God only to state itself in dogmatic formulae which no longer have behind them any living conviction. . . . It is time for Christianity to examine itself and see whether we really still have faith in the Kingdom of God, or whether we merely retain it as a matter of traditional phraseology.[60]

Schweitzer stands against the Ritschlian ahistorical reduction of the kingdom into ethical values alone. Such *Kultur-protestantismus* was driven by "ideas of the time," or, in other words, a secular agenda. For Schweitzer, Weiss's view also falls short: Weiss's idea that "the Kingdom is something to be waited for has an unfortunate corollary. It compels humans to do nothing but wait for the Kingdom which comes entirely of itself . . . [and] to refrain from all efforts to improve the present situation."[61] As Schweitzer sees it, the ethic that emerges from this view of the coming kingdom is "completely negative . . . in character; it is, in fact, not so much an ethic as a penitential discipline."[62] Opposing Weiss's future focus, Schweitzer sees humans as participants in the inauguration of the kingdom and gives human moral action a meaning not found in Weiss's apocalyptic scenario.

In "Compelling Hope," Schweitzer preaches that humans must be "conscious of our responsibility to our Lord for what our existence means to the people around us and what it means for the coming of the Kingdom of God in the world."[63] Likewise, his Pauline scholarship draws him to the conclusion that "to be a Christian means to be possessed and dominated by a hope of the Kingdom of God, and a will to work for it [in this world]."[64] This theme can be further deduced from Schweitzer's philosophically masked references to the human person as "an active, purposeful force in the world" and "our co-operation with the activity which the World-Spirit wills for us."[65] Far from an ethic of withdrawal, the kingdom of God leads Schweitzer to action in this world. His fear over what he perceived to be a loss of commitment to the kingdom's realization led him to take up battle against yet another opponent:

> I feel alienated from the whole new trend of ideas because all these people no longer carry with them the idea of the Kingdom of God. They fail to see the goal, without which civilization goes astray, but that is why we must carry this yearning and assurance all the more solidly.
>
> How well I now understand the prophets who, in the time of the coming and the destruction of Jerusalem, thought about and looked forward to the subsequent future, transcending the present.[66]

Here, Schweitzer appears to be taking issue with Rudolf Bultmann, whose eschatology was divested of ethical engagement. Historically Schweitzer and Bultmann did not see eye to eye. Bultmann excises history from Christology; historical investigation is reduced to *das Dass*, the mere fact *that* a historical figure existed. Real knowledge of Christ is through encounter with him in the word of the kerygma. Bultmann seeks to extract what he sees as the essence of what the mythology of eschatological discourse seeks to convey. His explicit counter-thesis to the *Quest*'s Jesus is: "History is swallowed up by eschatology."[67] The "meaning of history" is found in each individual person's present experience. The result is an individualistic encounter—a message about the demand for authentic existence in the face of God's crises. In this, the historical, social, and cosmic referents of eschatology are in effect reduced to a disposable alien mythological shell. For Bultmann, God's kingdom was not of this world. The kingdom was "that eschatological deliverance which ends everything earthly"; it was meaningless to call the kingdom the "highest value," "if by this is meant the culmination of all that human beings consider good....The Kingdom of God as eschatological deliverance is diametrically opposed to all relative values."[68] Like Schweitzer, Bultmann opposes the Ritschlian reduction of the kingdom into cultural values. But Bultmann is resolute in excluding an ethical dimension from the kingdom: "Whoever seeks it must realize that he cuts himself off from the world, otherwise he belongs to those who are not fit....The future Kingdom of God is not something which is to come in the course of time, so that to advance its coming one can do something in particular, perhaps through penitential prayers and good works."[69] Bultmann's kingdom (like his teacher Weiss's) robbed human activity of positive meaning.

Responding to this Bultmannian antithesis, Schweitzer returned to the union of the ethical and the religious and gave what he saw as his historical eschatology a distinct emphasis on activity:

> The abandonment of Jesus' *ethical eschatology* is avenged.... Instead of fighting for the triumph of the ethical spirit of God, through which individuals ... might be filled with sustaining inspiration, mankind today is on the verge of delivering itself to the stagnation and *decline of civilization*. Those who experience the woe that hangs over the future of the world are ready to encounter the historical Jesus and understand what He has to say. With Him they perceive that we shall be saved from present conditions through a mighty hope for the Kingdom of God and a will dedicated to it.[70]

The connection between the loss of an "ethical eschatology" and the "decline of civilization" is made explicit. Schweitzer is intent on retaining eschatological ethics, an eschatological worldview that advances action in anticipation of the kingdom, at the fore of Christian thought. But what was expressed in his academic theology was present all along in his sermons. The sermons give expression to personal specificity of Christian eschatology in Schweitzer's thought.

In his 1913 sermon "Preparing for the Kingdom of God," Schweitzer closes with the following words: "During these Sundays of Advent, think with us of what must come [the kingdom of God] and pray that God will send it soon."[71] Almost two decades later, an active call for the kingdom is still invoked:

> [The Lord's] prayer tells us that it is always necessary to hope and believe that one day ... the Kingdom of God will be here. Ever since Jesus was on earth and spoke to men and preached ... all the men who know the Word of God pray everyday, "O God, may thy Kingdom come!"
>
> This is why I say to all of you today, "Pray that the Kingdom of God may come into the world!" ... O God, we all pray unto thee. Send thy Kingdom into world![72]

The idiom of prayer is retained with seriousness, and not simply regarded as liturgical decoration lacking propositional form. It is "God" who is "our hope"; Schweitzer prays to God that "the Kingdom may come into the world!" Significantly, *God* ultimately accomplishes the kingdom's inauguration; there is a strong emphasis on eschatological transcendence. Schweitzer looks for the action God and implores God to take the initiative. *Prayer* for the coming kingdom suggests that the advent of this is not wholly within the sphere of human action; the impossibility of an earthly fulfillment is implicit.

The way in which Schweitzer addresses the theme of eschatology is helpful in gaining a clearer picture of his view of human moral agency. At one level, he is placing limitations on the import of human action by distinguishing it (like Weiss and Bultmann) from God's decisive act. But it is notable that Schweitzer develops his eschatology (like Ritschl) in an ethical context, for by so doing he emphasizes that eschatology evokes human acts. He sees the coming kingdom being prepared in a double movement in heaven and on earth, the actual decision lying not with this world but resting on God. If the kingdom is to come, God ultimately has to bring this about, but humans can do their part through moral action. The kingdom did have ethical and social implications for life in the present. But it could not be reduced to these as in liberalism.

Schweitzer does not limit the choice to either God's action or humans' action. Prayer to God to establish the kingdom cannot be separated from praxis. His prayerful mode of speech is a call to real activity. This may not be Schweitzer trying to correct others' use of the word *prayer*, but at least it announces that *he* proposes to use the word differently. He invites (indeed expects) humans to work in this realm for what is fitting in the light of the action of God to whom prayer is offered: "Don't forget this. Start right now, become active for the Kingdom of God."[73] Against the kingdom of human disorder stands the kingdom of divine order. Prayers that call for God to usher in a kingdom that overcomes "injustices, cruelties and wickedness," and instead manifests "forgiveness," "justice," and "peace,"[74] become a call for humans to enact such ideals in the present. In one sense, the more other-worldly Schweitzer focuses his prayer, the more this-worldly its relevance becomes for him.

Third, in opposition both to Ritschl and Weiss (among countless other liberals), who focused on a *human* moral community, and Bultmann, who reduced eschatology to an *individualistic* existential encounter and disregarded world history and the history of nature, Schweitzer's *kingdom in the heart*, though anthropocentrically grounded, is *cosmically* oriented. Schweitzer seeks to correct their eschatological underemphasis. The kingdom is not just for the individual (Bultmann) or for the human community (Ritschl and Weiss), but for the community of life. For Schweitzer, the eschatological field has been a playground for anthropocentricism: it is "a great weakness for man to be wholly concerned with his own individual redemption, and not equally with the coming of the Kingdom of God . . . in regard to the future of the world."[75] Ritschl saw humans rising above nature when they appropriated the message of the kingdom. Christianity establishes the belief that "personal life is to be prized above the whole world of nature. The world, viewed as distinct from the world of man, . . . must be regarded as a means to the Divine end [i.e., the kingdom]."[76] Standing in line with Ritschl, Bultmann distinguishes between an abstract *world-view* and a personal *self-understanding*. God, he argues, cannot be seen to be active throughout the cosmos. Such an understanding would conflate self-understanding with world-view: "Only statements about God are legitimate as expressing the existential relation between God and man. Statements which speak of God's actions as cosmic events are illegitimate."[77]

As we saw with Brunner's and Barth's theology, the natural world is for these theologians mere scenery for the Divine-human drama. Belief in the kingdom of God, Schweitzer observes, has "changed": Christians "no longer look for a transformation of the natural circumstances of the world; we take the continuance of the evil and suffering which belong to the nature of things, as something appointed by God."[78] The separation between the spheres of human history and nonhuman nature, Schweitzer tells us, is an artificial one:

> Originally the dominant thought of the Kingdom of God meant that believers shared with one another the blessings of a new creation. But now the experience of the individual took precedence....Each separate believer is now concerned with his own redemption. He cares nothing for the future of mankind and of the world.[79]

The emphasis is not on an individual doctrine of redemption or even on one that includes all humanity, but on a universal one. As with the universality of reverence for life, our conception of the kingdom should be cosmic in scope.

Schweitzer's discussion of cosmic eschatology appears connected with his understanding of the Fall. Though he does not directly address the subject, implicit in his description of the world as a "ghastly drama of the will-to-live divided against itself" (*Selbstentzweiung*, literally "self-cutting-in-two") is a sense of disorder, fragmentation, and cosmic estrangement. His sense of discord in the present alongside his vision of a peaceable future for all creation points back to the notion of a cosmic Fall. Schweitzer's conception of human redemption (*kingdom in the heart*) is an integral part of the redemption of all creation (*kingdom in the world*). The redemption of the human person draws in its wake the redemption of nature. This displays the cosmic eschatological framework in which Schweitzer's conception of human moral action stands.

Lastly, it may be interesting to note some of the personal consequences of each theologian's eschatology. For all his talk about ethics and the kingdom, Ritschl enjoyed an easy life as a European intellectual. As for Weiss, there is no evidence that his eschatological discovery led him to asceticism or profligacy. He, too, led a comfortable life as a career academic.

At the age of thirty-one, Bultmann took up a chair in New Testament studies in Marburg where he would remain until retirement at sixty-seven. In

1931, Bultmann gave a public lecture titled "The Crisis of Belief."[80] He shared the opinion of his Marburg colleagues that Germany was facing serious difficulties. But, for him, Christian belief entailed perpetual crisis. His lecture was a plea to relegate ethical, religious, and social crises to a subordinate position. Although an active member of the Confessing Church in Germany from its founding in 1933, Bultmann's opposition to National Socialism (unlike other members of that confession) was never so intense as to cause him trouble.

Schweitzer's understanding of Jesus' ethical eschatology led him to the greatest practical expression of his faith. In his own acted-out interpretation of the Bible, Schweitzer gave up his teaching at the University of Strasbourg, as well as his post at St. Nicholas Church, and left his father's manse in Günsbach on the afternoon of Good Friday 1913, the first stage of a journey to Lambaréné where he was to be, until his death in 1965, a medical missionary. As we will see in the next chapter, ethical activity was his *practical eschatology*.

More Misconceptions

Notwithstanding Schweitzer's determination to uphold an eschatological ethical worldview, *The Philosophy of Civilization* does not allude at all to the kingdom of God or eschatology in connection with the decay of civilization. But this was his philosophy; religious terminology and theological justification were not allowed. It is largely due to this omission (or tactical retreat) that his eschatological views are misunderstood by critics who have not examined the full range of theological writings. Indeed, one of most common criticisms of his theology is that it is insufficiently eschatological.

In *Theology of Hope*, Jürgen Moltmann does indeed laud Schweitzer's rediscovery of "eschatology for our age" as "undoubtedly one of the most important events in recent Protestant theology."[81] But the object of Moltmann's praise is the mere fact that Schweitzer raised the issue. For Schweitzer's treatment of eschatology, Moltmann's criticism could hardly be sharper: "The startling thing about Schweitzer's work . . . is that he had no eschatological sense at all—neither for theological nor for philosophical eschatology."[82] Moltmann acknowledges Schweitzer's *consistent eschatology* to be innovative. But what he praised was a sort of caricature, which, understandably, pointed to inconsistencies so enormous that a more charitable critic might have been led to suspect a misreading on *his* part, and seek clarification in other available writings. Instead, Moltmann was content to leave it as incomprehensible, preferring the all-too-easy victory. "None of the discoverers [Schweitzer and Weiss] took his discovery [i.e., eschatology] seriously. . . . The so-called 'consistent eschatology' was never really consistent."[83] Moltmann takes this criticism to the extreme: "The experience of two thousand years of delayed *parousia* makes eschatology *impossible today* [for Schweitzer]."[84] Moreover: "All that remains [for Schweitzer] of the hope against history aroused by Jesus and his followers is resignation.... History buries every hoped-for end of history."[85]

Oscar Cullmann put forth a similar view in *Christ and Time*:

> It is hard to understand the attitude of Albert Schweitzer ... and the representatives of the so-called consistent eschatology: they reject in their theological position that which they have recognized to be the centre of the New Testament faith.[86]

This perspective has become deeply entrenched in contemporary Schweitzer scholarship.

In *A New Quest of the Historical Jesus*, James Robinson had this to say about Schweitzer's regard for eschatology: "Schweitzer had little personal sympathy for eschatology, and saw in it no potentiality for theology today."[87] Astonishingly, J. C. O'Neill perpetuates the fantasy that Schweitzer does not see God as one "who answers prayers" and considers Schweitzer's God incapable of "interven[ing] supernaturally in history, from the outside" to inaugurate the kingdom. Moreover, he maintains that Schweitzer is a "Stoic" and, as such, "cannot allow anyone [i.e., Jesus or God] to be anyone else's helper or savior."[88] Even more: "Schweitzer clearly did not believe in such a God, and held that the fact that Jesus, who did believe in such a God, was proved wrong (because his God did not bring in the Kingdom at or soon after his death) *closes the issue for him.*"[89] Indeed, O'Neill goes so far as to claim that "Schweitzer *never* uses the word God except to indicate this mysterious life-force before which we have to bow."[90]

With such widely held misconceptions, one can begin to understand why Schweitzer so soon fell out of favor in some academic circles.

Schweitzer has a greater appreciation of the import of eschatology than Moltmann concludes. First, Schweitzer does not assert that Jesus' death was a total failure because the kingdom was not fully consummated when he "threw" his body on the "wheel of the world." In Jesus' death, defeat and victory are paradoxically related. Jesus may have been "crushed" by the wheel of the world, but his life and death *inaugurated*, even if not fully actualized, the kingdom and continues to do so through his Spirit "which goes forth from Him and in the spirits of men strives for new influence and rule."[91] For Schweitzer, devotion to the kingdom is categorical; we cannot escape the *wheel of the world*. Instead of seeking its release, we should—in the spirit of Jesus—throw ourselves on it in an effort to direct it to the kingdom and, if need be, suffer its crushing weight.

Second, far from Moltmann's claim of an "illusionary eschatology,"[92] the kingdom is for Schweitzer the core of the historical Jesus' ministry. Jesus' notion of the imminent end of the world was time-conditioned, but the ethical will expressed in his interim ethic is valid timelessly. This ethical will is the basis of Schweitzer's eschatology: Jesus "lays on us the task of striving to make more profound . . . our belief in the Kingdom of God and to become constantly more strongly established in [its realization]."[93]

Third, Moltmann's statement that for Schweitzer the "delayed *parousia* makes eschatology impossible today" is also fallacious. Schweitzer's under-standing of the delay, far from making the coming of the kingdom impossible, "requires us to invest ourselves earnestly in its realization."[94] Though he does not directly adopt (his historical) Jesus' apocalyptic outlook, far from abandon-ing eschatology, he seeks to elucidate the ethical import of Jesus' eschatology for all times. The abiding core of eschatological hope, which is not altered by the failure of the *parousia* to come, is the faith that Jesus inaugurated the kingdom. So long as the kingdom is inaugurated as Schweitzer stresses, belief in the future kingdom does not necessarily lose its intensity.

Contrary to Moltmann's and Cullmann's critiques, the twin themes of the kingdom and ethical eschatology are what Schweitzer stresses humans must strive most to realize. His eschatology promotes an all-encompassing expec-tation horizon of ethical action for world-transformation. Moltmann's criti-cisms are all the more surprising in that his own conclusions can be seen by the outsider to follow Schweitzer's emphasis on *working* and *living* for the realization of the kingdom (articulated sixty years earlier). Moltmann describes the Christian's vocation as "a fellow worker participating in the building of the Kingdom,"[95] and says of Christian life:

> The hope for the *parousia* is not a flight from the world . . . not a
> matter of mere "waiting." It becomes a life which is committed to
> working for the kingdom of God through its commitment to justice
> and peace in this world.[96]

For Schweitzer, a commitment to justice and peace in this world is mani-fested through the practice of reverence for life (a theme which, we will see, Moltmann also directly adopts). Schweitzer's thoughts on the kingdom and the atomic bomb also anticipate Moltmann's views on this matter:

> We are no longer content to believe in the Kingdom that comes of
> itself at the end of time. Mankind today must either realize the
> Kingdom of God or perish. The very tragedy of our present situa-
> tion compels us to devote ourselves in faith to its realization. We are

at the beginning of the end of the human race.... Our only hope is that the Spirit of God will prevail.[97]

Following Schweitzer's lead, Moltmann notes:

At issue is an orientation of all spheres of life toward the coming kingdom of God.... Today, life itself is in mortal danger. Since Hiroshima in 1945, humankind as a whole has become mortal. We are living in a time in which the nuclear end of humankind can happen at any moment. Tens of thousands of nuclear weapons are available for this "final solution" to the question of human-kind.... The consequences of this for the church of the kingdom of God [are] a "reverence for life" (Albert Schweitzer) and a fellowship with the earth and with all living creatures.... The future of the kingdom of God in this dying world begins with the presence of the Spirit, and hope in this kingdom is grounded in the experience of the Spirit that vivifies.[98]

As seen above, Schweitzer's Lambaréné sermons on the Lord's Prayer present several instances of petitionary prayer to God to consummate the kingdom. Clearly Robinson and O'Neill have misunderstood Schweitzer's eschatology. But to hammer one more nail in the coffin, we may cite Schweitzer's sermon "Thy Kingdom Come!" which concludes with the following prayer: "Let us pray unto God. God our Father send thy Kingdom speedily."[99] Once again, we are confronted with the transcendent character of Schweitzer's eschatology. The future kingdom comes from God. In the meanwhile, we are to live and labor in the world.

Cynics might view the more orthodox eschatological language exhibited in Schweitzer's sermons as a ploy to appease the Paris Mission Society, who helped to fund his hospital. But the evidence is against this. Having initially prohibited Schweitzer from preaching, it was the Mission Society who then asked him to preach, only a few months after his arrival in Lambaréné. Also, he notes that for his first trip to Lambaréné "the financial problem was solved," which meant that he was no longer dependent on the Mission for funding. By 1930 (when his sermons were most clearly eschatological), Schweitzer was, in effect, running his own hospital and preaching *his own* views.

Far from being eschatologically unfocused, his sermons reveal, in a rather pious—even charismatic—manner, an attempt to convert his hearers to Jesus and make the kingdom real in their hearts. For Schweitzer, Jesus is the bearer of an eschatology in which reverence finds its proper place. "The ethic of reverence for life *is* Jesus' ethic of love widened to universality."[100]

5

Knowing the "One Unknown"

Historical research could not deliver Jesus. That, tragically, was Schweitzer's conclusion of the historical *Quest*. And it is the reason why he ends his volume with these most well-remembered and poignant words:

> He comes to us as one unknown, without a name, as of old
> by the lakeside. He came to those men who knew Him
> not. He speaks to us the same words: "Follow thou me," and
> sets us to the same task which He has to fulfill for our
> time. He commands. And to those who obey Him, whether
> they be wise or simple, He will reveal Himself in the toils, the
> conflicts, the sufferings which they shall pass through in
> His fellowship and, as an ineffable mystery, they shall learn
> in their own experience who He is.[1]

These are not just the words of a biblical scholar whose work has ended in failure. While historical research cannot provide the biography of Jesus' life (as many of his contemporaries thought), it can liberate us to encounter Jesus by other means. Chief among these was the possibility of mystical union, "by the lakeside." Mysticism, for Schweitzer, is the means of knowing the "one unknown."

Schweitzer's poetic and subtle words were a provocation to the theological community. His very use of the word *mysticism* was suspect to German Neo-Lutheran theology in which he was cradled. The mystical path was held to be at variance with the assurances of reformed theology, most notably, justification by faith. Of course, it was from Paul that the Reformers gained their insight. How treacherous, then, that Schweitzer should extract from the same Paul a doctrine of Christ mysticism that displaced the venerable "by faith alone" doctrine of the Reformers.

Not least of all in the passage above is the emphasis on fellowship with Jesus through "toils, conflicts and sufferings," and thereby learning "who He is." Therefore there is an unmistakable ethical content to the "being with Jesus," what Schweitzer was later to call the "fellowship of those who bear the Mark of Pain."[2] In other words, a living encounter with Jesus should lead us to a deepened sensitivity not only to life, but also to the burden of suffering which is placed on life itself.

Immediately on finishing *Quest*, Schweitzer turned to Paul. The connection might not seem immediately obvious. But, for Schweitzer, Paul's mystical doctrine of "dying and rising again" with Christ is the process through which we come to know Christ in the heart and begin to realize the kingdom. As with his work on Jesus, a religio-ethical hermeneutic is evident from the outset: "I believe I am serving in this work the cause not only of sound learning but also of religious needs."[3]

The Influence of Paul

If Schweitzer found his (ethical) eschatology in Jesus, then Paul appeals to the (ethical) mystic in him. In *The Mysticism of Paul the Apostle*, Schweitzer sought specifically to answer the question of how Paul, beginning with primitive eschatological Christianity, arrived at a mysticism of dying and being born again in Jesus Christ. We may take as our starting point the meaning of *mysticism* with regard to Paul. Schweitzer opens with this description of the term:

> We are always in the presence of mysticism when we find a human
> being looking upon the division between earthly and super-earthly,
> temporal and eternal, as transcended, and feeling himself, while
> still externally amid the earthly and temporal, to belong to the super-
> earthly and eternal.[4]

While physically amidst the world, the mystic has a sense of transcending it. Schweitzer distinguishes two basic types of mysticism: *primitive*, or *early*, and *developed*. Early mysticism views union with the divine by "means of a magical act", namely, the performance of rites and efficacious ceremonies such as sacrificial feasts whereby the individual becomes one with the supernatural mode of existence of the "divine being."[5] Developed mysticism seeks union with the divine by means of an "initiation" whereby the participant is "born again" into a higher eternal and immortal state of being for which he or she yearns. There is yet a higher type of mysticism:

> When the conception of the universal is reached and a man re-
> flects upon his relation to the totality of being and to Being in
> itself, the resultant mysticism . . . then takes place through an act of
> thinking. The conscious personality . . . is able to conceive the mate-
> rial as a mode of manifestation of the Spiritual. It has sight of the
> Eternal in the Transient. Recognizing the unity of all things in
> God . . . it is conscious of itself as being in God, and in every moment
> eternal.[6]

In this *intellectual mysticism*, Schweitzer apprehends an immanence of the temporal in the eternal and the eternal in the temporal—a direct experience of the presence of God. Intellectual mysticism wherein the individual conceives the relation of the personality to the universal is evidenced among the "Brah-mans, in Platonism and Stoicism," as well as in the thought of "Spinoza, Scho-penhauer, and Hegel." Such a *God-mysticism*, or direct monistic union, is char-acterized negatively as "a sinking into the ocean of the Infinite."[7] Schweitzer utilizes his Pauline scholarship as an opportunity to reject identification of the self with the "Infinite." For him, God is both immanent and transcendent. God is transcendent in unknowable nature, yet immanent in love: "All living knowl-edge of God rests upon this foundation: that we experience Him in our lives as Will-to-Love."[8]

God-mysticism is also regarded problematic because instead of being a means, it can make the spirituality associated with the being-in-eternity "an end in itself." Spiritual absorption is held to result in a withdrawal from active engagement in worldly matters. Schweitzer makes this sweeping (if not wholly accurate) assessment of Spinoza's God-mysticism:

> How difficult it is for the intellectual mysticism of being-in-God to
> reach an ethic is seen in Spinoza. . . . There is always the danger
> that the mystic will experience the eternal as absolute passivity, and
> will cease to regard ethical existence as the highest manifestation
> of spirituality.[9]

This passive harmony with God is an intellectual affair that reaches the ethics of "inward liberation from the world, never at the same time the ethics of working in the world."[10] God-mysticism (as he says repeatedly of Schopen-hauerian and Jain life-negation, as well as of Weiss' and Bultmann's escha-tologies) lacks an impetus to activity. This negative mysticism appears to be the only mysticism Schweitzer knows, except, of course, his own. Following his conception of Paul, Schweitzer strives for a *deed mysticism* that endeavors to realize service to others.

Schweitzer had good reason for trying to distance his understanding of mysticism from a quietist interpretation. At the time he was writing, the liberal Protestant position had no sympathy for mysticism, which they understood as *quietism*. Ritschl, for example, believed that "the Christian life is quite opposed to mysticism. . . . [Mysticism] teaches escape from the world and renunciation of the world, and it places the value of the ethically good activity of human beings and of the formation of virtue far beneath the ecstatic union with God."[11] Some mystics have laid themselves open to such charges. But Schweitzer is certainly not one of them. He is careful to emphasize the ethical focus of Pauline Christ-mysticism, as well as of his own ethical mysticism.

Paul's mysticism is neither a primitive concept of union with the Divine through rites, nor is it a developed, intellectual concept of the oneness of all in God. On the contrary, there is not a God-mysticism, "only a Christ-mysticism by means of which man comes into relation to God."[12] For Schweitzer, Paul's exposition of union with Christ affords us the *only* sort of mysticism that is available, being superior to monistic mysticism on the one hand and a dualism on the other:

> The fundamental thought of Pauline mysticism runs thus: I am in Christ; in Him I know myself as a being who is raised above this sensuous, sinful, and transient world and already belongs to the transcendent. . . . This "being-in-Christ" is the prime enigma of Pauline teaching: once grasped it gives the clue to the whole.[13]

Pauline mysticism is not characterized as an immediate mystical relation to God, but, rather, as mediated by an experience of Christ, a *being-in-Christ* mysticism. Schweitzer cites twelve New Testament passages that underscore this mysticism: Galatians 2:19–20, 3:26–28, 4:6, 5:24–25, 6:14; 2 Corinthians 5:17; Romans 6:10–11, 7:4, 8:1–2, 8:9–11, 12:4–5; and Philippians 3:1–11. A collection of proof texts that (as Schweitzer would have been only too well aware) paralleled, if not exceeded, those which serve other key reformed doctrines, such as justification. These passages underscore that direct monistic union with Being (God-mysticism) is unrelated to Paul's thought, in that he never speaks of being "one" with God, or of being "in God." The apostle is "far removed from the *Deus sive natura*. His world-view is of a transcendent God."[14]

It is evident that Schweitzer's own ideas run parallel to his reading of Paul. Schweitzer dismisses any notion of "absorption" into Being, with a consequent loss of individual personality. Mystical union does not mean that one becomes

God. Rather, mystical relation to God is "mediated and effected" by union with Christ. Like his Paul who "knows only Christ-mysticism, unaccompanied by God-mysticism,"[15] Schweitzer maintains that "we all have to achieve fellowship with God through Jesus."[16] He underscores this belief dogmatically: "In union with Christ, union with God is realized in the *only* form available to us."[17] The transcendent essence of God is abrogated by being-in-Christ.

All in All

The consummation that Paul anticipates "when God shall be all in all" is explicitly eschatological.[18] In Schweitzer's reading of Paul (as well as in his own eschatology), it is only at the end of all things that there will be a direct *being-in-God*. Christ-mysticism is not equivalent to God-mysticism inasmuch as they are "chronologically successive."[19] The kingdom of God enters into the human heart through Christ-mysticism. But that does not constitute its final consummation.

A hint of Ritschl's religious (redemption through Christ) and ethical (the kingdom of God) foci appear again in Schweitzer's thought. From his standpoint, Paul's blend of mysticism and eschatology is able to balance redemption-through-Christ mysticism with kingdom-of-God theology:

> Paul has thought out his conception of redemption through Christ within the sphere of belief in the Kingdom of God. In Paul's mysticism the death of Jesus has its significance for believers, not in itself, but as the event in which the realization of the Kingdom of God begins. For him, believers are redeemed by entering already, through union with Christ, by means of a mystical dying and rising again with Him during the continuance of the natural world-era into a supernatural state of existence, this state being that which they are to possess in the Kingdom of God.[20]

Through Pauline Christ-mysticism, believers "already" possess an anticipation of the kingdom in the heart. The kingdom, which finds its fulfillment in the future, begins to be realized now in the "natural world-era." Christ-mysticism maintains present redemption (kingdom in the heart) and future kingdom of God (kingdom in the world). As seen, the failure to accomplish this synthesis of inauguration and transcendence (Ritschl, Weiss, and Bultmann) has moved civilization in the direction of its "decay."

Schweitzer's understanding of Christ-mysticism centers on a realized/anticipatory conception of the kingdom. The Christian is caught between the "already" of Jesus' resurrection (inauguration) and the "not-yet" of his *parousia* (consummation). Schweitzer credits Paul with giving "the Christian faith . . . the *eschatological mysticism* of 'being in Christ.' " Emphasis is equally placed here on participation (mysticism) and on anticipation (transcendent eschatology). In Schweitzer's judgment, Paul's eschatological mysticism has solved the "pressing problem" of the Christian faith, namely, that "although Jesus Christ has come His Kingdom is still delayed." As he sees it, eschatological mysticism allows "a faith of the present [mysticism] to arise within the faith of the future [eschatology]."[21] To put it in Schweitzer's own terminology, a faith in kingdom in the heart" is able to arise within a faith of the future kingdom in the world.

Implicit in Schweitzer's Christ-mysticism is yet another mysticism: eschatological mysticism. Christ-mysticism, as an eschatological mysticism, introduces the kingdom into the believer's heart: "Through mystical fellowship with the crucified and risen Jesus Christ, believers already share with Him the supernatural quality of life in the Kingdom."[22] Eschatological mysticism mediates between Schweitzer's two key conceptions—the "now already" of the inaugurated interpretation and the "not yet" of transcendent eschatology. It is no longer a time of pure expectation. But it is not as yet the completion of the kingdom.

Although Paul believed the kingdom would be postponed only for a short time, through Christ-mysticism, he and Schweitzer perceive the kingdom as a state of existence in which individuals can participate in the present. Christ-mysticism, as participation in the death (dying) and resurrection (rising) of Jesus, has three notable bearings in Pauline thought, each of which can also be found in Schweitzer's own theology: suffering, newness of life in the Spirit, and ethics. These will be examined in turn.

But it is worth noting that Schweitzer's conceptualizations have not gone unrecognized in subsequent New Testament study. His characterization of Paul's thought as an eschatological mysticism is reflected in what E. P. Sanders calls the apostle's "participationist eschatology." Indeed, Sanders's appreciation is explicit: "Schweitzer was completely correct in emphasizing that the 'mystical' and the 'eschatological' conception are intimately related." Likewise, R. Barry Matlock maintains that in this "eschatological participation" the "distinctive voice of Paul is heard."[23] Derided though he was by his fellow Reformed Christians, Schweitzer is still being re-discovered by New Testament scholars.

Cross and Kingdom

Schweitzer maintains that suffering, as a mode of manifestation of "dying with Christ," was Paul's "lot from the moment of his beginning to preach Christ and helped him to arrive at this conception."[24] Pauline teaching is not to be explained solely by the experience of Paul's conversion on the Damascus road "to which the apostle rarely makes reference in his letters." It is "better understood" by his suffering: "Again and again . . . he speaks of his [sufferings] so numerous and so heavy."[25] But suffering is not particular to Paul. For Schweitzer, the fellowship of Christ's sufferings, as depicted in Philippians 3:10, transcends Paul's tribulations and includes the community of believers, where it witnesses to Christ.

Before continuing, Schweitzer's understanding of suffering needs some clarification. As it stands, his emphasis on suffering runs the risk of turning Christianity into what G. B. Shaw considered "Crosstianity."[26] Suffering plays a creative role in both Paul's and Schweitzer's thought. But it is not in and of itself good. Schweitzer does not propose seeking suffering for its own sake nor uphold its nobility in the Christian endurance of suffering. As we will see, the positive significance attached to suffering directs the Christian both to union with Christ in the present as well as beyond the present to the eschatological kingdom where suffering will be abolished and the whole creation will be redeemed. An important differentiation is made between redemptive or creative suffering and tragic or meaningless suffering. In fact, Schweitzer makes an implicit (though unclear) distinction between three dimensions of suffering: suffering at the hands of death, suffering on account of our "selfish preoccupations," and physical suffering due to human injustice.

Schweitzer sees prolonged or intense physical suffering as "a more terrible lord of mankind than even death," and he speaks of his service in Lambaréné as a response to the "cry of the Fellowship of those who bear the Mark of Pain."[27] To apply Jesus' response to suffering for the inauguration of the kingdom to the pain that stems from physical sickness is to neglect Jesus' healing ministry. Schweitzer's medical mission work stands testimony to such a distinction. Even on his seventieth birthday, he was performing surgery on strangled hernias—at the core of his mission to be actively engaged in the relief of physical pain and suffering.

By *suffering*, Schweitzer also refers to *dying* away from our selfish preoccupations or detaching ourselves from the possessions of life: "We can gradually detach ourselves from those things which hold our senses captive here below and set our eyes on the eternal."[28] To accept suffering in this sense is not entirely passive.

To the suffering from human injustice, Schweitzer adopts Paul's response: Christians are called to redemptive suffering to overcome injustice in this world. Such suffering serves as a witness for the kingdom and becomes a mark of those who share fellowship with Christ. This is not detached Pauline scholarship on Schweitzer's part. In his sermon "Creative Suffering," he adopts the view that suffering is a "mark of true apostleship": "Those very ones who confess their faith in the Lord and his kingdom must suffer more than the rest."[29] But as Schweitzer makes clear in "We Shall Be Exalted," the power of Jesus' resurrection manifests itself, among other ways, through *fellowship* in suffering.

> Just as Jesus was exalted on the cross at Golgotha above the world, awaiting the consummation and transfiguration which the heavenly Father would grant him, so we too must suffer in order to be exalted above the world.... We must know that this misfortune is part of what it means to be a Christian and that Jesus draws us with him into his suffering.[30]

As Schweitzer sees it, Paul breaks with the view that suffering is a sign of abandonment or punishment by God; on the contrary, the tie of faith is a tie of "blood," implying suffering and "dying" with Jesus.[31] Schweitzer certainly utters the cry of Abba together with Jesus. But he also calls upon the name of Christ: "Whatever we suffer and endure, the hand of the Savior grasps us and his voice says to us: 'When I am lifted up, I will draw all men to me.' "[32] Christ lifts one above fear and trembling; there is peace in Jesus amid tribulation: "Infinite comfort floods over everyone who lives in communion with Him."[33] Like his picture of the "victory" and "reign" of Jesus' "mangled body" on the wheel of the world, the crucified Christ and the exalted Christ go together yet again in Schweitzer's thought.

Pauline thought stresses for Schweitzer not so much the mysticism of suffering or its nobility as it does the "newness" of the Christian experience:

> The Cross of Jerusalem remains always right in the centre of our religion. We gaze upon it with the same sense of being gripped by it as our fathers did.... Our thoughts turn to the words which Jesus spoke to his disciples on the way to Jerusalem: suffering is a baptism, a holy event.[34]

Suffering, or as Paul says, "dying" with Christ, signals the foundation of a "new creation." Following the apostle, Schweitzer maintains that in dying and rising with Christ one no longer lives in "the flesh" but receives new life "in the Spirit."[35] Life in the Spirit is a thoroughly ethical concept, but it is also an eschatological notion.

By highlighting the eschatological woes necessary for Jesus' martyrdom, Schweitzer's *wheel of the world* emphasizes that the kingdom cannot come without suffering. Philip West's reading of Jesus in the *Quest* reaches the following summary judgment: "God calls us to the way of the cross, which is suffering so that the Kingdom may come."[36] Christopher Rowland similarly notes that Schweitzer's portrait of Jesus "has the merit of taking seriously those twin themes of the Gospels"—the cross and the kingdom:

> Jesus is presented as one committed to the Kingdom but recogniz-
> ing the cost to himself that this realization involved, faced as he was
> with opposition and rejection of his message. There is an acceptance
> of the reality of the struggle and turmoil which must be gone
> through.[37]

Sufferings in pursuit of the kingdom are not meaningless, but are, rather, the cost of the transformation toward that end. Dying with Christ involves sharing the way of the cross—the cup of suffering—as Jesus goes to Jerusalem. Christ-mysticism, says Schweitzer, is "just that experience expressed in terms of universal application."[38] As he makes clear, there can be no escape from the painful reality (dying with Christ) which precedes vindication (rising with Christ). This challenge confronts those who wish to be "in Christ." No short cuts to rising with Christ are found here.

Constant rejuvenation of mystical fellowship through suffering (dying) allows Schweitzer to liken mystical union with inward renunciation from the world, and to equate rising with Christ with active (sometimes suffering) striving for the kingdom of God. To say that the theme of *imitatio Christi* is present in his thought is an understatement. The voluntary self-sacrifice of *his* Jesus apparently made a great impression on him. Schweitzer's Jesus set the example for all those who would (like Schweitzer) devote themselves to the realization of the kingdom for the world. Like Schweitzer's Jesus, one may be wrong about exactly when the kingdom will come, yet one is similarly called to place faith in and struggle for the eventual consummation of God's kingdom.

Some commentators have suggested that Schweitzer's picture of Jesus and his understanding of suffering are reminiscent of the central role suffering plays in the development of Nietzsche's *Übermensch*. Nietzsche's image conveys the idea of human life transformed and enhanced in such a way as to render it worthy of higher life-affirmation. His Übermensch stands in direct opposition to Schopenhauer's view that "suffering is the process of purification by which alone man is . . . led back from the path of the error of the will-to-live."[39] For Nietzsche, the "discipline of *great* suffering" engenders opportunities for higher creation by furnishing greater obstacles to overcome.[40] Suffering drives Nietzschean Übermenschen to greater heights of self-overcoming, and in this way, is a good to the ascending life.

Schweitzer's Jesus, it is argued, is a kind of good-willed Übermensch. As early as 1912, B. H. Streeter recognized the Nietzschean strand in the *Quest's* Jesus, remarking that Schweitzer's "boldly-outlined portrait is a little like the Superman of Nietzsche dressed in Galilean robes."[41] More recently, Grässer presented Schweitzer's portrait of Jesus as revealing a Nietzschean *"überirdische Persönlichkeit."*[42] But this characterization needs strong qualification.

As with Ritschl's and Bultmann's eschatologies, Schweitzer deems Nietzsche's conception of suffering and its relation to life-affirmation as preoccupied with human existence. According to Nietzsche, accepted ethics that promote "self-sacrifice" are deficient. In his scheme, or at least as Schweitzer sees it, individual development is distinct from social concerns: "Not what it means for society, but what it means for the perfecting of the individual, is the first question which has to be put."[43] The Übermensch is one who "asserts himself triumphantly against all fate, and seeks *his own ends* without any consideration for the rest of mankind."[44] This understanding stands in stark contrast to Schweitzer's picture of Jesus' "self-sacrifice" for the kingdom "in the world." In this scheme, suffering is directed to the realization of the kingdom where suffering will be eliminated. Schweitzer tells us to listen to the witness of Paul who, together with creation, "yearns for redemption from creaturehood . . . and from the body which is in thrall."[45]

Newness of Life

Schweitzer holds that a distinctive characteristic of Pauline thought is the way the apostle "develops his mysticism and his ethics side by side."[46] Paul "neither renounces nor forsakes the world, . . . the exoteric and the esoteric go hand in hand."[47] The last two quotations could have been taken from Schweitzer's description of ethical mysticism in *The Philosophy of Civilization* where he asserts that "the struggle of thought must be directed upon ethical mysticism. We must rise to a mysticism which is ethical, and to an ethic which includes mysticism."[48] This is not the only line of correspondence between Schweitzer's Pauline Christ-mysticism and his own thought.

Schweitzer's primary interest in Paul's dying and rising with Christ (Christ-mysticism) is its association with ethics and eschatology. He sees Paul's ethical exhortation founded upon the position that believers are no longer in flesh but in Spirit: "It is a 'simple logical consequence' that we should walk in accordance with the physical newness of life in order to show that the fleshly, *sarkic,* body has been put off."[49] Revealingly, flesh (*sarx*) is not the body; it is humanity in opposition to God. It is a matter of drawing the imperative from the indicative: because believers are no longer in flesh, they must no longer live according to it.

The idea, therefore, of a transfer from the old to the new is also evident. Christ-mysticism manifests itself in the actions of the believer: there is a "passing from natural being to being in the Spirit."[50] As examined, being, or life in the Spirit, marks a new pattern of ethical attitudes. The advent of the Spirit has a direct implication on ethical behavior: "Everyone who is moved by His Spirit should become capable of helping in the world."[51] More specifically, the mystical experience of redemption in Christ is manifested in eschatological action: Christ-mysticism enables "the redeemed man to manifest in it [the world] the Spirit of the Kingdom of God which is in him."[52] The connection in the last two quotations underscores that Schweitzer sees the characteristic Pauline distinction between flesh and Spirit as not just moral but also eschatological.

In what reads like a personal testimony, he states: "If we want to 'live a quiet life,' it [dying and rising with Christ] attacks us with the question whether the being possessed by Christ is living itself out in us, or whether it is merely a distant echo on the horizon of our lives."[53] Paul affirms for Schweitzer that the eschatological change that has taken place in Christ's death will have its effect in daily life. We are back to working for the kingdom and, thus, suffering with Christ. Paul's Christ-mysticism "does not urge those who have been redeemed by Christ to withdraw from the world; he bids them take their place in it."[54] The correspondence between this passage and Schweitzer's philosophical notion of ethical life-affirmation is readily apparent: "Ethical life-affirmation demands of man that he should interest himself in the world and in what goes on in it; and, what is more, simply compel him to action."[55]

We are now in a position to refine the provisional summary in chapter 1 on what ethical mysticism as an *eschatological* Christ-mysticism means to Schweitzer: human moral action serves not only to help realize union with Christ but also to realize the kingdom. His insight into the connection between Jesus' teaching and death can be seen to serve as the basis for his view of human willing for and working for the kingdom. John Cooper has described this "reformulation" of Jesus' significance as a "functional Christology,"[56] which speaks of "the meaning of Christ on the basis of what he did and what he still does through the Spirit," and tries to produce "a theology of full involvement in the needs of the world." He continues: "A functional Christology would be the impetus for Christians to make their morality and theology the same thing."[57] A Christology of this type is little different from Schweitzer's Christ-mysticism: "It is through the most thoroughgoing morality [ethics] that the highest spirituality [mysticism] is attained."[58]

Like Jesus, Schweitzer calls on us to practice an *eschatological ethic*:

> So long as the earthly world with all its circumstances still subsists,
> what we have to do is to live in it in the spirit of unworldliness ... to
> live with eyes fixed upon eternity, while standing firmly on the
> solid ground of reality.[59]

Christians (still) find themselves in the interim. As such, they are to live as if the eschatological moment was imminent and thereby capture the same pitch of eschatology that energized Jesus and Paul. In a letter to Walter Lowrie (the translator of *The Mystery of the Kingdom of God*), Schweitzer says of his work in Lambaréné: "The days are devoted to helping in the name of Jesus, to fighting for the Kingdom of God—actions that I call 'practical eschatology'."[60]

A Village of the Kingdom

Practical eschatology is the term given to those ethical actions undertaken by humans in this world seeking to anticipate the kingdom. The key word is *practical*: "Become active," Schweitzer beseeches his parishioners. "Persevere in action for the Kingdom of God."[61] In several letters, practical eschatology is described as work "for the coming of the Kingdom of our Lord Jesus."[62] It pertains, most often, to Schweitzer's medical service:

> I feel I've done the right thing in coming here [to Lambaréné], for
> the misery is greater than anyone can describe.... Evenings I go to
> bed dead-tired, but in my heart I am profoundly happy that *I am
> serving at the outpost of the Kingdom of God!*[63]

> Abscesses, leprosy, sleeping sickness with their dreadful pains.
> I am profoundly happy that I can help where there was no one
> else.... I do not regret coming here. It feels good to help, to be at the
> outpost of the Kingdom of God.[64]

The hospital is an "outpost of the Kingdom of God" because it seeks to uphold his same ethic of self-sacrifice and compassionate care for others that he believes to be central to Jesus' "ethic of active love."

Some readers may be struck by the rather lofty, indeed grandiose, aims articulated here that seem to speak of another world where ordinary human constraints do not apply. The reality was, however, very different. Schweitzer penned these lines in 1913 from the heart of equatorial Africa, where he was daily confronted with the problem of sheer survival: "Malaria, leprosy, sleeping sickness, dysentery, framboesia, phagedenic ulcers . . . elephantiasis tumors, pneumonia, and heart disease."[65] What is astounding, then, in this context, is that he could not only contemplate eschatological visions of the good but also come to a conception of reverence for life, which he regarded as the crown of all his accomplishments, amid the very threats of disease and death which other forms of life carried:

> I saw a man lying on the ground with his head almost buried in the
> sand and ants running all over him. It was a victim of sleeping
> sickness whom his companions had left there, probably some days
> before, because they could not take him any further. He was past
> all help, though he still breathed. While I was busied with him
> I could see through the door of the hut the bright blue waters of
> the bay in their frame of green woods, a scene of magic beauty,
> looking still more enchanting in the flood of golden light poured over
> it by the setting sun. To be shown in a single glance such a para-
> dise and such helpless, hopeless misery, was overwhelming.[66]

It should not be forgotten that when pressed in later life about his achievements, Schweitzer was adamant that his "primary contribution" was not as "the doctor who ministers to the sick," but, rather, as the author of the ethic of reverence for life.[67]

In his sermon "Compelling Hope," he preaches that "hope is the prerequisite of it [work]. . . . We accomplish nothing without hope, without a sure inner hope that a new age is about to dawn. Hope is strength."[68] Schweitzer places *hope* among the dispositions that shape moral agency and undergird moral selfhood. Practical eschatology is hopeful activity for change in the present. Indeed, for Schweitzer our hope is in vain if the possibility of sharing "with one another the blessings of a new creation" does not work in our midst now.[69] In such a context, eschatology not only serves to stimulate action, but is also the very basis of ethics.

Schweitzer's belief that "modern Kingdom-of-God religion calls on men to do Kingdom-of-God work"[70] is closely echoed in Moltmann's eschatology. Moltmann maintains that those who have "fellowship with Jesus are called to do the same messianic work as Jesus himself: 'Go and preach: the kingdom of God is at hand. Heal the sick, raise the dead, cleanse the lepers, cast out demons.'" He continues:

> In nineteenth-century Germany, "kingdom-of-God work" was the
> description given to missionary and diaconic ministries carried out by
> Christians in the world. . . . I could give as examples Kagawa's

"kingdom-of-God movement" in the Tokyo slums, the base communities in Latin America, and the peace movement in Germany. Everywhere God's kingdom takes us beyond the frontiers of the church.[71]

Moltmann could also have pointed to Schweitzer's medical work in Lambaréné as an example of "kingdom-of-God work," or practical eschatology. But Moltmann gives Schweitzer his due when he suggests that "the ethic reverence for life, an ethic taught by Albert Schweitzer" should be seen as integral to kingdom-of-God work.[72] Indeed, Moltmann borrows Schweitzer's term *practical eschatology* while in the same breath somehow contriving to deny that there was anything there to borrow: "The Christian life and conduct to which Christian ethics are supposed to lead are nothing other than *practical eschatology* and lived hope."[73] We might call this a kind of left-handed appreciation. With Schweitzer's practical eschatology in mind, we return with incredulity to Moltmann's remark that "the startling thing about Schweitzer's work . . . is that he had no eschatological sense at all—neither for theological nor for philosophical eschatology."[74] The startling thing about Moltmann's work is that he had no appreciation for Schweitzer's eschatological sense at all.

The same can said for others. "Ethics as practical eschatology," is how Meeks describes Moltmann's attempt to write a "historical ethic of hope." Reminiscent of Schweitzer's practical eschatology, Braaten refers to ethics in context of the kingdom as *eschatopraxis*, namely, seeking to live the future ahead of time. "In proleptic ethics it may truly be said that the end justifies the means, because the end is proleptically present and operative beforehand, rehearsing the qualities of the eschatological kingdom—peace, love, joy, freedom, equality, unity—in the course of history."[75] Braaten would have done well to add reverence for life.

All Creation Groans

In Schweitzer's theology work for the kingdom encompasses a cosmic element: it seeks to assist all life. It is important to recall his universal understanding of salvation; he emphasizes the need not just for "a personal doctrine of redemption," but one that includes the "transformation of the natural circumstances of the world."[76] By offering hope for the ultimate redemption of all creation, he places human moral action (practical eschatology) within a teleological context.

As with other aspects of Jesus' inauguration of the kingdom, the consummation of the kingdom will only be realized in the eschatological future.

But the question remains: how are humans to live in the interim time between creation and consummation, seeking to anticipate the biblical vision of universal peaceableness? Schweitzer believes that such peace can be anticipated between humans and other life in the present expressing "love in action, not only on behalf of human beings, but also on behalf of all living things."[77] As he sees it, hope is in vain if the possibility of sharing "with one another the blessings of a new creation" does not work in our midst now. Every act that preserves life from destruction is seen as a prelude to the new creation.

Like other aspects of Schweitzer's theology, his practical eschatology has suffered from misunderstanding among his fellow theologians. In fact, the perceived lack of connection between his eschatology and ethical thought has provided a source for another series of criticisms articulated by his contemporaries as well as by more recent commentators. Cullmann's and Barth's criticisms on the relationship between Schweitzer's exegesis and his ethics are perhaps the clearest expressions of this view. Cullmann claims:

> [Schweitzer did not] base his own philosophy of life . . . on Jesus' eschatology. . . . Schweitzer founded his own personal attitude on "reverence for life." For Schweitzer, this went hand in hand with a practical Christianity. But theoretically it was neither rooted in the eschatology of Jesus . . . nor in the eschatological mysticism of Paul. An impassable gap opens between his exegetical and his religious-philosophical attitudes. . . . In the case of Albert Schweitzer the results of his exegetical research [i.e. the central role of eschatology in Jesus and Paul] are out of balance with his philosophy of "reverence for life."[78]

Along similar lines, Barth's critique of Schweitzer does not read him very accurately at this point:

> Schweitzer (Von Reimarus zu Wrede, 1906) built it [eschatology] up into the theory that the whole momentum of the New Testament message and the New Testament faith lay in the hope that Jesus' return and the setting up of the kingdom of God on earth—a hope that had not been fulfilled and was therefore erroneous.
>
> Schweitzer himself was influenced by this view to the extent that he gave his positive teaching the form of an ethic of philosophy of culture [reverence for life] in which the Gospel lives on only in the form of the doctrine (identical with all kinds of Eastern wisdom) that the fashion of this world passes away and our portion can only be active sympathy with its irremediable misery.[79]

Following along this trodden path, Timothy Gorringe contends that Schweitzer did "nothing with his rediscovery of eschatology, but retreated to the calmer waters of liberal theology and the edge of the primeval forest [Lambaréné]."[80] The common consensus is that Schweitzer left the eschatological findings of his exegesis off to one side, articulating his ethic without them. These critiques hardly begin to understand the decisive role of eschatology in Schweitzer's ethical thought. They saw two bits of Schweitzer's thought, but not the interplay between them or the derivability of one from the other.

It is noteworthy that Cullmann refers to reverence for life as a "philosophy," suggesting unfamiliarity with its theological roots. Far from creating an "impassable gap" or being "out of balance" with the findings of Schweitzer's New Testament scholarship, Schweitzer's ethical mysticism is based on an eschatological Christ-mysticism which developed out of his studies of Jesus and Paul. Gorringe also misses the mark to the extent that he fails to appreciate how it was Schweitzer's understanding of Jesus' eschatological mission which drove him to take up service "at the edge of the primeval forest." This could hardly be considered a "retreat."

Barth's criticisms are even more puzzling. Like Moltmann, he sees the *Quest's* Jesus on the wheel of the world as a failed prophet. Of course, this is far from Schweitzer's understanding of the passage, as he makes clear:

> Those who continue to preach an ethic based on the words of historic Jesus are guilty . . . of leaving out of account the enablement towards the good, which God has since then bestowed upon believers through the death and resurrection of Jesus, and the consequent gift of the Spirit.[81]

Jesus' death and resurrection inaugurate the kingdom and deliver the Spirit which works in the human heart to help actualize the kingdom.

Next, Schweitzer never suggests that the "fashion of this world passes away" or that the world is illusory. On the contrary, he speaks of redemption from transience and death. Reverence for life is not merely to be seen, as Barth suggests, as an "active sympathy" with the "misery" of creation. Rather, Schweitzer's ethic, as a practical eschatology, stands in a much larger context: reverence for life is work for the kingdom where the "irremediable misery" of creation is *transformed*. At such a point, "the creatures [who] sigh with us," preaches Schweitzer, will "be freed from anxiety and perishability."[82] The whole community of created beings is destined for eschatological redemption. Practical eschatology is thoroughly a cosmic eschatology.

Living Nonviolently

It is likely that Barth, who objected to ethical "vegetarianism" on the basis "that it represents a wanton anticipation of what is described by Is. 11 and Rom. 8 as existence in the new aeon for which we hope,"[83] would have also opposed Schweitzer's practical eschatology on the same grounds. It was not that living nonviolently in peace with all creation was not God's will; rather the Christian's acts are "interim steps" with "no more than provisional and relative significance and range." Barth draws attention to the limitations of human agency; for our action, he insists, is never "more than a very feeble and not a perfect work."[84] His skepticism can be seen positively to challenge the notion of an upward progress to human history after witnessing the "decay of civilization." In *Ethics*, he sharpens his criticism: "It is not true that the pious man has to work at the coming of the kingdom of God. He has to pray for the coming of the kingdom of God—but this is something different."[85] Indeed, Barth deems prayer as "the most intimate and effective form of Christian action."[86] Schweitzer responds:

> In recent times a tendency has appeared in dogmatic religion which declares that religion has nothing to do with the world and civilization. It is not its business to realize the Kingdom of God on earth. This extreme tendency is mainly represented by Karl Barth.
>
> Barth says a religious person does not concern himself with what happens to the world. The idea of the Kingdom of God plays no part with him. He mocks at what he calls "civilized Protestantism [*Kulturprotestantismus*]." The church must leave the world to itself. All that concerns the church is the preaching of revealed truth. Religion is turned aside from the world.
>
> Yet Karl Barth—whom I, personally, value greatly—came to the point when he had to concern himself with the world . . . to defend the freedom of religion against the state. And he did it with courage. But it shows that his theory is false! It is something terrible to say that religion is not ethical. Karl Barth is a truly religious personality, and in his sermons there is much profound religion. But the terrible thing is that he dares to preach that religion is turned aside from the world and in so doing expresses what the spirit of the age is feeling.[87]

Presumably, Schweitzer is referring to Barth's work in helping to form the Confessing Church, as well as his significant contribution to the Barmen

Declaration of 1934, to suggest that faith and action merged for Barth. In the declaration, Barth pledged loyalty to Jesus Christ, thereby excluding the allegiance to Hitler that was demanded of all civil servants. While it is doubtful that Barthian theology advocates the quietism that Schweitzer portrays, Barth's statements on the "pious man" appear to reject the notion that human activity can significantly anticipate or participate in the consummation of the kingdom. This ambiguity in Barth's thought can be clarified.

In *Barth's Moral Theology*, John Webster argues that *prayer* should be understood as a "humble, confident, trustful assigning of priority to God's action."[88] Barth emphasizes that the kingdom will not be actualized without *God's* act. But there is more: "If this prayer is part of man's invocation of God, it does, of course, entail *doing* on man's part."[89] To this end, Barth remarks that there is "one thing . . . [the Christian] will never have cause to do, namely to refrain from action like the lazy servant."[90] Indeed, the action of those who invoke the kingdom of God should be "kingdom-like."[91] There is an ethical turning to "the great final day" for those

> who really press and involve God with this petition in the expectation
> that he will answer it, as people who are seriously and fundamen-
> tally disquieted and startled, press and involve themselves too in their
> own place and manner as people and within the limits of their
> own human capabilities and possibilities. They declare, and within
> their limits take on responsibility, that in the matter about which they
> pray to God something will be done correspondingly by them.[92]

Barth has a greater appreciation for hope and its attendant human moral action than Schweitzer suggests. As such, should we see practical eschatology as a "wanton anticipation" of the kingdom, a trivial activity? Barth is not very consistent. As Schweitzer helps to point out, Barth's work for international peace was based on the declaration of peace achieved through the reconciliation of the world by Christ, and its full realization in the eschatological future. And, as Barth proclaims, we have a "responsibility to witness to that peace and find ourselves called to do it."[93]

Still, Barth does not ascribe the same level of theological importance to ethical activity as does Schweitzer. Schweitzer's practical eschatology affords human moral action an important role in ushering in the kingdom. Barth underscores the fact that humans can only accomplish so much: hope "on the one side denotes a definite mode of human action, but on the other clearly expresses divine control of its ultimate quality."[94]

The way Barth distinguishes primary and secondary ethical action may help to elucidate his understanding of eschatology. "Primary ethical action" is repentance that follows from giving the glory to God, from worship. "Secondary ethical action," our actions toward our neighbor and in community, *follows* from this.[95] Similarly, Barth suggests that primary eschatological action involves prayer for God's action, while secondary eschatological action entails human moral activity in the light of that telos.

While Schweitzer understands the limitations of human activity and God's ultimate power to introduce the kingdom, he still stresses the positive function of ethical action. The ethical action proposed in reverence for life, as he sees it, is a response to the Spirit. But as Schweitzer makes clear, it is not the actualization of that promise itself for which he still waits in hope and offers prayer: "To Him [God] we yield our will; to Him we leave the future. . . . The ethical activity of man is only like a powerful prayer to God, that He may cause the Kingdom to appear without delay."[96] Schweitzer's emphasis on God is not meant to exclude social action but to relativist it. From this perspective, although Schweitzer and Barth hold some important differences, the two theologians' positions are much less far apart than each one presented it, or than one might have initially suspected.

For Schweitzer, the practice of reverence for life, when seen as the expression of practical eschatology, anticipates in some small way the peace of the kingdom. Schweitzer writes: "If I save an insect from a puddle, life has devoted itself to life, and the division of life against itself is ended."[97] "Life has devoted itself to life" and harmony has been achieved, if only for a moment in a microcosm; part of the future vision of redemption is already inaugurated in the present. Indeed, according to Charles Joy, the "wild creatures of the Lambaréné jungle often eat from Schweitzer's hand, or permit him to caress them freely."[98] "The nourishment of one creature at the expense of another," writes Barth, "does not correspond to an original order and will not therefore correspond to a final."[99] The violence of the natural world is seen by both to be characteristic of the fallen nature of creation and a disruption of the original peace amongst creatures. Barth's eschatological conception highlights that predation is not God's final order and his future vision takes an ethical form not dissimilar to Schweitzer's practical eschatology: "There is *another* world and *this* world is not yet this other world, which in the words: 'Be changed!' is set as a goal towards which we have to cast our eyes and direct our steps."[100]

This chapter has been concerned with the twin themes of mysticism and eschatology which dominate Schweitzer's thought. For many, these are otherworldly concerns, whereas—and this cannot be stressed enough—for him, they were sources of moral empowerment in this world. Specifically, they were among the key intellectual building blocks to the subsequent conceptualization of reverence for life.

Schweitzer refused to resign himself to the *Selbstentzweiung* that characterized the world, and especially in his frontline work in Lambaréné. What might appear to be esoteric themes of transcendence was the daily life-blood of his heroic work there. And heroic it was. That this practical service and healing of the sick was Christ-like cannot be gainsaid. Whatever its limitations or partialities, Schweitzer's life exhibits a moral heroism that few other theologians, let alone physicians, can match.

6

Rediscovering Lambaréné

Common opinion believes that reverence for life died with Schweitzer in Lambaréné in 1965. Don Cupitt delivers the usual verdict as follows:

> The religion of life is currently acquiring its saints as well as its prophets and teachers. Was Albert Schweitzer its John the Baptist? He probably was; but he too is out of fashion, and his own ethic of Reverence for Life is largely forgotten even as it has prevailed.[1]

There are a number of obvious misconceptions here. In the first place, Schweitzer never subscribed to a *religion of life*. Indeed, he would hardly have understood the term. As we have seen, reverence only emerged out of an intense intellectual struggle and a fascination with the persons of Jesus and Paul as well as the Jain conception of ahimsā. No pantheism (for that is arguably what a religion of life lapses into) could possibly be interested in transcendence, let alone an eschatological mysticism.

Secondly, the reference to Schweitzer as "out of fashion" is a curious argument from a theologian whose task should be concerned with discerning, even confronting, fashion, rather than subscribing to it. Truth, of course, cannot be established by popular votes. Schweitzer, like all of us, was historically conditioned: the specific missionary work to which he felt called was inevitably the product of a particular time and place, as is true of all human Endeavor. But that should not obscure what was necessary or laudable about his work, nor should it mean that we cannot appropriate the best of his example today.

There is an incongruity in Cupitt's view that Schweitzer's reverence is "forgotten even as it has prevailed." When Schweitzer indicated that he wished to be remembered by reverence for life as his crowning accomplishment, he was obviously not staking out the ground for a verbal formula. Rather, reverence was an experience, even a revelation, open to all. That the value of life is, to some extent, on the moral agenda, and that we now commonly debate, for example, abortion, euthanasia, capital punishment, nuclear weapons, ecology, and vegetarianism, is part of Schweitzer's rightful legacy of which he would have been proud. Cupitt overlooks that the strength of Schweitzer's position derives from his preparedness to confront fashion: tame though it might appear now, he risked public obloquy by his concern for insects, animals and the environment. He was also a source of ridicule by his colleagues who could not understand why he would give up an established academic career even to help humans suffering in Lambaréné.

Cupitt neglects the significance of Schweitzer as an iconic figure in the now burgeoning life-centered ethics movement. As evidence, this chapter selects for examination two strands of development of Schweitzer's work, *acknowledged* or *unacknowledged*, in liberal Protestant and process theology.

Ground of All Beings

In 1962, Lambaréné physician Richard Friedmann asked Tillich (1886–1965) why it was that he rarely mentioned Schweitzer in his books. Tillich responded that everything he wrote presupposed the influence of Schweitzer. "But shouldn't you publicly acknowledge this?" Friedmann asked. Tillich replied (somewhat disingenuously one might think) that it seemed to be

> a fact of life that the most important things are taken for granted.
> What is most important to life, for instance? We talk about food and
> water, but that which is most important, which we would not sur-
> vive for a few minutes without, air, we hardly ever refer to. We take for
> granted the air we breathe, as we do the great germinal thinkers
> who have become basic to our entire systems of thought.[2]

Tillich acknowledged his indebtedness more fully during a television program, *The Theological Significance of Schweitzer*.[3] In response to the first question from Jerald Brauer, as to whether he had ever met Schweitzer, Tillich replied:

No, I am sorry, I always missed him, although we were scheduled to meet several times.... But that doesn't mean that I really missed him. At least he didn't miss me, because he was with me all my life since my past student days in the year 1909.[4]

Tillich first recounts how for him, at the age of seventeen, Schweitzer's *The Quest of the Historical Jesus* "was like a revelation." Tillich claims, "[It] decidedly determined my whole theological career."[5] When asked about the influence of Schweitzer's picture of Christ, he remarks, "[If] this new reality [i.e., Christ] is in its very centre God's self-surrendering love [i.e., Will-to-Love] . . . then on this point we would come together."[6] Brauer questioned Tillich if this "new reality" was primarily an ethical principle as Schweitzer believed, or whether it was "something more basic than an ethical principle." Tillich does not rule out a connection: "I don't know [if] Schweitzer considers life . . . or the ground of everything living, in a similar way as I consider the divine Ground of all beings. There may be a similarity."[7] There may be indeed, and more than one, as Tillich's works show readily enough.

Elsewhere Tillich is more specific about the nature of these similarities and his indebtedness to Schweitzer's work. For example: "The unity of all life, as I like to call it, seems to me one point in which Schweitzer is of greatest importance and in which I follow him."[8] The verb *follow*, here, is usefully ambiguous, marking both dependence (follow-as-disciple) and independence (follow-as-developer). In the former sense, compare the following to passages:

Schweitzer: "God is the creative force which produces and sustains all that is."[9]

Tillich: God "is the creative Ground of life, the power of life in everything that lives."[10]

It is clear that both theologians understand God as the underlying creative principle in all things. But Tillich goes further. His essay "Nature and Sacrament" carries forward this trajectory by developing a sacramental theology of nature where the Divine is found not only in the traditional sacraments but also in natural reality. Stemming from this theology, Tillich develops his ontological concept of life.

If the actualization of the potential is a structural condition of all being, and if this actualization is called *life*, then the universal concept of life is unavoidable. Consequently, the genesis of stars and rocks, their growth as well as their decay, must be called a life process. The ontological concept of life liberates the word *life* from its bondage to the organic realm and elevates it to the level of a basic term that can be used within the theological system.[11]

Tillich rejects anthropocentrism claiming that "the inorganic has a *preferred* position among the dimensions in so far as it is the first condition for the actualization of every dimension. This is why all realms of being would dissolve were the basic condition provided by the constellation of inorganic to disappear."[12] When Tillich speaks of the inorganic dimension's preferred position he is not conferring on it an "ontologised, qualitative position of superiority." Rather, he is highlighting its status as "the fundamental conditioning dimension of all the other dimensions."[13] That is, the inorganic plays an essential role in supporting the life process. Tillich opposes the mechanistic view of so-called inanimate, inert matter: "Just like every other dimension, the inorganic belongs to life, and it shows the integratedness and the possible disintegration of life in general."[14] His perception highlights the interdependence of all life; all reality, to some important degree, participates in the life process.

We have already seen that one of Schweitzer's principal concerns is the issue of hierarchies and differential species valuation. He questions the anthropocentric standard by which humans differentiate life forms and suggests that *all* living beings have value *in themselves*. Though humans must make practical decisions about the priority of different life forms, such judgments should not be taken as an objective measure of the intrinsic value of other life. Hierarchies, or levels, cannot be defended by establishing the importance that different life forms hold in the universe, which is, of course, unknowable.

Tillich accepts this criticism of anthropocentrism. He too challenges anthropocentrism by recognizing perhaps even more clearly than Schweitzer (or indeed anyone else of Schweitzer's generation) the *interdependence* of the organic and inorganic dimensions and hence finds it impossible to differentiate between the organic and the inorganic in attributions of value. His preference for the inorganic dimension challenges the traditional hierarchy of life in nature, with humans at the top, reflecting varying degrees of value in creation. Tillich's conception of humans as the highest beings in creation is qualified with the notion that we are not necessarily the most perfect: "Perfection means actualization of one's potential; therefore a lower being can be more perfect than a higher one if it is actually what it is potentially. . . . and man can become less perfect than any other, because he not only can fail to actualize his essential being but can deny and distort it."[15] Following Schweitzer's lead, of such human-made systems of gradation, Tillich maintains:

In this view reality is seen as a pyramid of levels following each other in vertical direction according to their power of being and their grade of value.[16]

And Schweitzer:

The ethics of reverence for life makes no distinction between higher and lower, more precious and less precious lives.... For what are we doing, when we establish hard and fast gradations in value between living organisms, but judging them in relation to ourselves, by whether they seem to stand closer to us or farther from us.[17]

Tillich concludes that the metaphors *level, stratum,* or *layer,* should be excluded from any description of life processes. His critique encompasses more than a change of terminology: "The significant thing ... is not the replacement of one metaphor by another [*levels* with *dimensions*] but the changed vision of reality which such replacement expresses."[18] The importance of the metaphor *dimension* lies in its capacity to transform our perception of life. There's a sort of symmetry. No metaphor is safe if unwatched, but by the same token none is absolutely worthless when watched. Tillich could argue that level-metaphors are *currently* acting as a brake, but could afford to concede that they may once have been enlightening compared with the then alternative. Similarly, he cannot afford to imply that the dimensions-metaphor (or any other) is somehow exempt from itself going through this cycle. Perhaps more importantly, Tillich's aim in distinguishing the dimensions of life is to underscore the multidimensional *unity of all life* as well as the source and consequences of the *ambiguities* of all life processes. Schweitzer's and Tillich's thought stress the danger, epistemologically, ontologically, and ethically, in any systematic valuation.

Shared Convictions

Tillich's philosophy of life resonates with several other key Schweitzerian insights as can best be shown by parallel passages. There are three areas of thought where engagement appears likely.

First is the area of epistemology and specifically Schweitzer's emphasis that the knowledge one acquires inwardly (will-to-live) transcends what one sees outwardly in the world:

Schweitzer: "I can understand the nature of the living being outside of myself only through the living being within me.... Knowledge of [external] reality must pass through a phase of thinking about the nature of [personal] being."[19]

Tillich: "Man has become aware of the fact that he himself is the door to the deeper levels of reality, that in his own existence he has the only possible approach to existence itself.... The immediate experience of one's own existence reveals something of the nature of existence generally."[20]

In both cases, and in equivalent terms, their thought places the human subject firmly within the material world. Through our body, we each have inner awareness of something that is also part of the world. By making the fundamental force (*will* for Schweitzer and *being* for Tillich) in the natural world homogenous, the traditional division between humans and the world is rejected by both thinkers.

Second, Tillich's stress on the *unity*, or relatedness, of all life parallels Schweitzer's understanding of the self as "life which wills to live, in the midst of life which wills to live"[21] and his conception that "in the very fibers of our being, we bear within ourselves the fact of the solidarity of life."[22] The experiential identification of one's individual will-to-live with other life, and through life with God, is foundational to Schweitzer's mystical theology. The self, as will-to-live, exists in relation to other wills-to-live, both human and nonhuman:

The important thing is that we are part of life. We are born of other lives; we possess the capacities to bring still other lives into existence.... So nature compels us to recognize the fact of mutual dependence ... [and] the solidarity of all life.[23]

The correspondence with Tillich's thought in *The Shaking of Foundations* is evident: "We are bound to it [the "Ground of life"] for all eternity, just as we are bound to ourselves and to all other life."[24] For Schweitzer and Tillich, there is an ontological or chthonic link with all wills-to-live or life; all life has a common origin in the infinite Will-to-Live, or Ground of life. For both, the world is an important means of relationship with the Creator.

Third is the highly contentious perception, shared by both theologians, that all reality is animate. Schweitzer states: "Everything, accordingly, which meets me in the world of phenomena is a manifestation of the will-to-live."[25] The will-to-live is not limited to humans, but rather is discernible in "the flowering tree, in strange forms of medusa, in the blade of grass, [and] in the crystal."[26] As has been seen, Tillich similarly highlights the vitality of the "inorganic" dimension as well as the way in which the inorganic is present in the spiritual and vice versa.[27] Also of note is Tillich's defense of voluntarism, as found in Schweitzer's thought. He writes:

> How can there be a will in stones and crystals and plants and animals? They ... have no purpose which is directed by an intellect express- ing itself in language, using universals, etc. But this is not what will means if it is understood in an ontological sense. Will is the dynamics in all forms of life.... [Will] appears in man as conscious will, in an- imals as instincts or drives—these also appear in man—in plants as urges, and in material reality as trends such as gravitation, etc. If you understand will as the dynamic element in all reality, then it makes sense.... It is the universal driving dynamic of all life processes.[28]

This universal conception of vitality is perhaps the most striking of the features which, shared by Schweitzer and Tillich, distinguish them from most (if not all) of their contemporaries.

Brauer later questions Tillich about Schweitzer's ethic of reverence for life and asks whether he is "engaged in a theological construction that is moving in a somewhat similar direction?" Tillich responds:

> Yes, I think it's more moving in a similar direction. But I have the suspicion that Schweitzer and I have similar fathers in spirit. The first one ... is Schelling, who produced first in the development of Western philosophy a developed philosophy of nature. And that brought him very near to Goethe, about whom Schweitzer has writ- ten one of the most beautiful papers evaluating especially Goethe's philosophy of nature. Later on we come to the philosophy of life of the end of the nineteenth century with Bergson, who has influenced the British-American philosopher, Whitehead. And I feel myself very much in this line. And then much more than these two, Nietzsche, whose philosophy of life also has deeply influenced me.[29]

More important, Tillich summarizes the moral lesson impressed on him by these philosophers, and especially by Schweitzer:

> Out of these sources I have come to the idea that every theology which separates men from nature is completely mistaken. Nature participates in man and men participate in nature, and for this reason I feel now more than in earlier years the impact of Schweitzer's idea of the inviolability of life. I even have a large section in the forth- coming third volume of my *Systematic Theology* under the title, "The Inviolability of Life."[30]

Tillich did not produce a section "The Inviolability of Life"—which would have been a crass misinterpretation of Schweitzer's ethical mysticism of reverence—but entitled part IV "Life and Spirit" instead. Nonetheless, Schweitzer's impact on his understanding of human relations with the natural world is evident. Following Schweitzer, Tillich stresses the need for humans to respect those dimensions of being upon which their own being is predicated.[31] Durwood Foster recounted the following story in his address to the North American Tillich Society:

> Some of us wanted to go fishing.... They [the fish] were said to be
> biting over in the bay. We assumed Paulus was coming, and it
> seemed to be so when we met at the Tillich's house to deploy. But on
> hearing the talk of fishing, Paulus's mood changed. One could
> wonder if this was linked to other reactions of avoidance, or dread,
> toward the animal world. But the tack he took was to indict, quite
> vehemently, our Ritschlian attitude of callously exploiting nature,
> turning everything into a mere thing to be used. He was totally
> sincere about this.... We argued that we planned to eat the fish,
> if we caught any, and harvesting the game was essential for its own
> well-being. Paulus wasn't impressed. He stayed at home. And when
> we got to the water, no one wanted to fish.[32]

For Tillich, the "inviolability of living beings is expressed in the protection given to them in many religions ... and in the actual participation of man in the life of plants and animals."[33] Like Schweitzer, Tillich made a study of several world religions and as a matter of interesting convergence it is possible that he was similarly influenced by the extension of moral concern for non-human species as found in varying degrees in many Indian religions. Tillich notes that "in the relation of man to all other living beings a change took place only where the relation of man to some animals (or, as in India to animals in general) became analogous to the relation of man to man."[34]

Redeeming Ambiguities

Interaction with the natural world is for Tillich "so much a part of universal human existence that it does not require expanded comment." But the *ambiguities* in the relations between humans and the natural world "call for full discussion."[35] While discussing this aspect of their philosophies of life, Tillich renders an incorrect interpretation of Schweitzer's thesis:

A slight difference would be observed by the careful—certainly by
the future—observers, namely that in Schweitzer perhaps there is a
little bit more emphasis on the love element in nature and in man.
I would agree with him in this, but we also must see the destructive
element in all natural realities, and this destructive element has perhaps
been neglected not so much in Schweitzer's actions than in Schweitzer's thinking. Here seems to me the limit of his philosophy of life.

Certainly life is in principle holy and inviolate. But on the other
hand, life is violated all the time. It violates itself all the time and
has the ambiguity that it's both creative and destructive, and both
integrating and disintegrating, both manifesting the divine Ground
and hiding the divine Ground. And in these ambiguities, I am discussing my philosophy of life, and I am not sure how far Schweitzer
would follow me on this point. I have more the feeling that his
emphasis is on the positive side.[36]

More accurately, there is a striking similarity between Schweitzer's and
Tillich's view of cosmic reality. It may be Tillich's concern to emphasize his
independence which has led him to overlook numerous passages in Schweitzer's writings on nature's moral ambiguity. Indeed, Tillich could hardly have
made this criticism if he had been aware of Schweitzer's following remarks:

The world is horror in splendor, meaningless in meaning, sorrow
in joy.[37]

Nature is beautiful and sublime, viewed from the outside. But to read
in its book is horrible. . . . *Nature knows no reverence for life*. It produces life in thousands of most meaningful ways and destroys it in
thousands of the most senseless ways. . . . Creatures live at the
cost of the lives of other creatures.[38]

It remains a painful enigma for me to live with reverence for life
in a world which is dominated by creative will which is also destructive will, and destructive will which is also creative.[39]

Where Schweitzer notes the division of the will-to-live against itself, Tillich
writes of the estrangement of *being* from *Being* itself:

[Life] lives and grows . . . by suppressing or removing other life.[40]

Nature is not only glorious; it is also tragic. It is subjected to the laws
of finitude and destruction. It is suffering and sighing with us. . . . No

one who has ever listened to the sounds of nature with sympathy can forget their tragic melodies.... Separation constitutes the state of everything that exists; it is a universal fact, it is the fate of every life.... *Existence is separation!*[41]

Human existence, indeed, all reality, is characterized by *estrangement*. But Schweitzer's and Tillich's originality does not lie in their statements of the dilemma, whatever their tone or phrasing might imply. Seen from the outside, they both had trouble (as others still do) digesting Darwin's ideas. *Darwin* is shorthand here: of course, the world did not have to wait until 1857 to discover that nature was red in tooth and claw.

But, there is more. For the purposes of this examination, it is important to acknowledge that Schweitzer and Tillich are among the first thinkers to examine this issue from a *theological* (as opposed to evolutionary-biological) standpoint. Both are trying to find a way of accounting for and ultimately overcoming this division/estrangement. In Schweitzer's thought, the will-to-live is superseded by the will-to-love, which acts "always with special relations of solidarity with others."[42] "Love," as Schweitzer writes in what anticipates Tillichian terminology, "means harmony of being, community of being."[43] Tillich correspondingly discusses how the "Spiritual Presence" manifests itself as love. Because the "first mark of estrangement includes un-love," it is reconciled *by* love: "In love, estrangement is overcome by reunion."[44] Likewise, in *Love, Power, and Justice*, the "power of God is that He overcomes estrangement"; reconciliation takes "the form of reuniting love . . . and love is the power for reunion of the separated."[45] Love, says Tillich, "is the *reunion* of life with life. . . . For life belongs to life."[46] For both theologians, love is the means par excellence for reconciliation. Their "parallel" solutions are more than assertions of cosmic reconciliation by Divine intervention. Both Schweitzer and Tillich make an especial claim on the human person to serve as mediators of divine love in the world.

Lastly, although Tillich does not discuss eschatology in his interview, Schweitzer's and his understandings of cosmic reconciliation in the kingdom of God display a possible influence or at least a convergence on certain key points. Schweitzer's eschatology encompasses a cosmic framework: it seeks to overcome the division that characterizes the whole of creation. He rails against the individualistic reduction of the kingdom to personal salvation: it is "a great weakness for man to be wholly concerned with his own individual redemption, and not equally with the coming of the Kingdom of God . . . in regard to the future of the world."[47] Schweitzer's eschatology is rooted in his reading of Paul's "marvelous passage" (Romans 8:22) that "speaks of the longing of the whole creation for early redemption" and displays "his deep sympathy with the animal creation ... and natural world."[48] Elsewhere, he praises the letter to the Romans where Paul "describes how even the creatures sigh with us to be freed from suffering and perishability,"[49] and how the apostle, together with creation, "yearns for redemption from creaturehood ... and from the body which is in thrall."[50]

Tillich's understanding of the ambiguity of life leads to a similar quest for the *un*ambiguous kingdom of God. He, too, denounces a privatistic interpretation of the kingdom: "Man cannot claim that the infinite has entered the finite to overcome its existential estrangement in man alone."[51] On the contrary, Tillich's sermon "Nature, Also, Mourns for a Lost Good" offers an account of nature's "longing" for reconciliation, also based on Paul's letter to the Romans: the apostle "knows that we, with all other creatures, are in the stage of expectation, longing and suffering with all animals and flowers, with the oceans and winds."[52] Tillich likewise notes:

> Always mankind has dreamed of a time when harmony and joy filled all nature, and peace reigned between nature and man. ... In Paul's melancholic words this dream sounds. Man and nature belong together in their created glory, in their tragedy, and in their salvation. ... For there is no salvation of man if there is no salvation of nature, for man is in nature and nature is in man.[53]

Furthermore, Tillich acknowledges the import of Jesus' crucifixion for all creation: "We *should* ask whether we are able to feel ... that the event at Golgotha is one which concerns this universe, including all nature and all history."[54]

And, in *Systematic Theology*, Tillich writes:

> It is a Kingdom not only of men; it involves the fulfillment of life under all dimensions. ... The symbol of a "new heaven and a new earth" indicates the universality of the blessedness of the fulfilled Kingdom of God. ... All dimensions of life were included in the consideration of the ultimate *telos* of becoming.[55]

A comparison of Schweitzer's and Tillich's understandings of cosmic redemption displays a further similarity between the two thinkers. Schweitzer writes:

> The prophet Isaiah (11:6–9) proclaims that the Lord will save the world.[56]
>
> Originally the dominant thought of the Kingdom of God meant that believers shared with one another the blessings of a new creation.

But now the experience of the individual took precedence. . . . Each separate believer is now concerned with his own redemption. He cares nothing for the future of mankind and of the world.[57]

And similarly Tillich maintains:

And one thing is made very clear . . . that salvation means salvation of the *world*, and not of human beings alone. Lions and sheep, little children and snakes, will lie together in peace, says Isaiah.

Therefore commune with nature! Become reconciled with nature after your estrangement from it. . . . It will sigh with us in the bondage of tragedy. It will speak of the indestructible hope of salvation![58]

Their visions of the kingdom articulate and complete their consistent emphasis on the unity of life and especially of the human creature with the rest of nature.

Finally, in accord with Schweitzer's practical eschatology, Tillich fashions an eschatological dialectic: a relationship between our present existence and future hope. "The *eschaton* becomes a matter of present experience without losing its futuristic dimension."[59] Though the kingdom refers beyond history, "saving power [also] breaks into history, works through history."[60] Although Tillich does not give systematic content to the type of work he envisions resulting from such a future-oriented theology, it presumably encompasses the "reunion of the separated" through love in all dimensions. He points to the "biblical vision of peace in nature" envisaging "an unambiguous self-transcendence in the realm of the organic which would change the actual conditions of organic life."[61] This characterization of the kingdom when viewed alongside his understanding of the effect of the *eschaton* in the present, upholds the possibility of reconciliation, if only in a limited fashion, of the ambiguities of cosmic reality in the present and unconditionally in the future.

The similarities between Schweitzer's and Tillich's conceptions of the tragic (as elsewhere) are evident, and surely too numerous to be mere convergence. It seems fair to conclude that Schweitzer's legacy, imperfectly studied though it was, had a noteworthy impact on Tillich. Given fuller understanding and acknowledgement, it could well be of even greater resource in the future.

Process of Life

Schweitzer's thought can be seen more directly at work in *process thought*. The dominant thinker behind this field is the English mathematician-philosopher

Alfred North Whitehead (1861–1947), who proposed a *philosophy of organism* in *Process and Reality* (1929), where the relationship of one organism to another places humans in fellowship with all living things. As with the possible influence of Bergson's élan vital on Schweitzer's thought, Tillich notes Bergson's impact on Whitehead's philosophy. It is also noteworthy that Tillich lists Whitehead amongst those who influenced his thinking. All of these thinkers can be seen as part of a general movement of sensitivity in Western ethics in the twentieth century to address life-ethics. Although various presentations of process theology exist, three theologians in particular have developed Whitehead's process thought with a view toward ethical consideration of nonhuman species: John B. Cobb, Jr., Charles Birch, and Jay B. McDaniel.

In Cobb's earliest text on ecological-theology, *Is It Too Late? A Theology of Ecology* (1972), he proposes to develop a New Christianity based on process thought and Schweitzer's "vision of all life as worthy of reverence."[62] Cobb endorses Schweitzer's understanding of reverence for life as Jesus' "ethic of love widened to universality" and calls for the extension of Christian love beyond humans to other living beings.[63] But such enlarged ethical sensitivity is not founded by focusing on the will-to-live à la Schweitzerian metaphysics. Rather, an awareness of humans' kinship with other living things is a result of biological evolution: "We must come to experience ourselves as a part of that whole community of living things to which we point by speaking of the evolutionary process."[64] From this basis, Cobb seeks to develop an ethic to guide humans' actions toward other species.

In Cobb's development of an evolutionary philosophy of life, the intrinsic value of a creature is connected with its capacity for feeling:

> I do not believe that consciousness of any kind is necessary to feeling and to the value of feeling. Although conscious enjoyment is far richer than unconscious enjoyment, I believe the latter also has value. And I believe that unconscious feeling, and therefore some low level of value, pervades the universe.[65]

Process metaphysics, on the basis of early twentieth-century quantum physics and Darwinian thought, postulated fields of force and experience in all phenomena. Cobb argues that humans are not the only bearers of intrinsic value and claims that all beings are capable of some feeling *irrespective* of consciousness. For him, *varying* degrees of intrinsic value exist throughout creation. Based largely on this valuation of life, Cobb and Birch develop an *ethic of life* in *The Liberation of Life*.

They regard Schweitzer as "the one great Western twentieth-century thinker who took seriously the value of all living things" and acknowledge his

reverence for life as having "a spreading influence on others." But they claim
Schweitzer's ethic is deficient in one major area: it "did not gain expression in
practical ethical guidelines."[66] Birch and Cobb put their finger here on a "flaw"
(briefly raised by Brunner) in Schweitzer's ethics. But, as even they acknowledge, it was one of which Schweitzer was already aware. And it remains to be
seen whether their cure is worse than the disease:

> Schweitzer consciously opposed the development of a differentiated
> evaluation of forms of life which would make such guidelines pos-
> sible. Judgments of value among species will have a subjective
> element, and similarity to human beings is likely to play a distorting
> role at times. But it does not follow that no generalizations are pos-
> sible or that human beings will show greater wisdom in this area
> if they make decisions *ad hoc*. An adequate ethic of reverence
> for life requires the development which Schweitzer refused
> to give it.[67]

Birch and Cobb are able to articulate Schweitzer's objection to value
judgments and in the same breath give the impression that the force of his
critique is not powerful enough to deter their "differentiated evaluation" of life.
The dispute between the two sides boils down to the following quandary: either
one adopts a Schweitzerian pro-life (in the widest sense of the word) stance
which precludes theoretical claims for one life form over another, or following
Birch and Cobb, one accepts a pro-(some)life position and, as in their case,
develops a hierarchy of moral privilege.

Birch and Cobb's criticism would prove severe if Schweitzer had set out to
construct a systematic ethic. But he clearly did not. Schweitzer offers *reverence*
as a banner or touchstone—and perhaps should have done more to prevent it
from being taken for more, i.e. a practical, one-stop guide in all circumstances.
As such, the problem with their critique lies in the attempt to understand
reverence for life from a systematic standpoint. Schweitzer, as we have seen,
describes *reverence* as an "ethical *mysticism*"; that is, *not* in terms of systematic
ethics or moral commands. His emphasis on mysticism (no matter how much
he tries to affirm it as a public reality) signifies a moment of private revelation
and lies beyond rational justification as even he acknowledges: reverence for
life "ends in the irrational realm of mysticism."[68] Ethical mysticism is beyond
the nature of public debate, lending itself (despite Schweitzer's best efforts)
neither to rational justification nor to rational criticism. Either you get reverence or you do not: it proves difficult to reason about it. In the light of this, as
Birch and Cobb point out, reverence escapes interpretation in terms of moral

rules or principles which can be universally applied and debated. That is, his ethic precludes the formulation of precise moral guidance or normative ethics.

Birch and Cobb might have done well to point out that Schweitzer recognized the inevitability and necessity of a moral hierarchy in practice (and he himself appears to have exercised a tentative form of hierarchy by often affording humans and other animals moral priority over other life forms). But Schweitzer failed to formulate its relation to reverence in such a way as to maintain what he affirmed of it. In spite of all his practical affirmation of normative ethics, Schweitzer never ceases to think of this as incongruous with his mysticism. At least on this point, Birch and Cobb's complaint that Schweitzer's ethical mysticism effectively sidelines normative ethics is cogent.

Schweitzer saw matters differently; the mystical (nonsystematic) nature of his ethics (i.e., its lack of "practical" guidelines) was its strongest point, or perhaps more accurately the strongest point left to him. It is through mysticism, not following rules, that we are afforded union with the Divine. And as is made clear, he believes the mystical nature of reverence is derived from its relation to cosmic (not anthropocentric) reality. Furthermore, against those like Birch and Cobb who seek to develop strict moral hierarchies, Schweitzer's articulation of the moral in terms of reverence denies that our ethical role is primarily that of a technician applying expertise to a rule.

By refusing to be overly systematic in his treatment of exceptional cases, Schweitzer was, in effect, trying hard not to do casuistry which he viewed as a closed ethical system similar to legalism. He almost certainly shared the view that code-morality sought to "build a fence around the Law"; that is, offer more basic legalistic definitions of right and wrong. Attempts to define precisely and exhaustively the content of law, and to establish some rank among the laws in cases where conflict makes a necessary breach of it, were frowned upon because he feared that *law* lacked positive moral *will*. It may come as no surprise then that he takes pain to distinguish reverence from the casuistical creation of moral judgments about particular cases. For example, when asked if in laboratory experiments on animals there was "useful pain which causes good, and useless pain which leads to nothing," he simply replied, "Monsieur, do not ask me to discuss now the great problem of experiments on animals. I am not prepared, and it is a difficult question."[69] Such responses did little to mitigate criticisms of inconsistency and opened Schweitzer up to the legitimate charge that while denouncing moral hierarchies in theory, he adopted one in practice. The point is, of course, that while Schweitzer made judgments in practice (as we all have to do), what he was fundamentally disinclined to do was to enshrine such judgments as binding laws or codes—as though they were objective benchmarks in ethics, when in fact they were only (for him) subjective decisions determined by necessity.

But there is more. Through his studies of Kant, Schweitzer was only too well aware that reverence transcended rational assessment. So while it may be said that Schweitzer was not a systematic ethicist, it can also be said that he evidently neither tried to be, nor wanted to be, one. There is a sense in which the real question for him is not epistemic but pragmatic. By conceiving the ethical problem "in terms of knowledge rather than love and practice, 'ethics' . . . domesticates the good in such a way as to prevent it from presenting any challenge too disturbing."[70] By reducing *ethics* to a particular principle or set of principles (i.e., to "differentiate" as Birch and Cobb wish), the moral agent is distanced from the critical claim which the good makes. That is why Schweitzer thinks "the good conscience is an invention of the devil."[71] Aiding and abetting self-justification is the crime of which systematic, casuistic, legalistic ethics is, in his eyes, "guilty." Indeed, humans are forced "to live at the cost of other life and to incur again and again the guilt of destroying and injuring life."[72] Guilt was one feeling he did not want to blunt. Reverence and guilt go hand in hand.

In order to grasp this point more clearly, it is important to contextualize Schweitzer. He lived for most of his professional life in the Lambaréné jungle. He was daily presented with competing claims for his moral attention, both human and nonhuman. He could not practically live without killing, and rarely did so. As his description of life in the primeval forest makes clear, it was not even possible to live there without destroying poisonous spiders, fending off mosquitoes and clearing some forest.[73] To his credit, what Schweitzer fails to do (if a failure it is) is not to camouflage or rationalize his own practice by an appeal to some supposed objective hierarchy of moral worth. This is understandably frustrating for professional ethicists, but it arises, in context, more out of a sense of powerlessness and guilt than it does any attempt to pervert any existing system of ethics. As life there made plain, the world was a "ghastly drama of the will-to-live divided against itself."[74] No one rule, no differentiated ethic of life, could discriminate among all the competing claims. That is why Schweitzer sought to inculcate a moral sense, rather than a moral system. The force of this criticism is perhaps best illustrated by an examination of Birch and Cobb's hierarchical valuation of life.

Valuating Life

Birch and Cobb posit that feeling or "unconscious feeling" exists in all matter and, as such, "there is intrinsic value everywhere."[75] All life holds some irreducible worth. But that does not mean equality. In an attempt to provide reverence "the development Schweitzer refused to give it," they systematically differentiate the intrinsic value of various life forms. Differentiation of this sort is supposed to help humans to make decisions about the relative worth of different life forms and enable more consistent ethical practice.

Birch and Cobb hold broadly to a threefold ethical valuation of life. First, they find rocks', cells', and plants' experience to be "dim" and holding only "instrumental" value. Entities of this type can "appropriately be treated primarily as means." Second, in animal life, *conscious* feeling arises. With this "increased complexity of the central nervous system and the development of the brain," they "find every reason to suppose there is increased capacity for richness of experience." In contradistinction to other nonhuman life forms, animals "cannot rightly be treated as mere means"; animals "make a claim upon us," and we have "duties" to them in a way different to other nonhuman beings.[76] Third, human beings, because of their "explosion of intellectual activity" and highest degree of consciousness, are at the summit. Birch and Cobb's ethic of life concludes that although all beings possess feeling capacity to some degree, "it is much worse to inflict suffering on creatures with [a] highly developed capacity to suffer than those where this capacity is rudimentary."[77]

What might Schweitzer have said in reply? Birch and Cobb's thesis extends moral consideration to animals and rejects anthropocentrism (in the sense that humans alone hold intrinsic value and nonhuman life holds only instrumental value). But they adopt another species-informed hierarchy of life forms that are not conscious in a manner directly analogous to humans. From a Schweitzerian standpoint, Birch and Cobb have merely replaced one form of discrimination with another. For him, such hierarchical ethical schemes imply "the view that there can be life that is worthless [i.e., cells and plants for Birch and Cobb] which can be willfully destroyed ... according to circumstances."[78]

A limitation to Birch and Cobb's ethics is that it binds unconscious life to yet another anthropocentric hierarchy and commits a similar error to that which they accuse others of with regard to animals. Their ethic of life is mainly for vertebrates (principally for mammals), and offers little moral concern to beings with decreasing complexity in their central nervous system or who lack one altogether. But it is clear that all ethical systems discriminate against some species; all perspectives, in one sense, are anthropocentric. The key question is whether the preference Birch and Cobb's ethic extends to animals and humans is justifiable, that is, nonarbitrary? To find, from a Schweitzerian perspective, some of their insights unsatisfactory is not to neglect the ways in which they have benefited from and engaged with Schweitzer's insights.

God and Pelicans

McDaniel's process theology is deeply indebted to Birch and Cobb. He received his doctorate under Cobb's supervision, and has since worked with Birch to edit *Liberating Life: Contemporary Approaches to Ecological Theology*. He has followed with *Earth, Sky, Gods, and Mortals: A Theology of Ecology for the Twenty-first Century* and *With Roots and Wings: Christianity in an Age of Ecology and Dialogue*, both of which frequently refer to the work of Birch and Cobb and their ethic of life. The aim of his *Of God and Pelicans: A Theology of Reverence for Life* is to "link concern for individual animals...with a concern for the stability, beauty, and integrity of ecosystems."[79] Although these two concerns often converge, they can also come into conflict.

McDaniel begins discussion of his *life-centered ethic* with a notion of a "universalizing divine love." God's love is both "universal and particularized" and is "unsurpassably broad and, with respect to each creature, unsurpassably deep." "It is important," he writes, "to emphasize that divine love includes plants and inorganic realities such as mountains, rivers, stars, and wind."[80] God does not love "mere objects" or "vacuous actualities" in the material realm; informed by "speculative insights from the new physics, Christians can assume that sentience—understood in this context as the capacity of energy events to feel influences, albeit unconsciously, from submicroscopic environments—is itself characteristic of the submicroscopic energy of which mountains, rivers, stars, and wind consist." It should be noted that this is a radically new definition of sentiency. In McDaniel's scheme, there is no sharp dichotomy between sentient and insentient matter: "So-called 'dead' matter is simply less sentient—less alive—than 'living' matter." Accordingly, nothing is "really dead," and God's "love and empathy" extends to mountains, rivers, stars, and wind, "or at least to the momentary pulsations of unconscious and yet sentient energy of which these material forms are vast and dynamic expressions."[81]

Following Birch and Cobb's ethic of life, McDaniel suggests that animals, "amid their sentience" and with "advanced nervous systems," merit moral consideration above nonanimal species. Although all existents hold intrinsic value and deserve "respect, love, and preservation, ... only animals can possess moral rights."[82] The potential for animals to experience pain, raises their level of rights beyond those of other nonhuman species.

McDaniel's process theological worldview sets the stage for the development of his ethical thought. He acknowledges two figures influential to the articulation of his life-centered ethic. First, he sees Aldo Leopold's (1887–1948) *land ethic* as an important advancement in ecological ethics. Leopold was concerned with developing an ethic to guide humans' "relation to land and to [the] animals and plants which grow upon it."[83] In words highly reminiscent of Schweitzer's definition of the moral "It is good to preserve life, promote life, and develop life,... bad to destroy life, injure life, or repress life," Leopold's land ethic deems something "right when it tends to preserve the integrity, stability, and beauty of the biotic community. It is wrong when it tends otherwise."[84] As Leopold sees it, the good of the biotic community, the effect upon ecological systems, takes precedence and is the measure of an action's ethical quality.

Second, McDaniel sees Schweitzer as the "mentor of the animal rights movement,"[85] and his ethic as "an antidote" to points of view that emphasize systems but not individuals: "The 'land ethic' of Aldo Leopold, which has been taken up by many an environmentalist, needs to be complemented by the 'life ethic' of Albert Schweitzer."[86] McDaniel maintains that in advancing "his reverence for life ethic in the early part of our century, Schweitzer well anticipates the concerns of contemporary animal rights activists... in eliminating the unnecessary suffering of individual animals."[87] It is noteworthy that McDaniel, while he acknowledges Schweitzer's influence, reduces reverence to a concern strictly for "individual kindred creatures, particularly animals."[88] This shift in emphasis serves McDaniel's interests since, as we have repeatedly seen, Schweitzer was (in principle) interested in upholding the inherent value of all life.

McDaniel seeks to incorporate aspects of Leopold's land ethic along with Schweitzer's reverence for life into a "life-centered ethic that responds both to the abuse of individual animals under human subjugation and to the degradation of larger biotic wholes."[89] His life-centered ethic embraces three "moral virtues."

The "first moral virtue is reverence for life," which, following Schweitzer, means having an "inward disposition that is respectful of, and caring for, other animals, plants, and the Earth and that refuses to draw a sharp dichotomy between human life and other forms of life."[90] The second moral virtue cultivates the moral precepts in the Jain ethic of ahimsā and converges with Schweitzer's application of Indian ethical thought:

> Among the religions of the world the ones that have been most keenly reverential of life ... are the classical traditions of Jainism and Jain-influenced Buddhism, with their doctrines of ahimsā or non-injury to animals. As these Asian traditions make clear, the life of compassion rightly extends to animals as well as to people. It rightly leads to a progressive disengagement from injury to animals.[91]

It is worth pointing out that McDaniel, as with his treatment of Schweitzer's reverence for life, narrows the concern of ahimsā to humans and animals.

The third moral virtue is the exercise of *active goodwill*. Here again, McDaniel may be in dialogue tacitly with Schweitzer who maintained that the "ideal of inactivity [i.e., a negative duty to refrain from destroying] obstructs the way to the real ethics of active love," which seeks to promote and help other life.[92] Or, as McDaniel puts it, *active goodwill* implies not only an avoidance of harm to non-human creatures but also "the active fostering of opportunities for [a creature] . . . to realize its interests."[93]

In correspondence with Schweitzer's emphasis on the division of the will-to-live against itself, McDaniel sees the world as full of competing interests amongst species. Though his three moral virtues are applicable to all life in theory, humans must choose practically between different life forms, violating the interests of some and protecting the interests of others. To discern the interests of different species in a consistent fashion, he proposes a "ranking of interests." While all living things have intrinsic value, McDaniel (like Birch and Cobb) believes that some beings possess more intrinsic value, and therefore greater ethical consideration, than do others.

McDaniel's starting point is very much like that of Birch and Cobb. He shares with them a sort of sympathy with Schweitzer's dilemma, but a less than full appreciation of its true recalcitrance. The horns of the dilemma are *generality* and *validity*. For Schweitzer, being driven to an ad hoc solution (in the interests of validity) isn't very good. But the untenability of all the generality-arguments is worse. Birch and Cobb, and following them, McDaniel, see the same two horns, and simply prefer the other one. To that extent, what we have is a juxtaposition of assertions—which the protagonists might be tempted to mistake for a real controversy despite the absence of features usually considered desirable, such as a critique of older arguments and a minimum of novel ones. Indeed, McDaniel makes very little attempt to go beyond assertion, and shows no awareness of the temptation to understate the weakness of one's own "case."

There is, of course, a price to pay. Where Schweitzer is acutely sensitive to the dangers of anthropocentrism, McDaniel is committed, more boldly (or less cautiously) than Birch and Cobb, to deploying a series of theoretical propositions which, it is all too evident, are increasingly anthropocentric. In the attempt to provide a foundation for a hierarchy of values, McDaniel summons to his aid, successively, "complexity of the nervous system," existence of a "psyche," and "experiential richness."[94] The very variety of these props, their increasing pseudo-measurability, and the absence of critical or historical discussion of any of them, reflect adversely on the solidity that even their author seems to attribute to any one of them. Still, McDaniel approaches Schweitzer's judgment, when, in closing, he acknowledges that the "need for judgment on the basis of degrees of intrinsic value must be complemented by reverence for life."[95] But, in so doing, McDaniel only brings us back to the original dilemma; the tension between recognizing competing interests (Schweitzer) and ranking interests (Birch and Cobb, McDaniel) remains.

Several Christian theologians have responded to some of Schweitzer's key life-ethics ideas. This enduring, even burgeoning, interest is testament to the prescience of his concerns, present in varying degrees in contemporary ecological and animal ethics, as well as in cosmologies, ontologies, and philosophies of life. His direct and indirect influences on contemporary life-ethics debates provide a standard for gauging the capacity of reverence to generate significant response. Schweitzer's thought continues to challenge constricted ethical conceptions of life and offers some insights on how they might be enlarged. In that sense, there is a lot of engagement with Schweitzer left to do.

7

The Quest Goes On

Shortly before Schweitzer's wife, Helen, died in 1957, she asked him how long he planned to stay in Lambaréné. He replied: "As long as I draw breath." Indeed, after his revelatory moment on the Ogowe in 1915, Schweitzer lived along the banks of the river for a further half century, until his death on September 4, 1965.

Difficult though it may be for some to believe today, Schweitzer was lauded as one of the intellectual and moral giants of his age. His twenty-three books sold in the millions. His work in Lambaréné was regarded by many as the popular embodiment of Christianity in action. The scholarship on Jesus and Paul aroused intense academic debate. His study of Bach, which he himself conceived of as an interlude, was judged groundbreaking. International efforts for peace and vigorous opposition to atomic weapons helped to earn him the Nobel Peace Prize in 1952. No other person, it seems, has been so lauded and regarded as such an icon—in so many fields—of human endeavor.

Yet, this star which shone so brightly grew dim within one or two generations. Reverence for life suffered more misinterpretation than it did neglect. Le Grand Docteur possibly anticipated the malaise that would befall his intellectual child by indicating that if it "will ever emerge, the success will have to be credited to the many who have undertaken the responsibility of making the concept of reverence for life understood throughout the world."[1] If that is the case, Schweitzer has been poorly served by his followers. As we have seen, the misunderstandings of his ethic are manifold and constitute as large a misportrayal as almost any major figure in history has endured. It is worth concluding then by stating as sharply and succinctly as possible some of the continuing challenges of Schweitzer's thought to both theology and ethics.

Mystical Value

The first, and perhaps most important, contribution concerns *the mystical apprehension of the value of life*. At the center of many present controversies is the issue of value: whether beings outside of ourselves hold value, and, if so, what kind and why. What Schweitzer emphasizes is that the recognition and appreciation of the value of life is a mystical apprehension. This understanding is primary because all subsequent decisions and choices depend upon it.

To understand this point, it is perhaps best to recall Plato, who describes philosophers in a democratic state as those who "wrangle over notions of right in the minds of men who have never beheld Justice itself."[2] Likewise, Schweitzer would maintain that one can have no proper sense of oneself or other beings in the world unless, first and foremost, one has a sufficient sense of the value of life itself. Everything depends practically upon this prior recognition of value. In order to appreciate more fully Schweitzer's insight, it may be instructive to contrast his position with instrumentalist and utilitarian considerations of value as expounded by thinkers within the Christian tradition. Schweitzer affirms a positive view of each manifestation of "life" as "something possessing value *in itself*"[3] and believes "that the mystery of life is always too profound for us, and that its value is beyond our capacity to estimate."[4] His thought here is quintessentially Stoic in the sense that he refuses to add subjective value-judgments—such as, this is valuable, this is expendable—to any manifestation of life. As Pierre Hadot remarks, "The Stoics' notorious *phantasia kataleptike*— 'objective representation'—takes place precisely when we refrain from adding any judgment value to naked reality."[5] Each manifestation of the will-to-live, Schweitzer argues, is to be seen in and for itself, and separate from anthropocentric representations.

By contrast, many prominent Christian theologians have offered an instrumentalist understanding of life. Deeply entrenched in a theological tradition of the orders of creation, St. Augustine states in relation to the Old Testament prohibition against killing:

> When we say, "Thou shalt not kill," we do not understand this of the plants, since they have no sensation, nor of the irrational animals

that fly, swim, walk, or creep, since they are disassociated from us
by their want of reason, and are therefore by the just appointment of
the Creator subjected to us to kill or keep alive for our own uses;
if so, then it remains that we understand the commandment simply
of man.[6]

Augustine, in his rejection of fellowship with nonhuman life, is not alone
in the Christian tradition. St. Thomas Aquinas also feels that "dumb animals
and plants are devoid of the life of reason," which is "a sign that they are
naturally enslaved and accommodated to the uses of others."[7] Influenced by
Aristotelian notions of ordering, Aquinas endorses the notion that lower creation exists to serve the higher. Addressing the question whether it is lawful for
humans to kill living beings, he concludes:

There is no sin in using a thing for the purpose for which it is.
Now the order of things is such that the imperfect are for the
perfect...it is not unlawful if man uses plants for the good of animals, and animals for the good of man as the Philosopher [Aristotle]
states.[8]

In *Summa Contra Gentiles*, Aquinas again expounds an instrumentalist
and hierarchical understanding of creation:

Hereby is refuted the error of those who said it is sinful for a man to
kill dumb animals: for by divine providence they are intended for
man's use in the natural order. Hence it is not wrong for man to
make use of them, either by killing or in any way whatever.[9]

Aquinas understands the role of nonhuman creation almost strictly in
terms of its capacity to serve human wants. Creation, he insists, was created
solely for "intellectual creatures": "The Divine Ordinance of animals and plants
is preserved not for themselves but for man," and hence, "as Augustine
says...both their life and their death are subject to our use."[10] In his theology,
the value of nonhuman life is measured by its utility to human interests. Since
it lacks *rationality*, then nonhuman creation can be considered as an instrument for humans who alone possess such a capacity.

To be sure, though Aquinas and Augustine believe that human beings can
have *no* community with nonhuman creatures that lack rational souls, Aquinas
does not deny the existence of souls in plants and animals. Every living being
was believed to possess a "soul" of some kind. He does, however, make a sharp
distinction between different types of souls: "vegetative" for plants, "sensitive"
for animals, and "rational" for humans.[11] Rationality is regarded as the faculty

par excellence that determines our immortal soulfulness, a trait explicitly denied to nonhuman creation.

A similar instrumentalist understanding of nonhuman life is found in the Reformers, notably John Calvin and Martin Luther. Addressing the issue of the subjection of animals to human dominion in Genesis 1, Calvin remarks, "Hence we infer what was the end for which all things were created; namely, that none of the conveniences and necessities of life might be wanting to men."[12] Again, he writes, "Because we know that the universe was established especially for the sake of mankind, we ought to look for this purpose in his [God's] governance also."[13] Calvin believes that "men may render animals subservient to their own convenience, and may apply them to various uses, according to their wishes and their necessities."[14] For Calvin, nonhuman creatures are reduced to instruments to be used for human aims. Luther follows suit. After the fall and flood, "the animals are subjected to man as to a tyrant who has absolute power over life and death."[15] For Luther, this is God's "gift" to humans and it shows how God is "favorably inclined and friendly towards man."[16] Such understandings of nonrationality and nonfellowship have largely dominated Christian discussions of animal and plant life and have served as the justification for excluding other life forms from moral consideration.

These thinkers and two traditions, similar to most modern theology, unite in seeing nonhuman life as a utility device for the fulfillment of human aims. In contrast, Schweitzer locates the value of beings not in any specific faculty or capacity limited to a certain species, but rather in the will-to-live common to all life. He presents a rival idea to the scholastic and reformed views: *life* has inherent worth independent of human calculations. In his "Reverence for Life" sermons from Strasbourg (1918), Schweitzer addresses the conduct of humans to the life around them. He begins with a sweeping refutation of traditional Christian conceptions of humans' behavior toward nonhuman life: "Christianity, from the first centuries up until deep in the Middle Ages, did not ennoble people in their behavior toward living creatures. . . . Throughout the centuries one finds the greatest thoughtlessness and crudeness bound together with the most earnest piety." He continues with an attack on the theological rationale for neglect of nonhuman creatures:

> One thinks less about what we ought to be toward the poor crea-
> tures than again and again about how one can make the most
> of the difference between man and them: "You have an immortal
> soul. The animal does not. An unbridgeable chasm lies between
> us," as if we really knew something about it.[17]

The emphasis promulgated by Aquinas, Augustine, Calvin, and Luther, among others, that is placed on the *differences* between humans and other life forms has, Schweitzer claims, obscured humans' moral responsibility to reverence nonhuman life. Schweitzer also comments on the enormous difficulty even in the settling of these differences:

> *How far down does the boundary of conscious, feeling life reach?* No one can say. Where does the animal stop and the plant begin? And the plants: Is it possible that they feel and are sensitive even if we cannot demonstrate it? Is not every life process, right down to the uniting of two elements, bound up with something like feeling and sensitivity?[18]

However accurate Schweitzer's remarks on the sentiency of plant life may be, he does call attention to the point that humans' lack of definitive knowledge on such issues as souls or sentiency should not count against other life forms. Along these lines, R. G. Frey argued that to take sentiency as the basis of moral rights would "condemn the whole of non-sentient creation, including the lower animals, at best to a much inferior moral status or, at worst possibly to a status completely beyond the moral pale."[19] For instance, whereas Cartesianism saw animals largely as machines and devoid of sentiency, the Christian tradition now generally recognizes them to be sentient creatures.

But the very practice of selecting one quality that elevates humans above other life forms has, Schweitzer maintains, excluded from humans' moral concern those beings that lack such traits. Many life-ethicists who make a claim for animal rights (such as Birch, Cobb, and McDaniel) accept the ethical presupposition manifest in the Scholastics and Reformers, namely, that humans should extend moral consideration *only* to those beings who similarly possess such traits as sentiency or rationality. Utilitarian philosopher Peter Singer misses Schweitzer's point to reverence *life* when he states: "If a being is not capable of suffering, or of experiencing enjoyment or happiness, there is nothing to be taken into account [morally]."[20] Singer divides the world into self-conscious, sentient beings who merit moral consideration and (supposedly) nonsentient and less morally significant beings. Rather than offering a critique of this position, these thinkers have followed suit and simply extended the limit of moral concern a little further on the spectrum.

Instead of focusing on the differences among various forms of life, Schweitzer maintains that humans should seek to "experience the inner-relatedness that exists among all living things."[21] A utilitarian perspective of the world, he suggests, conceals from us our relation with it. A strong sense of interconnectedness among all life is encapsulated in his dictum: "I am life which wills to live in the midst of life which wills to live."[22] Self-consciousness goes hand in hand with moral consciousness; placing the self within a cosmic dimension (whereby the self becomes aware of its relation to other wills-to-live) transforms humans' perception of themselves and of other life. As such, Schweitzer defines the human person in terms of relationality, not juxtaposition, to other life. From such an ontology of sociality, he emphasizes that the "dissimilarity, the strangeness, between us and other creatures is here removed," and he enjoins humans to hold a "love and reverence for all being . . . no matter how externally dissimilar to our own."[23]

The mystical apprehension of the value of life, or will-to-live, as Schweitzer would say, becomes the central linking concept of ontological continuity among humans, nonhuman species, and the infinite Will-to-Live (God). It is this sense of connection, not difference or utility, that Schweitzer challenges us to find with other manifestations of life.

Expanding Horizons

The resourcefulness of Schweitzer's above-mentioned insights can be more clearly understood if we are prepared to bear with him as he questions some of the most established principles of Christian theology. The second challenge concerns expanding the horizon of moral responsibility by *moving from a humanocentric to a theocentric view of the universe.* In a 1919 sermon, he questioned whether humans should be considered the goal of creation:

> The purpose of nature, with her thousands of appearances of life, is not understood as . . . merely the presupposition of man's existence. When I lift my eyes to the sky and say to myself that these luminous points up there mean an infinity of worlds, then my existence and that of humanity become so small by comparison that I am unable to think of the fulfillment of this human being as the purpose of the world. Nature is not the presupposition of humanity, and humanity may not conceive of itself as the purpose of the infinite world. . . . That the world should exist for the sake of paltry little humanity, where we appear to ourselves in the infinity of being as something infinitesimally small, is the offence we have already felt as children when our thought process awoke.
>
> . . . [While] man and humanity can be understood as the end purpose of the world, this is true only as in dreamlike guesses, for the enigmas that pile up against us here are not explained.[24]

In his essays "Religion in Modern Civilization" (1934) and "The Ethics of Reverence for Life" (1936), he again proposes changing our view from a preoccupation with human beings to a wider focus:

> Look to the stars and understand how small our Earth is in the universe. Look upon the Earth and how minute man is upon it. The Earth existed long before man came upon it. In the history of the universe, man is on the Earth for but a second. Who knows but that the Earth will circle around the sun once more without man upon it? Therefore we must not place man in the centre of the universe.
>
> We like to image that Man is nature's goal; but facts do not support that belief. Indeed, when we consider the immensity of the universe, we must confess that man is insignificant. And certainly man's life can hardly be considered the goal of the universe. Its margin of existence is always precarious. Study of the geologic periods shows that. So does the battle against disease. When one has seen whole populations annihilated by sleeping sickness, as I have, one ceases to imagine that human life is nature's goal.[25]

Schweitzer starkly presents the idea that humans are not the "center" or "goal" of the whole universe. As seen throughout most of his writing, he places humans in the unique role of moral agents working with the Will-to-Love to reduce suffering and help bring about eschatological redemption. But he maintains, here, that we cannot equate the arrival of human beings on earth with the sole purpose of creation. The significance of Schweitzer's attempt to make room for what may be called *cosmic consciousness* determines the way in which the human person views his or her relation to the world. Two Christian theologians in particular have further developed this insight: John Burnaby and James Gustafson take up a similar critique of humanocentric views of life and carry forward the trajectory Schweitzer began.

Almost half a century after Schweitzer first presented this notion, Burnaby presented his protest against an anthropocentric view of creation in *The Belief of Christendom: A Commentary on the Nicene Creed* (1963). The "assumption" that other life forms in universe were created for humankind is not, he claims, a position "required by the Christian faith." Burnaby's discussion of this insight warrants extended quotation:

> We easily read [the first chapter of Genesis] as though the whole structure of the universe had no other purpose but the production of the human species and that all things in it had been made for the use of man. And we may slip from there into the further assumption

that the "use" of man can only mean his happiness or even his material comfort.

Now the human species...has "all things in subjection under his feet...sheep and oxen and the beasts of the field." Yet the Psalmist can still exclaim: "What is man, that thou art mindful of him?" And the Book of Job enforces the counsel of humility from the sheer mystery of creation, and the limits to all human powers of understanding or controlling it....Mankind is the product not only of this earth but of the whole stellar universe, which is the setting, the cosmic order that has made possible the evolution of humanity on this particular planet....Nevertheless, these considerations do not justify us in affirming that the universe was made for man.

...We cannot then assume that even if the things that are "in subjection under our feet" extend far more widely than the author of Job supposed, it follows that God's universal purpose reaches no further than ourselves. The purpose of creation as a whole must be beyond our comprehension....And this should make it impossible for us to think that God has created all things with no other purpose than the satisfaction of men's natural desires and needs. We need not abandon the ancient insight, whereby the purpose of man's being, that in which he is to find his fulfillment, is embraced in the purpose of all creation—the *glory* of God....God is glorified on earth when the eyes of men are enlightened, when they see his goodness in his works and come to worship him. But it would be presumptuous to imagine that the glory of God *depends* on the existence of the human eye.[26]

Burnaby's commentary on the Creed echoes and extends Schweitzer's insights. Both share the view that humans cannot assume that they are the goal of creation. Related to this, the two thinkers maintain that God's purpose extends to all creation: all life, the whole universe, exists principally not for humans' wants but for "the glory of God." Related to this notion is the idea that the import of creation is not dependent on humans' assessment of its worth, as it holds value to God irrespective of its utility to humans. Burnaby, here, shifts from an anthropocentric species valuation to one that is theocentric and renders the theological basis to Schweitzer's insight explicit.

Building again on Schweitzer's thought from a theological context, Burnaby contends that a Christian understanding of creation must engage more widely than the human species alone. As the Nicene Creed states, God is the Maker of heaven and earth "and of all things visible and invisible." Whereas

"heaven and earth" in the language of the Creed-makers described the material
world as perceived by *our* senses, the added clause ("visible and invisible") elucidates that the range of God's creation is not so limited: "It widens out to
embrace things beyond the reach of our powers of perception."[27] Burnaby helps
us to see that our value-perceptions are corrigible. His reading of the Creed in
this light has consequences for the moral status of creation: by rejecting an
instrumentalist view of life where species valuation is dependent on human
"perception," Burnaby adopts a theocentric perspective of creation that upholds its own intrinsic value to God. Burnaby's commentary highlights how an
anthropocentric theological perspective prevents us from understanding the
value of other beings to God.

In *Theology and Ethics*, James Gustafson develops what he calls *theocentric
ethics*. Although a theocentric perspective of the universe does not reject a
distinctive view of human dignity to God, it does, he argues, deny that humans
are the sole bearers of value: "*All* things are 'good,' and not just good for us."[28]
"If one's basic theological perception is of a Deity who rules all creation, and
one's perception of life in history and nature one of patterns and interdependence," writes Gustafson, "then the good that God values must be more
inclusive than one's normal perceptions of what is good for me, what is good
for my community, and even what is good for the human species."[29] Here, he
argues Schweitzer's point theologically: the boundaries of our moral concern
should not be limited to humans insofar as God's purpose extends to the whole
of creation. Building on Schweitzer's thought, Gustafson's critique questions
whether humans can be considered God's "chief" concern:

> If God is "for man," he may not be for man as the chief
> end of creation. The chief end of God may not be the salvation of
> man. Man's place in the universe has to be rethought, as does
> man's relation to God. The moral imperative that I shall de-
> velop in due course is this: we are to conduct life so as to
> relate to all things in a manner appropriate to their relations to
> God.[30]

Gustafson holds that human conduct is to be evaluated not on the basis of
what "guarantee[s] benefits to man," but, instead, in relation to humans' "place
in the universe."[31]

Like Burnaby, he maintains that humans can no longer be the measurers
of the value of all beings, as their interests are not the entire purpose of God's
creation. Theocentric ethics do not therefore confine notions of the right and
the good to anthropocentric terms alone, but, rather, expand the context in
which human moral action is to be assessed.

Schweitzer's rejection of the elevation of humans in the universe can be seen to offer Christian ethics a new understanding of humans' relationship with creation where species value is independent of its usefulness to human purposes. Jürgen Moltmann and Hans Küng have developed a similar theme:

> Ever since the beginning of modern Western civilization we have been accustomed to viewing nature as the environment *for us*; it is related to ourselves. We look at all other natural beings with an eye solely to their utility value where we are concerned. Only human beings are there "for their own sake." Everything else is supposed to be there "for the sake of human beings." This modern anthropocentrism has robbed nature of its soul. We should respect the earth, plants and animals for themselves, before weighing up their utility for human beings.[32]

At the very least, what can be said at this juncture based on the ideas put forth by Schweitzer, and developed by Burnaby and Gustafson (if not Moltmann and Küng), is that there is a serious question to be asked with respect to humans' understanding of their position in creation. It cannot be assumed that God is solely, or even chiefly, concerned with the human species. Although Christian theology involves anthropology, Schweitzer challenges us to see that it should not end there.

Neighbors in Creation

Schweitzer's next contribution concerns seeing *one's attitude to "life" as a touchstone of Christian ethics.* The way humans relate to even the smallest manifestation of life is seen as a reflection of one's attitude to the Creator. Such a view firstly affirms the value of all life and incorporates consideration of non-human species in theological discourse: "To think out in every implication the ethic of love for all creation—this is the difficult task which confronts our age."[33] We may recall that Brunner and Barth, though skeptical of certain aspects of Schweitzer's thesis, lauded his concern for the lack of attention shown to nonhuman species in ethical discourse. To take seriously a theocentric ethical view of creation is to affirm that all life holds value to the Creator and merits reverence: "We reject the idea that man is 'master of other creatures,' 'lord' above all others. We no longer say there are senseless existences with which we can deal as we please."[34] Schweitzer objects to the long tradition of moral hierarchy which places humanity at the top of the pyramid of descending worth. He suggests a transformation of our relationship to the universe: we are to perceive each manifestation of life for *itself*, and no longer for *ourselves*.

A second and related view concerns nonviolence and assistance to life as the central ethical imperative. "A man is truly ethical," Schweitzer writes, "only when he obeys the compulsion to help all life which he is able to assist, and shrinks from injuring anything that lives."[35] This thoroughgoing nonviolent position has been adopted more recently by Stanley Hauerwas, for whom "nonviolence is not just one implication among others that can be drawn from our Christian beliefs; it is at the very heart of our understanding of God."[36] For Schweitzer, a commitment to living peaceably cannot be that of a stoic acceptance of the world; rather, it extends beyond the confines of human boundaries and encourages us to attempt to make reconciliation wherever there is discord in creation.

Third, Schweitzer's view challenges the idea that humans' sole responsibility in the world is to take care of their own species. Refusing this position constitutes the continuing resourcefulness of his ethical thought. Both in prayer[37] and in deed,[38] humans are called to a concern for all creation. He believes that reverence for life offers "something more profound and mightier than the idea of humanism. It includes all living beings."[39] Ethical concern for human life is seen to be part of a wider moral horizon that encompasses all life. In his exegesis of the parable of the Good Samaritan, Schweitzer seeks to expand our understanding of neighbor to include nonhuman creation:

> Formerly, people said: Who is your neighbor? Man. Today we must
> no longer say that. We have gone further and we know that all
> living beings on earth who strive to maintain life and who long to be
> spared pain—all living beings on earth are our neighbors.[40]

By extending the category of *neighbor* to include all life, Schweitzer's reading of the parable develops Jesus' refusal to limit the extent of neighbor love. As Richard Hays writes in *The Moral Vision of the New Testament*: "The point is that we are called upon to become neighbors to those who are helpless, going beyond conventional conceptions of duty to provide life-sustaining aid to those whom we might not have regarded as worthy of compassion."[41] Schweitzer rejects the same limiting question that the lawyer asked Jesus; rather than narrowing the scope of *neighbor*, he recasts the issue.

Schweitzer includes nonhuman life in the category of neighbor. He rejects attempts to circumscribe the boundaries of moral concern: reverence for life "does not draw a circle of well-defined tasks around me, but charges each individual with responsibility for all life within his reach and forces him to devote himself to helping that life."[42] He reads the parable as a metaphor for moral inclusivity that corresponds analogically to nonhuman species. In his discussion of Schweitzer's ethic of reverence for life, Moltmann develops this theme of extended neighborly care. "We might do well," he writes, "to extend the double commandment of love to the earth, the partner which has hitherto been only tacitly presupposed: you shall love God your Lord with all your heart, and with all your soul, and with all strength, and your neighbor as yourself—and this earth as yourself."[43] Like Jesus' rejection of a racially restrictive criterion of neighborly discrimination, Schweitzer seeks to counter the limiting structures of communal proximity by emphasizing humans' participation in the *community of life*.

As Schweitzer's convictions deepened, some of the practical implications of his thinking began to catch up with him. One change was his adoption of a vegetarian diet later in life. Erica Anderson, his photo-biographer narrates:

> No bird or animal in the hospital village—hen or pig or sheep—is killed for food. Fish and crocodile meat brought by fishermen are occasionally served at table, but Schweitzer himself in recent years has given up eating either meat or fish, even the liver dumplings he used to relish and enjoy.
>
> "I can't eat anything that was alive any more" [Schweitzer said]. When a man questioned him on his philosophy and said that God made fish and fowl for people to eat, he answered, "Not at all."[44]

During Schweitzer's final illness, his daughter, Rhena, offered him beef broth. He declined.[45]

Readers of *On the Edge of the Primeval Forest* might have first been scandalized by stories of Schweitzer killing poisonous spiders, dining on monkey flesh, and even carrying a gun. But what critics overlook is that these activities belong to his pre-gestational Ogowe experience. When Schweitzer spoke of guilt, he never excluded himself.

One should not overlook both the development of thought and the development of practice in Schweitzer's life. He became deeply critical of animal experimentation and opposed all forms of hunting for sport. It follows that he was even more rigorous with his dietary habits at ninety than he was at thirty, when he first determined: "[I will make] my life my argument."[46] Not incidentally, we should note in passing how grueling such dietary restrictions would have been not only in the 1950s but especially when confronted with the restraints of life in an equatorial forest. Instead of criticizing Schweitzer's early use of meat and fish products, it is critical to grasp how deeply counter-cultural and practically burdensome vegetarianism was at that time.

Schweitzer did not stop with changing his dietary habits. His hospital at Lambaréné was a model of ecological responsibility: he went out of his to preserve trees and flora, re-used every piece of wood, string, paper, and glass, and rejected modern technological developments which would have resulted in environmental degradation. Long before notions of *sustainability, wise-use,* and *intermediate technology* became known, he was already practicing them and, in so doing, inspired Rachel Carson's *Silent Spring* in 1962 and helped to usher in the modern environmental movement.

The mission of *reverence* continued to expand. In the late 1950s and early 1960s, Schweitzer became most vocal and active internationally against nuclear weapons. Regarded as one who avoided political controversy, he considerably developed his public commitment during this period. When he received his Nobel Prize for Peace, he gave three radio addresses, later published as *Peace or Atomic War?* calling for the cessation of all nuclear tests: "The renunciation of nuclear weapons is vital to peace."[47] After the Geneva Conference in 1962–1963, when the test ban treaty was signed among nuclear powers, Schweitzer wrote to President Kennedy on 6 August 1963: "The treaty gives me hope that war with atomic weapons between East and West can be avoided." Schweitzer viewed the treaty as "one of the greatest events, perhaps the greatest, in the history of the world" and gave personal thanks to Kennedy's "foresight and courage" and his being "able to observe that the world has taken the first step on the road leading to peace."[48]

Schweitzer was a pioneer of an inclusive, nonviolent ethic and prophetic of many contemporary concerns in life-centered ethics. He repeatedly drew attention to the inadequacy of humanocentric thought as a rational critique of the world and sought to widen the scope of ethics to incorporate concern for all manifestations of life.

Schweitzer predicted that future ages will look back with shock at our neglect of other life forms:

> Today it is thought to be going too far to declare that constant regard
> for everything that lives ... is a demand made by rational ethics.
> The time is coming, however, when people will be astonished that
> mankind needed so long a time to learn to regard thoughtless injury
> to life as incompatible with ethics.[49]

He challenges us to see that our moral community is not simply composed of humans: " 'What you have done to one of the least of these, you have done to me.' This word of Jesus is valid for us all, and it ought to determine what we do also to the least among living creatures."[50] The Samaritan is a paradigm of love that shatters conventional responsibility and thus for Schweitzer *creates* a new set of neighbor relations where previously there were none. And certainly for him, the concluding words of the parable stand as a challenge to Christian ethics: "Go and do likewise."

The Mark of Pain

The way Schweitzer's fourth insight can contribute to ethics is the directing of *moral sensitivity to suffering life*. He repeatedly draws attention to "the cry of the Fellowship of those who bear the Mark of Pain."[51] Who are the members of this Fellowship?

> Those who have learnt by experience what physical pain and
> bodily anguish mean, belong together all the world over; they are
> united by a secret bond. One and all they know the horrors of suf-
> fering to which man can be exposed, and one and all they know the
> longing to be free from pain.[52]

The Fellowship of Pain certainly included the human community. But it also extended beyond humankind. For Schweitzer, life and suffering were not two separate things, but rather one notion: "All life is suffering. The [human] will-to-live . . . experiences not only the woe of mankind, but [also] that of all creatures with it."[53] When Schweitzer's favorite pelican died, he said, "He didn't have to suffer. *Scheiden ohne Leiden*—to part without suffering—is al-ways beautiful."[54] In a passage from his autobiography, he speaks again of his sensitivity to the prevalence of suffering and the costly, sacrificial kind of loving it engenders:

> Only at rare moments have I felt really glad to be alive. I cannot help
> but feel the suffering all around me, not only of humanity but of
> the whole of creation.
>   I have never tried to withdraw myself from this community of
> suffering. It seemed to me a matter of course that we should all take
> our share of the burden of pain that lies upon the world.[55]

Schweitzer's comments draw attention to the recognition of the tragedy of life in conflict with itself. Four implications follow from this key theme in Schweitzerian thought.

The first motif pertains to theological orientations or perspective. The starting point of reflection is a practical, ethical step to identify with suffering. Involvement in the sufferings of others is seen as a prerequisite for insight in theological conceptualization. In this scheme, the transformative nature of suffering gives rise to a theological account of reality as understood by members of the Fellowship:

> He who has been delivered from pain must not think he is now
> free again, and at liberty to take life up as it was before, entirely
> forgetful of the past. He is now a "man whose eyes are open" with
> regard to pain and anguish, and he must help to overcome those two
> enemies (so far as human power can control them) and to bring to
> others the deliverance which he has himself enjoyed.[56]

Although not a direct source for contemporary liberation ethics, Schweitzer in his own way and time provided insight into the theological vision that support liberation thought. Feminist and liberationist theological perspectives have, for example, similarly drawn attention to the importance of not isolating theory and practice, or seeing the former as theologically superior. Dietrich Bonhoeffer's writings also represent this Schweitzerian shift in theological orientation. In an essay for members of the conspiracy he stated:

> It remains an experience of inestimable value that for once we
> have learned to see the great events of world history from below, from
> the perspective of the excluded, the suspected, the ill-treated, the
> powerless, the oppressed and despised, in short, *the suffering.* . . .
> Personal suffering is a more useful key, a more fruitful principle
> for viewing and actively understanding the world than personal
> happiness.[57]

Such liberationist-oriented theologies, like Schweitzer's, open up the way for the lived experience of the *community of suffering* to shape theological reflection. Both Schweitzer and Bonhoeffer speak to the eye-opening perspective such identification affords theology. And if commitment to suffering is a starting point of theologizing, then a Fellowship theology requires the incorporation of the collective experience of all "those who bear the Mark of Pain." Schweitzer suggests that members of the Fellowship gain a quality of understanding that goes beyond individual thinking; as a Fellowship, they develop an additional insight into God and the world. What he highlights is a participatory model of revelation in conjunction with and not in opposition to a propositional one. In a key passage from his sermon on Romans 14:7, Schweitzer seeks to foster an appreciation of the notion that theologizing "involves the compassionate one in suffering":

> Once one has experienced the suffering of the world in himself, he
> can never again feel the superficial happiness that mankind

desires.... He thinks of the poor whom he has met, of the sick who
he has seen, of the people of whose difficult fate he has read, and
darkness falls across the light of his joy.... Then comes the voice of
the tempter, "Why torment yourself, then? Don't be so super-
sensitive. Learn the necessary indifference." These temptations un-
obtrusively ruin the presupposition of all goodness.

So I say to you: Don't become indifferent. Remain alert! It
is a matter of your souls! If I—and here in these words I expose my
innermost thoughts—were only able to destroy the deception with
which the world wants to sleep! If only... you could flinch no
more before reverence for life... Ordinarily, I shrink from in-
fluencing people because of the responsibility it entails, but...
[may] each of you experience the great suffering from which
one can never get free and gain the wisdom that comes
of compassion.[58]

Schweitzer moves from a personal (and potentially self-preoccupying)
understanding of pain to an understanding that emerges from a sharing of and
reflection on the sufferings of others. He seeks to reshape theology from this
perspective: from this Fellowship, we "feel that we know by experience the
meaning of the words: 'And all ye are brethren.'" Schweitzer's call to Fellowship still stands as a challenge to contemporary theology: "Would that my gen-
erous friends in Europe could come out here [to Lambaréné] and live through
one such hour!"[59]

A second feature of Schweitzer's reflection on the community of suffering
is the communal and relational basis of suffering in the body of Christ. His
remark that it seemed to him "a matter of course that we should all take our
share of the burden of pain that lies upon the world" is reminiscent of Paul's
epistle to the Galatians (6:2) where the apostle writes of love bearing the "burdens" of others as fulfilling the law of Christ. He takes Jesus' pattern of costly
self-sacrifice and projects it into a moral imperative for the community to serve
other life. This position finds expression in Moltmann's theology which has a
distinctly Schweitzerian accent:

Whatever reason we may find for this vulnerable condition of
creation between its origin and its consummation, the only important
thing is the fellowship of suffering which human beings share
with other earthly creatures. In our present condition, the community of creation is a community of suffering....
    ... [The] Christian's suffering is thus a loving solidarity with the
whole of the suffering creation."[60]

Moltmann's links to Schweitzer's community of suffering are evident. Indeed, the ethical consequence Moltmann draws from this realization is one of reverence for life which "requires us to renounce violence against life."[61]

Third, Schweitzer advances the related insight: the knowledge that comes from suffering is a sharing in the bodiliness of Jesus. He appears to develop Hegel's concept of *God existing as community* (the dwelling of the Holy Spirit as *Absolute Spirit* in the community) by turning this formula into a Christological one in the community of suffering with Christ. People come to know God not strictly as individuals, but (amid other ways) by participating in the Body of Christ: "We too must pass through suffering. We must know...that Jesus draws us with him into his suffering."[62] As with St. Paul's reference in Philippians 3:10 to "the fellowship of Christ's sufferings," the Fellowship of Pain transcends the particular sufferings of the individual and comprises the entire community. This infuses a more participatory, communal theologically available dimension to Schweitzer's ethical/Christ mysticism.

Schweitzer's attention to the community of suffering involves the human self in sharing this *burden of pain* in the world. This entails the abandonment of oneself in service to the other:

> However concerned I was with the suffering in the world, I
> never let myself become lost in brooding over it. I always held
> firmly to the thought that each one of us can do a little something to
> bring some portion of it to an end. Thus I gradually came to the
> conclusion that all we can understand about the problem is that we
> must follow our own way as those who want to bring about
> redemption.[63]

While Schweitzer believed suffering was ineluctably a feature of his life, he never allowed it sovereignty over his own existence. The fourth implication, then, that he draws from this insight is that human responsibility in the world involves seeking to release others from suffering. Prolonged or intense physical suffering is seen as "a more terrible lord of mankind than even death itself."[64] This especial emphasis on the debilitating nature of pain that exists in both the human and nonhuman world focuses attention on the problem of redemption:

> And we all, when we see suffering, must be challenged by a desire
> for redemption, to help all creatures. There is always mystery,
> we move within the midst of a great mystery: the mystery of pain.
> And we come to be always conscious of our great responsibility
> to alleviate it.[65]

Sensitivity to the suffering in the world requires humans not only to renounce violence against life (insofar as it is possible to do so) but also to alleviate it. This involves a costly self-sacrifice on behalf of others and finds expression for Schweitzer in reverence for life. Perhaps more than any other theologian, he connects the suffering in the world with service to other life.

There is an implicit Christological reference that underscores Schweitzer's thought. After all, who is the pre-eminent example of the suffering servant who bears the marks of pain? We discover, as Schweitzer tells us, who "He is" in the toils, struggles and conflicts of life by being drawn into his fellowship. Following on from Schweitzer, there has been a growing strand in modern theology that emphasizes the suffering of God. Moltmann's work makes explicit the link between the suffering of God and the liberation of all life in his remarkable line: "God has made the suffering of the world his own in the Cross of his Son."[66] The radical insight from this is that God, too, shares in the Fellowship of those who bear the Mark of Pain.

Liberating Life

The problem of suffering cannot be resolved in this world. Schweitzer's insight into the Fellowship of Pain necessarily concerns an eschatological hope for the redemption of creaturely suffering. His *practical eschatology* can contribute to contemporary theological ethics by offering an *eschatology of liberation* (a universal redemption of all beings from the bondage of suffering and death) as well as a *liberation eschatology* (an eschatological ethic which seeks to realize the future peace of the kingdom of God in the present).

Schweitzer's eschatology of liberation draws on both Old and New Testament visions of universal redemption. His perception of the kingdom stems from his reading of "the prophet Isaiah" (11:6–9) who proclaims "the Lord will save the world."[67] St. Paul's "marvelous passage"[68] (Romans 8:22) that "speaks of the longing of the whole creation for early redemption" and displays "his deep sympathy with the animal creation and natural world"[69] is also formative in his eschatology. Schweitzer praises Paul's letter to the Romans where the apostle, together with creation, "yearns for redemption from creaturehood . . . and from the body which is in thrall."[70]

Schweitzer's vision of redemption is as comprehensive as creation itself. It is perhaps the intellectual legacy of Platonism in the Christian tradition (i.e., the belief in the immortality of the soul rather than in bodily resurrection) that has largely obscured this all-encompassing image of the kingdom. Richard Bauckham and Trevor Hart put it thus: "The bulwark which the dogmatic affirmation of bodily resurrection has with difficulty maintained against the complete spiritualizing of human destiny has been less effective against the persistent tendency to understand human destiny as a destiny apart from the rest of creation."[71] Schweitzer writes of the cosmic scope of Christian eschatology, highlighting the import of God's future as one not merely for humans but for the whole creation. Eschatology serves as a source of hope and liberation for the whole creation which groans and sighs. The dichotomy between individual and cosmic eschatology, personal and universal hope, is, he tells us, a false one. This cosmic eschatology has taken root most prominently in Moltmann's writing:

> If God's future, as the future of the Creator, has to do with the
> whole creation, then wherever eschatology is narrowed down
> to merely one sector of that creation, . . . that has a destructive effect
> on the other sectors, because it deprives them of hope. The escha-
> tological field of human hopes and fears has always been a favorite
> playground for egocentricism and anthropocentricism. But true
> hope must be universal, because its healing future embraces every
> individual and the whole universe. If we were to surrender hope
> for as much as one single creature, for us God would not be
> God.[72]

As Moltmann points out, there are not two Gods, a Creator and a Redeemer. Rather, creation and redemption stand in unity. The notion of human solidarity with the rest of material creation embedded in Schweitzer's definition of the self (as will-to-live amidst wills-to-live) is reaffirmed eschatologically: the essence of the kingdom consists "in the rule of the Spirit . . . in our hearts and through us in the whole world."[73] He challenges us to find a doctrine of human redemption *with* the world, not from the world.

Although images of eschatological salvation can lead to a transcendent eschatology, Schweitzer's emphasis on *practical* eschatology combats such a wholly otherworldly conception by affirming a more immanent eschatological hope. Though Schweitzer is by no means the first theologian to discuss the cosmic aspect of redemption, his ethical eschatology offers a powerful model for humans to begin to realize such universal redemption in the present. This thrust inspires our ethical vision to be inclusive of all life. Integrally related, therefore, to Schweitzer's eschatology of liberation is his *liberation eschatology*.

One question raised by an eschatological conception such as Schweitzer's that places an emphasis on human moral action is the relationship between future and present. In contemporary theology, there are several ways to conceive of the relationship between ethics and eschatology. On the one hand, it can be seen as disjunctive, in which the eschatological future will be so different from the present that there will be little or no continuity between the two. On the other hand, it can be understood as conjunctive, where present human actions hold significance for the future. A disjunctive relationship suggests that present ethical action will have little impact on the inauguration of the kingdom of God. In such a case, eschatology could not serve as a foundation for an intrahistorical ethic. By contrast, if the relationship is conjunctive, then present human moral action could be seen to influence the eschatological future. A conjunctive eschatological theory, however, risks collapsing eschatology into human actions and losing an emphasis on God's action.

Schweitzer's practical eschatology has the merit of affirming both sides in a mutually complementary fashion. The *practical* denotes a definite mode of human action (conjunction), but its corresponding *eschatology* expresses divine control of its ultimate consummation (disjunction). In so doing, Schweitzer keeps this-worldly and other-worldly, present and future, and historical and eschatological concerns together. He does not suggest that reverence for life will in itself bring the kingdom of God into existence. It seeks to anticipate a peace, which is yet outstanding. By stressing the future, Schweitzer maintains an emphasis on the initiation of God's eschatological act and prevents himself from conflating eschatological salvation with intrahistorical transformation:

> We are familiar with the idea that by the active ethical conduct of individuals the Kingdom of God may be realized on earth. Finding that Jesus speaks of ethical activity and also of the Kingdom of God, we think that He, too, connected the two in the way which seems so natural to us. In reality, however, Jesus does not speak of the Kingdom of God as of something that comes into existence in this world through a development of human society, but as of something which is brought about by God when He transforms this imperfect world into a perfect one.[74]

The kingdom cannot be fully actualized prior to God's act, and the eschatological act brings something which human action alone cannot deliver. But the conjunction in a practical eschatology of reverence for life affords human action meaning in the present to prepare the way for the coming kingdom. "The essence of Christianity," says Schweitzer, "is world-affirmation which has gone through an experience of world-negation. In the eschatological world-view of world-negation, Jesus proclaims the ethic of active love."[75] What this passage means can perhaps best be understood by highlighting how Schweitzer's practical eschatology affirms a this-worldly, active eschatological ethic as well as the ultimate consummation of God's kingdom.

Schweitzer maintained commitment to the kingdom of God to be "the greatest and most important thing which is asked from Christian faith."[76] He believed that once the perception of an imminent end is removed, eschatology's ethical energy is enfeebled: "Both their [humans'] rejection of this world and the idea that the Kingdom of God will come of its own accord condemn them to do nothing to improve the present."[77] An eschatological ethic of world transformation is stressed here. When eschatological belief in the kingdom recedes into a distant expectation, so eschatology is transformed and, as a consequence for Schweitzer, becomes unethical. The eschatological kingdom is seen to impart now its power to create the new kingdom; that is, the power of the not-yet shapes ethical principles in the present.

Schweitzer was a pioneer in viewing eschatology as an engine for moral action. It is striking how various subsequent versions of liberation theology employ eschatology. Letty Russell employs the term *advent shock* to address the sense of disorder in the present in comparison with the anticipated future fulfillment: "Because of advent shock we seek to anticipate the future in what we do, opening ourselves to the working of God's Spirit and expecting the impossible." Following Schweitzer's practical eschatology of reverence for life, Russell has called for a shift in theological/eschatological ethics to "search out alternative way[s] of ordering our reality and our world that [are] less harmful to human beings, to nature, and to all creation."[78] Gustavo Gutierrez comments that "the attraction of 'what is to come' is the driving force of history."[79] Rosemary Radford Ruether assigns a utopian function to eschatology: a prophetic "vision of the new age to come in which the present system of injustice is overcome and God's intended reign of peace and justice is installed in history."[80] Similarly, eschatology also has a prominent role in the work of James H. Cone's *A Black Theology of Liberation*.[81] Such images serve to challenge the present and offer an alternative ethical vision towards which one should strive.

In this sense, eschatology speaks not only to the future, but for Schweitzer also relates to the significance of the kingdom at the present moment. Such a this-worldly eschatology holds a liberating function—in Schweitzer's case, striving to realize his understanding of Isaiah's and St. Paul's visions of universal peaceableness to the greatest extent possible. Schweitzer's practical eschatology of reverence for life provides a challenging call to move into this future-made-present.

Lastly, perhaps Schweitzer's greatest contribution lies not in his words, but in the application of his ideas. When Hippias demanded from Socrates a definition of justice, Socrates replied: "Instead of speaking of it, I make it understood by my acts."[82] What Socrates shows us is that we can never understand justice if we do not *live* it. *Mutatis mundi*, Schweitzer would want to say much the same thing about theology and ethics. Indeed, the *full* force of his challenges remains undiscovered unless he is encountered as a person. He wanted his thought, in the final analysis, to direct us to praxis—for us to take up our "share of the burden of pain that lies upon the world."[83] With him, *reverence for life* and *practical eschatology* are a call to action. Schweitzer's decision to make his life his argument continues to provoke us to question what it means to do ethics. And he provides us with a response as relevant and unsettling today as it was for his time.

The Ogowe: A Tributary

Schweitzer's body was buried on the hospital grounds under the palm trees just off the shores of the Ogowe. He left strict instructions that he be placed in a bare pine coffin and that the grave be marked with a simple wooden cross which he had made himself. In his coffin were placed his battered pith helmet and a bag of rice that he used to carry to feed the animals. The funeral was attended by fellow hospital workers, lepers, cripples, and other patients who were well enough to walk. Reportedly, groups in the hundreds from throughout Gabon journeyed to his grave on flotillas of pirogues from up or down the river.

"River and forest! Who can really describe the impressions they make?" Schweitzer meditated. "It is impossible to say where the river ends and the land begins . . . at every bend in the river a new tributary shows itself. The Ogowe is not a river but a river system, three or four branches, twisting themselves together, and in between are lakes big and little."[84] The same could be said of the origin, development, and future of his ethical thought. Like the river, our quest for Schweitzer's reverence for life has winded and snaked, reached forward and back in fits and starts, traveled up and downstream.

And the Ogowe? It continues to flow for those who wish to make the journey.

Notes

ABBREVIATIONS

The following abbreviations have been made in the notes referring to primary works by Schweitzer and selected works by others that are repeatedly cited. Full documentation for each publication is provided at first mention.

By Albert Schweitzer:

CRW	*Christianity and the Religions of the World*
EDGE	*On the Edge of the Primeval Forest*
GOETHE	*Goethe: Five Studies*
IND	*Indian Thought and Its Development*
LEBEN	*Die Geschichte der Leben-Jesu-Forschung*
LETT	*Letters 1905–1965*
LIFE	*"The Ethics of Reverence for Life"*
MCY	*Memoirs of Childhood and Youth*
MKG	*The Mystery of the Kingdom of God*
MYST	*The Mysticism of Paul the Apostle*
OMLT	*Out of My Life and Thought*
PAUL	*Paul and His Interpreters*
PC	*The Philosophy of Civilization*
QUEST	*The Quest of the Historical Jesus*
REV	*A Place for Revelation: Sermons on Reverence for Life*
RFL	*Reverence for Life*
SPIRIT	*"The Tornado and the Spirit"*
TEACH	*The Teaching of Reverence for Life*

Selected works:

CD   *Church Dogmatics*, Karl Barth
ChrL   *The Christian Life* (vol. 4, pt. 4, *Church Dogmatics*),
        Karl Barth
DI   *The Divine Imperative*, Emil Brunner
ETHICS *Ethics*, Karl Barth
GAP   *Of God and Pelicans*, Jay B. McDaniel
LIB   *The Liberation of Life*, Charles Birch and John B. Cobb, Jr.
PATH   *The Jaina Path of Purification*, Padmanabh S. Jaini
SOULS   *Harmless Souls*, W. J. Johnson
SOURCE *The Source of Life*, Jürgen Moltmann
ST   *Systematic Theology*, Paul Tillich
WWR   *The World as Will and Representation*, Arthur Schopenhauer

PREFACE

1. Elaine Kaye, *Mansfield College, Oxford: Its Origin, History, and Significance* (New York: Oxford University Press, 1996), 179.

INTRODUCTION

1. Albert Schweitzer, *Out of My Life and Thought: An Autobiography*, trans. Antje Bultmann Lemke (New York: Henry Holt & Company, 1990), 154–55. Hereafter cited as *OMLT*.

2. Rachel Carson, *Silent Spring* (New York: Houghton Mifflin, 1962), v.

3. Linda Lear, *Rachel Carson: Witness for Nature* (London: Allen Lane, 1997), 438, 440.

4. George Seaver, *Albert Schweitzer: The Man and His Mind* (London: A. & C. Black, 1947), 305.

5. Magnus Ratter, *Albert Schweitzer: Life and Message* (Boston: Beacon Press, 1950), 232.

6. Schweitzer, in Oskar Kraus, *Albert Schweitzer: His Work and His Philosophy*, trans. I. G. McCalman (London: A. & C. Black, 1944), 171.

7. John Everett, "Albert Schweitzer and Philosophy," *Social Research* 33, no. 4 (Winter 1966): 513.

8. *Out of My Life and Thought: An Autobiography*. Translated by Antje Bultmann Lemke (New York: Henry Holt & Company, 1990), 185.

9. *The Philosophy of Civilization*. Vol. 1, *The Decay and Restoration of Civilization*. Vol. 2, *Civilization and Ethics*. Translated by C. T. Campion (New York: Macmillan, 1950; reprint New York: Prometheus Books, 1987), 312.

10. *Liberating Life: Contemporary Approaches in Ecological Theology*, ed. Charles Birch, William Eaken, and Jay B. McDaniel (Maryknoll, N.Y.: Orbis Books, 1990), 148.

CHAPTER I

1. Gabriel Langfeldt, *Albert Schweitzer: A Study of His Philosophy of Life* (London: Allen & Unwin, 1960), 14, 115; D. E. Rölffs, "Briefe," *Deutsches Pfarrblatt* 35 (30 December 1931): 824; Kraus, *Schweitzer: His Work and His Philosophy*, 49; Jackson Lee Ice, *Schweitzer: Prophet of a Radical Theology* (Philadelphia: Westminster Press, 1977), 176.

2. See Schweitzer, *Reverence for Life*, ed. Ulrich Neuenschwander, trans. Reginald H. Fuller (New York: Harper & Row, 1969). Hereafter cited as *RFL*. See also Schweitzer, *A Place for Revelation: Sermons on Reverence for Life*, ed. Martin Strege and Lothar Stiehm, trans. David Larrimore Holland (New York: Macmillan, 1988). Hereafter cited as *REV*.

3. *OMLT*, 25.

4. Emil Brunner, *The Divine Imperative: A Study in Christian Ethics*, trans. Oliver Wyon (London: The Lutterworth Press, 1937), 195. Hereafter cited as *DI*.

5. Schweitzer, *The Philosophy of Civilization*, trans. C. T. Campion (New York: Macmillan, 1950; reprint, New York: Prometheus Books, 1987), 304. Hereafter cited as *PC*; page numbers reference the date edition.

6. *OMLT*, 232.

7. Schweitzer, *The Mysticism of Paul the Apostle*, trans. W. Montgomery (London: A. & C. Black, 1955), 297. Hereafter cited as *MYST*.

8. *PC*, 302.

9. Schweitzer, *Christianity and the Religions of the World*, trans. Joanna Powers (London: Allen & Unwin, 1939), 84. Hereafter cited as *CRW*.

10. *PC*, 305.

11. Schweitzer, "The Ethics of Reverence for Life," *Christendom* 1 (Winter 1936): 229. From a transcript of Schweitzer's Gifford Lectures made by Reverend Dwight C. Smith, ed. and rev. Schweitzer. Hereafter cited as *LIFE*.

12. Albrecht Dihle, *The Theory of Will in Classical Antiquity* (Berkeley: University of California Press, 1982), 123.

13. Ibid., 127.

14. Arthur Schopenhauer, *The World as Will and Representation*, 2 vols., trans. E. F. J. Payne (Dover, New York 1958), 1:126; see also 2:293. Hereafter cited as *WWR*, with volume number.

15. *PC*, 282.

16. See Schweitzer, *Die Religionsphilosophie Kants* (Tübingen: J. C. B. Mohr, 1899).

17. *WWR*, 2:293.

18. *WWR*, 2:350 (Schopenhauer's emphasis).

19. *PC*, 55.

20. *PC*, 236. Schopenhauer repeatedly affirms that the thing-in-itself is the will-to-live; see *WWR*, esp. 2:14, 16, 18.

21. Henri Bergson, *Creative Evolution*, trans. Arthur Mitchell (New York: Dover, 1998) p. 6, 17, 22, 24, 29, 30.

22. *PC*, 264–65.

23. Ibid., 308.

24. *WWR*, 1:362; *PC*, 241.

25. *WWR*, 2:576.

26. Albert Schweitzer, *Indian Thought and Its Development*, trans. Mrs. C. E. B. Russell (Boston: Beacon Press, 1936) p. 7.

27. *PC*, 279.

28. *The Philosophy of Civilization*. Translated by C. T. Campion. New York: Macmillan, 1950; reprint, New York: Prometheus Books, 1987. p. 279.

29. Ibid., 281–82, 285.

30. Christopher Janaway, *Self and World in Schopenhauer's Philosophy* (Oxford: Clarendon Press, 1989), 266.

31. Schweitzer, *Indian Thought and Its Development*, trans. Mrs. C. E. B. Russell (Boston: Beacon Press, 1936), 1–2. Hereafter cited as *IND*.

32. Ibid., 2.

33. *PC*, 76.

34. *IND*, 263.

35. *PC*, 271.

36. *REV*, 15–16.

37. *PC*, 312, 78 (my italics).

38. *OMLT*, 104.

39. Arthur Schopenhauer, *Manuscript Remains*, vol. 1, trans. E. F. J. Payne (Oxford: Berg, 1988), 466.

40. *WWR*, 1:104–5 (Schopenhauer's italics).

41. John Atwell, *Schopenhauer: The Human Character* (Philadelphia: Temple, 1990), x.

42. *PC*, 281–82.

43. Ibid., 310.

44. Ibid., 310.

45. Schweitzer, *The Teaching of Reverence for Life*, trans. Richard and Clara Winston (New York: Holt, Rinehart & Winston, 1965), 27. Hereafter cited as *TEACH*.

46. *PC*, 282.

47. Ibid., 237.

48. *The Philosophy of Civilization*. trans. C. T. Campion. New York: Macmillan, 1950; reprint, New York: Prometheus Books, 1987. p. 237.

49. *LIFE*, 239 (my italics).

50. *IND*, 264.

51. Kraus, *Schweitzer: His Work and His Philosophy*, 42.

52. *WWR*, 2:164, 168.

53. Ibid., 2:349–50.

54. *CRW*, 66, 83.

55. *REV*, 22.

56. *CRW*, 84.

57. *MYST*, 379.

58. Schopenhauer, *On the Basis of Morality*, trans. E. F. J. Payne (Oxford: Berghahn, 1995), 54 (my italics).

59. *MYST*, 379.

60. Schweitzer, *Goethe: Five Studies*, ed. and trans. Charles R. Joy (Boston: Beacon Press, 1948), 76. Hereafter cited as *GOETHE*.

61. Langfeldt, *Albert Schweitzer: A Study of His Philosophy of Life*, 52–53.

62. *OMLT*, 158.

63. *PC*, 313.

64. Ibid., 314.

65. *OMLT*, 242.

66. *CRW*, 51.

67. *PC*, 312.

68. Ibid., 284.

69. *WWR*, 1:379.

70. Ibid., 283.

71. *IND*, 118.

72. *CRW*, 75.

73. *MYST*, 379.

74. Schweitzer, sermon, quoted in Fritz Wartenweiler, *Der Urwalddoktor Albert Schweitzer* (Aargau, Switzerland: Freuden Schweitzer Volksbildungsheime, 1950), 113–14.

75. *MYST*, 378.

76. Schweitzer, *The Forest Hospital at Lambaréné* (New York: Henry Holt & Company, 1931), 77.

77. Schweitzer, *From My African Notebook*, trans. Mrs. C. E. B. Russell (London: Allen & Unwin, 1938), 112.

78. *CRW*, 83.

79. Kraus, *Schweitzer: His Work and His Philosophy*, 42.

80. Schopenhauer, *On the Basis of Morality*, 54–55.

81. Ibid., 103.

82. Schweitzer, correspondence with D. E. Rölffs (1931), in *Letters 1905–1965*, trans. Joachim Neugroschel (New York: Macmillan, 1992), 123. Hereafter cited as *LETT*.

83. Schweitzer, correspondence with Josselin de Jong (28 November 1930), in *LETT*, 113.

84. *CRW*, 80.

85. *MYST*, 378.

86. *CRW*, 90 (my italics).

87. *OMLT*, 235.

88. *OMLT*, 153.

89. *LIFE*, 236.

90. See Nietzsche, *The Will to Power*, trans. W. Kaufmann and R. J. Hollingdale (London: Lowe & Brydone, 1968), 689; Nietzsche, *Beyond Good and Evil*, trans. Helen Zimmern (New York: Dover, 1997), 36.

91. Nietzsche, *Will to Power*, 550 (Nietzsche's emphasis); see also 333, 366, and 369.

92. Nietzsche, *Beyond Good and Evil*, 259 (Nietzsche's emphasis).

93. Nietzsche, *Will to Power*, 689. For Schweitzer's critique of Nietzsche's philosophy, see *PC*, 243–49.

94. Schweitzer, conclusion in *Die Geschichte der Leben-Jesu-Forschung* (hereafter cited as *LEBEN*), in Henry Clark, *The Ethical Mysticism of Albert Schweitzer* (Boston: Beacon Press, 1962), appendix 2, 197.

95. *OMLT*, 58 (my italics).

96. *PC*, 290.

97. Ibid., 323.

98. Schweitzer, 'Ethics of Compassion', Strasbourg (23 February 1919) in *RFL*, pp. 118–119. His sermons 'The Life of Service' and 'The Call to Mission' also discuss this theme. See *RFL*, pp. 58–66, 50–57.

99. Schweitzer, in Hermann Hagedorn, *Prophet in the Wilderness* (New York: Association Press, 1939), 137.

100. Schweitzer, "The Tornado and the Spirit," *Christian Register* (September 1947): 328. Hereafter cited as *SPIRIT*.

101. *SPIRIT* p. 328.

102. *MYST*, 303.

103. *PC*, 332, 77.

104. *GOETHE*, 97, 98.

105. Schweitzer, correspondence with D. E. Rölffs (1931), in *LETT*, 123.

106. *SPIRIT*, 328.

107. *IND*, 259, 260.

108. *PC*, 309.

109. Ibid., 310.

110. Ibid., 311.

111. Ibid., 310.

112. Schweitzer, correspondence with Oskar Kraus (7 November 1931), in *LETT*, 124 (Schweitzer's emphasis).

113. Lois K. Daly makes an important contribution concerning the relationship between Schweitzerian and feminist ethics, especially their convergence on non-hierarchical relationships. See Daly, "Ecofeminism, Reverence for Life, and Feminist Theological Ethics," chap. 7, *Liberating Life: Contemporary Approaches in Ecological Theology*, ed. Charles Birch, William Eaken, and Jay B. McDaniel (Maryknoll, N.Y.: Orbis Books, 1990).

114. *TEACH*, 47.

115. *PC*, 305.

116. Ibid., 57 (my italics).

117. *LIFE*, 188.

118. *PC*, 325.

119. Ibid., 318.

120. Ibid., 344.

121. Ibid., 83.

122. Ibid., 316.

123. *OMLT*, 237; *PC*, 313.

CHAPTER 2

1. George Marshall, *An Understanding of Albert Schweitzer* (New York: Philosophical Library, 1966), 22.

2. OMLT, p. 236.

3. *PC*, 297.

4. *DI*, 195.

5. Ibid., 125.

6. Ibid., 195.

7. Ibid., 612.

8. Ibid., 126.

9. Ibid., 124; 195, 602 (Brunner's italics).

10. Kraus, *Schweitzer: His Work and His Philosophy*, 5.

11. Ice, *Schweitzer: Prophet of a Radical Theology*, 92 (Ice's emphasis).

12. *CRW*, 36.

13. *OMLT*, 241.

14. *CRW*, 29 (my italics).

15. Ibid., 75.

16. Ibid., 60.

17. *REV*, p. 23.

18. *DI*, 126, 127.

19. Ibid., 128, 129.

20. Brunner, *Man in Revolt: A Christian Anthropology*, trans. Olive Wyon (Philadelphia: Westminster Press, 1939). Brunner offers a fuller discussion on the "orders of creation" in *The Christian Doctrine of Creation and Redemption: Dogmatics* vol. 2, trans. Olive Wyon (London: Lutterworth Press, 1952), esp. 24–36.

21. Hans Leisegang, *Religionsphilosophie der Gegenwart* (Berlin: Junker & Dunnhaupt, 1930), 87–89.

22. PC, p. 311 (*Ethik ist in grenzenlos erweiterte Verantwortung gegen alles, was lebt*).

23. Schweitzer, correspondence with Jack Eisendraht (1951), in *LETT*, 218.

24. *REV*, 11.

25. *OMLT*, 236.

26. *DI*, 196, 130.

27. Schweitzer, *On the Edge of the Primeval Forest*, trans. C. T. Campion (London: A. & C. Black, 1922; New York: Macmillan, 1948), 70. Hereafter cited as *EDGE*; page numbers reference the 1948 edition.

28. *IND*, 83 (my italics).

29. Ibid., 5.

30. *REV*, 37

31. *OMLT*, 236.

32. *PC*, 317.

33. *OMLT*, 236 (my italics).

34. Schweitzer, correspondence with Jack Eisendraht (1951), in *LETT*, 218.

35. *PC*, 318.

36. *TEACH*, 23.

37. *LIFE*, 187 (Schweitzer's emphasis).

38. *IND*, 187.

39. Karl Barth, in *Briefwechsel Karl Barth—Eduard Thurneysen 1921–1930* (Zurich: Evangelischer Verlag, 1974), 628. Also cited in Eberhard Busch, *Karl Barth: His Life from Letters and Autobiographical Texts*, trans. John Bowden (London: SCM Press, 1976), 183.

40. Seaver, *Schweitzer: The Man and His Mind*, 42–43.

41. Barth, *Ethics*, ed. Dietrich Braun, trans. Geoffrey W. Bromiley (New York: Seabury Press, 1981), 141. Hereafter cited as *ETHICS*.

42. Barth, *Church Dogmatics*, 14 vols., trans. Geoffrey W. Bromiley (Edinburgh: T & T Clark, 1961), 3:4:349. Hereafter cited as *CD*, with volume and part numbers.

43. Ibid., 354–55.

44. *ETHICS*, 141 (Barth's emphasis).

45. *CD*, 3:4:380.

46. Ibid., 3:4:339.

47. Ibid., 3:4:341 (my italics).

48. *ETHICS*, 337.

49. Ibid., 140.

50. *CD*, 3:4:349.

51. Ibid., 3:4:349–50; cf. *ETHICS*, 140.

52. *ETHICS*, 141.

53. *CD*, 3:4:351, 343.

54. *ETHICS*, 141.

55. *CD*, 3:4:352.

56. *CD* III/4, 351.

57. Ibid., 3:4:350.

58. Charles R. Joy, *The Animal World of Albert Schweitzer* (Boston: Beacon Press, 1950), 11.

59. Ann Cottrell Free, *Animals, Nature, and Albert Schweitzer* (Washington, D. C.: Flying Fox Press, 1993), 50–51.

60. *CD*, 3:4:351.

61. Ibid., 3:4:352.

62. Ibid., 3:4:332–33 (my italics).

63. Ibid., 3:1:16, 18 (my italics).

64. Brunner, *Man in Revolt*, 414.

65. *CD*, 3:4:324.

66. For a discussion of nonhuman species in Barth's theology, see Andrew Linzey, "The Neglected Creature: The Doctrine of the Nonhuman Creation and its Relationship with the Human in the Thought of Karl Barth," PhD dissertation (University of London, 1986). See also Linzey's *Animal Theology* (London: SCM Press, 1994), 9–11, for his discussion of Schweitzer and Barth. I am indebted to his work in the discussion that follows.

67. *CD*, 3:2:6.

68. *CD*, 3:4:337.

69. Brunner, *Reason and Revelation*, trans. Olive Wyon (Philadelphia: Westminster Press, 1946), 33.

70. *CD*, 3:2:3 (my italics).

71. *CD*, 3:3:43.

72. Schweitzer, in Werner Picht, *Albert Schweitzer: The Man and His Work*, trans. Edward Fitzgerald (London: Allen & Unwin, 1964), 73.

73. Brunner, *Man in Revolt*, 414.

74. Philip Sherrard, *Human Image: World Image; The Death and Resurrection of Sacred Cosmology* (Ipswich: Golgonooza Press, 1992), 164. In 1 Corinthians 15:39, Paul suggests that not all flesh is the same. The meaning that *sarx* holds for Paul is quite different; flesh (*sarx*) is opposed to spirit.

75. Sherrard, *The Rape of Man and Nature: An Enquiry into the Origins and Consequences of Modern Science* (Ipswich: Golgonooza Press, 1987), 64.

76. John Muddiman, "A New Testament Doctrine of Creation?" in *Animals on the Agenda: Questions about Animals for Theology and Ethics*, ed. Andrew Linzey and Dorothy Yamamoto (London: SCM Press, 1998), 32.

77. Jürgen Moltmann, *The Source of Life: The Holy Spirit and the Theology of Life*, (Minneapolis: Fortress Press, 1997), 12. Hereafter cited as *SOURCE*.

78. John B. Cobb, Jr., "All Things in Christ?" in *Animals on the Agenda*, 177.

79. Schweitzer, sermon, "Second Sunday of Pentecost," Lambaréné (24 May 1914),unpublished sermon located in the Albert Schweitzer Institute for Humanities archive at Quinnipiac University (my italics). See *The African Sermons*, edited and translated by Steven E. G. Melamed (Syracuse: Syracuse University Press, 2001), "The Temple of the Holy Spirit," Second Sunday of Pentecost (24 May 1914), 33.

80. *ETHICS*, 139.

81. *CD*, 3:4:324.

82. Harvey Egan, *An Anthology of Christian Mysticism* (Collegeville, Minn.: Liturgical Press, 1991), xxv.

83. Evelyn Underhill, *The Essentials of Mysticism and Other Essays* (London: Dent, 1904), 4.

84. Egan, *Christian Mysticism*, xxv.

85. Barth, *The Epistle to the Romans* (New York: Oxford University Press, 1968), 109–10.

86. Barth, *The Christian Life*, trans. J. Strathhearn McNab (London: Student Christian Movement Press, 1930), 50–51.

87. *CD*, 3:4:333. Barth's section on "Respect [Reverence] for Life" repeatedly refers to the affirmative nature of the will-to-live. See especially "Freedom for Life," 3:4:324–470.

88. *PC*, 79.

89. *LIFE*, 188.

90. *TEACH*, 47.

91. *CD*, 3:2:78; see also *CD*, 3:4:19–21.

92. *LIFE*, 239; *ETHICS*, 58.

93. *ETHICS*, 121.

94. *OMLT*, 104; see also 233.

95. *LIFE*, 233.

96. *CD*, 3:4:341.

97. *ChrL*, 52 (my italics).

98. Barth, *The Holy Ghost and the Christian Life*, trans. R. Birch Hoyle (London: Frederick Muller, 1938), 22.

99. *ETHICS*, 142 (Barth's emphasis).

100. *CD*, 3:4:397–98.

101. *ChrL*, 57.

102. Ibid., 168 (my italics).

103. Ibid., 264; see also 212–13.

104. *CD*, 3:4:355.

105. *LIFE*, 239.

106. Schweitzer, sermon, "Ethics of Compassion," Strasbourg (23 February 1919), in *RFL*, 118–19. His sermons "The Life of Service" and "The Call to Mission" also discuss this theme; see *RFL*, 58–66, 50–57.

107. "Questions for the Seminar with Professor Karl Barth," twelveth session (1 October 1963–15 February 1964), in J. A. Lyons, *The Cosmic Christ in Origen and de Chardin* (Oxford: Oxford University Press, 1982), 95; *CD*, 3:4:383.

108. *MYST*, 54.

109. Ibid., 54 (my italics). See also Schweitzer, *Paul and His Interpreters: A Critical History*, trans. W. Montgomery (London: A. & C. Black, 1948), 96–97, 103–4. Hereafter cited as *PAUL*.

110. *ChrL*, 101 (my italics).

111. *REV*, 23; Schweitzer, *The African Sermons*, "Preparing for the Kingdom of God," Lambaréné (first Sunday in Advent, 30 November 1913), 15. Unpublished sermon located in the Albert Schweitzer Institute archive at Quinnipiac University.

112. *ETHICS*, 121 (my italics).

113. Barth, *Holy Ghost*, 24.

114. *CD*, 1:2:859; see also 868.

115. Barth, "Conversations with Youth Chaplains from the Rhineland" (4 November 1963), in Busch, *Karl Barth: His Life from Letters*, 466.

116. *CD*, 3:4:324.

CHAPTER 3

1. Unpublished correspondence between Jackson Lee Ice and Albert Schweitzer (7 July 1952) from the archives of the Albert Schweitzer Institute for the Humanities (Connecticut, U.S.).

2. Joy, in *GOETHE*, 24.

3. *GOETHE*, 24.

4. GOETHE, p. 27.

5. Ibid., 27.

6. Joy, in *GOETHE*, 25.

7. *GOETHE*, 25.

8. *IND*, vi. For an account of the influence of Indian thought on Schopenhauer, see Moira Nicholls, "The Influences of Eastern Thought on Schopenhauer's Doctrine of the Thing-In-Itself," in *The Cambridge Companion to Schopenhauer*, ed. Christopher Janaway (Cambridge: Cambridge University Press, 1999), 171–212; Dorothea Dauer, *Schopenhauer as Transmitter of Buddhist Ideas* (Berne: Herbert Long & Company, 1969); and Bryan Magee, *The Philosophy of Schopenhauer* (Oxford: Clarendon Press, 1983), 14–15, 316–321. Also, a discussion of Schopenhauer's introduction to the study of Indian antiquity is found in Ludwig Schemann, ed., *Schopenhauer-Briefe* (Leipzig: 1893), 332.

9. Schweitzer, correspondence with Asiatic Society, Calcutta, India (10 February 1965), in *LETT*, 351.

10. For a treatment, see H. G. Rawlinson, "India in European Literature and Thought," in *The Legacy of India*, ed. G. T. Garratt (Oxford: Clarendon Press, 1937); Rawlinson, "Indian Influence on the West," in *Modern Indian and the West*, ed. L. S. S. O'Malley (London: Oxford University Press, 1941); and P. J. Marshall and G. Williams, *The Great Map of Mankind* (London: Dent, 1982).

11. Georg Wilhelm Friedrich Hegel, *The Christian Religion: Lectures on the Philosophy of Religion*, vol. 2, trans. Peter Hodgson (Missoula, Mont.: Scholars Press, 1979), 43.

12. *WWR*, 2:608.

13. Schopenhauer, *Werke in zehn Bänden*, vol. 5, ed. Arthur Hübscher, trans. E. F. J. Payne (Zurich: Diogenes Verlag, 1977), 40.

14. Schopenhauer, *Manuscript Remains*, vol. 1, 467.

15. Schweitzer, correspondence with Prime Minister Lal Bahadur Shastri, New Delhi, India (12 June 1960), in *LETT*, 348.

16. Schweitzer, *Memoirs of Childhood and Youth*, trans. Kurt and Alice Bergel (New York: Syracuse University Press, 1997), 37. Hereafter cited as *MCY*.

17. Ibid., 41.

18. *IND*, vi (my italics).

19. Ibid., 10.

20. Ibid., 83 (my italics).

21. Ibid. (my italics).

22. Ibid., 78.

23. Ibid., 79.

24. Ibid., 83.

25. Ibid., 10.

26. Ibid., 84.

27. Ibid., 234.

28. Moritz Winternitz, *A History of Indian Literature*, 3rd ed., vol. 1 (Calcutta: University of Calcutta, 1962), 1.

29. Some of the major works in German and French at the time include Ernst Leumann, *Das Aupapatike Sutra, erstes Upanga der Jaina* (Leipzig: Brockhaus, 1883); August Friedrich Rudolf Hoernle, *Jaina Agama* (Calcutta: Bilbiotheca Indica, 1888); Hermann Jacobi, "Mahavira," *Indian Antiquary* 9 (1880): 158–63; *Eine*

Jaina-Dogmatik: Umāsvāti's Tattvārthādhigama-Sutra (Leipzig: Brockhaus,1906); *Ubersicht uber die Avasyaka-Literatur* (Hamburg: Friederichsen, 1934); Arman Albert Guérinot, *Repetoire d'Epigraphie Jaina* (Paris: Geuthner, 1908) and *La religion djaina* (Paris: Geuthner, 1926); Helmuth von Glasenapp, *Der Jainismus: Eine indische Erlö-sungs-Religion* (Berlin: Hayer, 1925); and Walther Schubring, *Acaranga-Sutra* (Leipzig: Brockhaus,1910), *Worte Mahaviras* (Gotingen: Vandenhoeck, 1926), and *Die Lehre der Jainas* (Berlin: Walter De Gruyter and Company, 1935). For an extensive bibliography on Jainism, see Padmanabh S. Jaini, *The Jaina Path of Purification* (Berkeley: University of California Press, 1979).

30. Schweitzer, correspondence with Prime Minister Lal Bahadur Shastri, New Delhi, India (29 November, 1964), in *LETT*, 349.

31. *IND*, 43.

32. *TEACH*, 13.

33. *IND*, viii.

34. *WWR*, 2:170 (Schopenhauer's emphasis).

35. *IND*, 1.

36. Ibid., 1–2.

37. Ibid., 42.

38. Ibid., 7–8.

39. Ibid., 117.

40. Ibid., 8–9 (my italics).

41. Schopenhauer apparently suffered from this same problem. See Christopher Janaway, ed., *The Cambridge Companion to Schopenhauer* (Cambridge: Cambridge University Press, 1999), 171–212.

42. Padmanabh S. Jaini, *The Jaina Path of Purification* (Berkeley: University of California, 1979), 1. Hereafter cited as *PATH*.

43. See *Acārānga Sutra*, 1.1.2, 1.5.5.

44. *PATH*, 167.

45. As cited in W. J. Johnson, *Harmless Souls* (Delhi: Motilal Banarsidass, 1995), 63. Hereafter cited as *SOULS*.

46. Mahavira, quoted in Gurudeva Chitrabhanuji, "Jainism as a Religion of Nonviolence," in *Jainism in a Global Perspective*, ed. Sagarmal Jain and Shriprakash Pandey (India: Parsuanatha Vidyapitha, 1998), 1.

47. Jain Yogasastra, quoted in N. P. Jaina, "Jaina Religion," in *Jainism in a Global Perspective*, 88, 110.

48. Sadhvi Shilapiji, "*Ahimsā Dharma*" [The Religion of Nonviolence], in *Jainism in a Global Perspective*, 27.

49. *LIFE*, 188.

50. Ibid., 181 (Schweitzer's emphasis).

51. Ibid. (Schweitzer's emphasis).

52. *PC*, 309.

53. *LIFE*, 181.

54. *TEACH*, 39.

55. *PC*, 297.

56. Hermann Jacobi, *Sacred Books of the East*, vol. 22 (Oxford: Clarendon Press, 1884), 3.

57. *PATH*, 103.

58. Ibid.

59. *REV*, 10.

60. *Acārānga Sutra* 1:2:3; *Kritānga Sutra*, bk. 1, lecture 11:33, in Jacobi, *Sacred Books*, 314; *SOULS*, 10.

61. *REV*, 10.

62. Schweitzer, "The Revival of Falconry," in Joy, *Animal World of Albert Schweitzer*, 177. Originally published as *Nochmals Falkenjägerei* (Zurich: Atlantis, May 1932).

63. See Max Scheler, *The Nature of Sympathy*, trans. Peter Heath (New York: Archon Books, 1970) 17f.

64. *REV*, 10–11, 14.

65. *PC*, 236–37.

66. *IND*, 83–84

67. Jagmanderlal Jaini, *Outlines of Jainism* (Cambridge: Cambridge University Press, 1916), 71.

68. *REV*, 15.

69. Ibid., 26.

70. *IND*, x.

71. Ibid., 81.

CHAPTER 4

1. Schweitzer, in Theodore Siebert, "Unerwartete Begegnung im Elsass," *Runderbrief* 9 (January 1956): 48. (author's translation)

2. See Seaver, *Schweitzer: The Man and His Mind*, 206–7.

3. Schweitzer, *The Mystery of the Kingdom of God*, trans. Walter Lowrie (London: A. & C. Black, 1914), 274. Hereafter cited as *MKG*.

4. Schweitzer, *The Quest of the Historical Jesus*, trans. W. Montgomery (London: A. & C. Black, 1910; reprint, London: SCM Press, 1996), 4. Hereafter cited as *QUEST*; page numbers refer to the 1996 edition.

5. Schweitzer, *The Kingdom of God and Primitive Christianity*, trans. L. A. Garrard (New York: Seabury Press, 1966), 128n (my italics). Schweitzer's remarks here pertain to a passage from pages 378–79 in *QUEST*.

6. *OMLT*, 48.

7. *QUEST*, 357.

8. Ibid., 388, 389–90.

9. Ibid., 368–69.

10. Ibid., xi.

11. Ibid., 399.

12. *OMLT*, 59.

13. *QUEST*, 397.

14. J. C. O'Neill, *The Bible's Authority: A Portrait of Thinkers from Lessing to Bultmann* (Edinburgh: T & T Clark, 1991), 261.

15. *LEBEN*, 201.

16. *QUEST*, 397.

17. Ibid., 170.

18. Ibid.

19. *MYST*, 174; see also *QUEST*, 399, and *LETT*, 85.

20. *MYST*, 172.

21. Schweitzer, correspondence (Rhineland, 1954), in *LETT*, 254.

22. Friedrich von Hügel, *The Mystical Element of Religion: As Studied in Saint Catherine of Genoa and Her Friends*, 2nd ed. (London: J. M. Dent & Sons, 1923), 3.

23. *QUEST*, 400.

24. Ibid., 254; see also 400.

25. *IND*, 4.

26. *LEBEN*, 201.

27. Schweitzer, sermon, "Compelling Hope," Strasbourg (18 December 1902), in *RFL*, 47.

28. Schweitzer, "Religion in Modern Civilisation," in Seaver, *Schweitzer: The Man and His Mind*, appendix 3, 338.

29. See Schweitzer, *From My African Notebook*, trans. Mrs. C. E. B. Russell (London: Allen & Unwin, 1938), 112. Schweitzer's sermons were translated by his daughter, Rhena Schweitzer Miller. They were compiled and appeared as part of Steven E. G. Melamed's doctoral dissertation at Florida State University (awarded spring semester, 1997). The titles of the seven sermons, in chronological order, are: "Our Father," "Thy Kingdom Come!" "Send Thy Kingdom!" "The Will of God Is Already in Your Heart," "A Happy Heart," "Our Daily Bread," and "Deliver Us From Evil."

30. *OMLT*, 93.

31. Schweitzer, "Sunday in Lambaréné," in *From My African Notebook*, 112.

32. Erich Grässer, *Albert Schweitzer als Theologe* (Tübingen: J. C. B. Mohr, 1979), 210.

33. *MYST*, 394 (my italics); ibid., 380.

34. Schweitzer, sermon, "Thy Kingdom Come!" Lambaréné (3 August 1930), in shortened publication name from note 75, chap. 2, page(s) (my italics).

35. Schweitzer, sermon, "Send Thy Kingdom!" Lambaréné (10 August 1930), in shortened publication name from note 75, chap. 2, page(s) (my italics).

36. Schweitzer, in *The African Sermons*, "Thy Kingdom Come!" (3 August 1930), 97. Unpublished sermon located in the Albert Schweitzer Institute for Humanities archive at Quinnipiac University.

37. *MYST*, 294.

38. Ibid., 304; see also *OMLT*, 219.

39. Schweitzer, in Kraus, *Albert Schweitzer: His Work and His Philosophy*, 42.

40. *MCY*, 90.

41. Schweitzer, in *The African Sermons*, "Sermon on the Good Samaritan," Lambaréné (9 November 1930), 126. Unpublished sermon located in the Albert Schweitzer Institute for Humanities archive at Quinnipiac University.

42. Albrecht Ritschl, *The Christian Doctrine of Justification and Reconciliation: The Positive Development of the Doctrine*, trans. H. R. Mackintosh and A. B. Macaulay (Edinburgh: T. & T. Clark, 1900), 11.

43. Ritschl, *Three Essays*, trans. Philip Hefner (Philadelphia: Fortress Press, 1972), 86, 87

44. Ibid., 13.

45. Ibid., 11.

46. Johaness Weiss, foreword to *Die Predigt Jesu vom Reiche Gottes* (Göttingen: Vandenhoeck and Ruprecht, 1892), v, trans. Mark Chapman, appearing in Chapman, "The Kingdom of God and Ethics: From Ritschl to Liberation Theology," in *The Kingdom of God and Human Society*, ed. R. S. Barbour (Edinburgh: T & T Clark, 1993), 150.

47. Weiss, *Die Idee des Reiches Gottes in der Theologie* (Giessen: J. Ricker, 1901) 113, trans. Mark Chapman, also in Chapman, "The Kingdom of God and Ethics," 151.

48. Weiss, *Die Idee des Reiches Gottes in der Theologie*, 155, also in Chapman, "The Kingdom of God and Ethics," 152.

49. Weiss, *Jesus' Proclamation of the Kingdom of God*, trans. Richard Hiers and David Holland (London: SCM Press, 1971), 132 (Weiss's emphasis).

50. *MYST*, 393.

51. *OMLT*, 235.

52. Ibid., 52.

53. *QUEST*, 483 (my italics).

54. Schweitzer, "Spirit of Christ Vital to World in Distress", unpublished essay located in the archives Albert Schweitzer Institute for Humanities at Quinnipiac University (my italics).

55. Schweitzer, in E. N. Mozley, *The Theology of Albert Schweitzer for Christian Inquirers* (New York: Macmillan, 1951) 101.

56. *CRW*, 85.

57. Ibid., 75.

58. See chap. 17 in *OMLT*.

59. *QUEST*, 283–84 (Schweitzer's italics).

60. *MYST*, 382, 385.

61. Schweitzer, in Mozley, *The Theology of Albert Schweitzer for Christian Inquirers*, 82–83.

62. *QUEST*, 239.

63. Schweitzer, "Compelling Hope," in *RFL*, 48.

64. *MYST*, 384.

65. *OMLT*, 151; *PC*, 216.

66. Schweitzer, correspondence with Baron Lagerfelt and Greta Lagerfelt (10 April 1938), in *LETT*, 159.

67. Rudolf Bultmann, *History and Eschatology* (Edinburgh: University Press, 1957), 16.

68. Bultmann, *Jesus and the Word*, trans. Louise Smith and Erminie Lantero (London: Charles Scribner's Sons, 1958), 33.

69. Ibid., 34–35; Ibid., 44.

70. *LEBEN*, 200. (my italics)

71. Schweitzer, in *The African Sermons*, "Preparing for the Kingdom," First Sunday in Advent (30 November 1913), 15. Unpublished sermon located in the Albert Schweitzer Institute for Humanities archive at Quinnipiac University.

72. Schweitzer, in *The African Sermons*, "Send Thy Kingdom!," (10 August 1930), 100–101. Unpublished sermon located in the Albert Schweitzer Institute for Humanities archive at Quinnipiac University.

73. *RFL*, 81.

74. Schweitzer, Lambaréné sermons, in *The African Sermons*, unpublished sermons located in the Albert Schweitzer Institute for Humanities archive at Quinnipiac University: "Thy Kingdom Come!" (3 August 1930), 97; "Forgive! And be Forgiven" (6 July 1930), 86; "Thy Kingdom Come!" (3 August 1930), 98; "The Parable of the Prodigal Son" (14 September 1930), 114.

75. *MYST*, 384.

76. Ritschl, *The Christian Doctrine of Justification and Reconciliation: The Positive Development of the Doctrine*, 222, 279.

77. Bultmann, *Jesus Christ and Mythology* (New York: Charles Scribner's Sons, 1958), 69.

78. *MYST*, 384.

79. Schweitzer, in Mozley, *The Theology of Albert Schweitzer for Christian Inquirers*, 83.

80. Bultmann, "Krisis des Glaubens—Krisis der Kirche—Krisis der Religion: Drei Marburger Vorträge von Rudolf Bultmann, Hans Freiherr von Soden, Heinrich Frick" (lecture, Giessen: 1931).

81. Moltmann, *Theology of Hope: On the Ground and the Implications of a Christian Eschatology*, trans. J. W. Leitch (London: SCM Press, 1967), 37.

82. Ibid., 38–39.

83. Ibid., 37.

84. Ibid., 39 (my italics).

85. Moltmann, *Hope and Planning*, trans. Margaret Clarkson (London: SCM Press, 1971), 167.

86. Oscar Cullmann, *Christ and Time: The Primitive Christian Conception of Time and History*, 2nd ed., trans. Floyd Filson (London: SCM Press, 1962), 30.

87. James M. Robinson, *A New Quest of the Historical Jesus and Other Essays* (Philadelphia: Fortress Press, 1983), 34.

88. O'Neill, *Bible's Authority*, 265.

89. Ibid., 256 (my italics).

90. Ibid., 263. (my italics)

91. *QUEST*, 399.

92. Moltmann, *Theology of Hope*, 39.

93. *MYST*, 384.

94. Schweitzer, *Schweizerische Theologische Umschau* (1953), in *A Treasury of Albert Schweitzer*, ed. Thomas Kiernan (New York: Gramercy Books, 1994), 207.

95. Moltmann, "The Future as Threat and Opportunity," in *Contemporary Religion and Social Responsibility*, ed. N. Brockman and N. Piediscalzi (New York: Alba House, 1973), 112.

96. Moltmann, *The Way of Jesus Christ: Christology in Messianic Dimensions*, trans. Margaret Kohl (London: SCM Press, 1990), 340–41.

97. Schweitzer, in Mozley, *The Theology of Albert Schweitzer for Christian Inquirers*, 107.

98. Moltmann, *A Passion for God's Reign: Theology, Christian Learning, and the Christian Self*, ed. Miroslav Volf (Grand Rapids, Mich.: William Eerdmans, 1998), 54–55.

99. Schweitzer, in *The African Sermons*, "Thy Kingdom Come!" (3 August 1930), 99. Unpublished sermon located in the Albert Schweitzer Institute for Humanities archive at Quinnipiac University.

100. *OMLT*, 235 (my italics).

CHAPTER 5

1. *QUEST*, 401.
2. *EDGE*, 11, 70, 124.
3. *MYST*, x.
4. Ibid., 1.
5. Ibid.
6. Ibid., 1–2.
7. Ibid., 378.
8. *OMLT*, 241.
9. *MYST*, 297.
10. *PC*, 301.
11. Ritschl, *Three Essays*, 76.
12. *MYST*, 3.
13. Ibid.
14. Ibid., 8.
15. Ibid., 5.
16. Schweitzer, correspondence with the Reformed Church of the United States (1930s), in *LETT*, 144.
17. *MYST*, 380 (my italics).
18. 1 Corinthians 15:24–28.
19. *PAUL*, 223.
20. *MYST*, 380.
21. Ibid., 380.
22. Schweitzer, "The Conception of the Kingdom of God in the Transformation of Eschatology," in Mozley, *The Theology of Albert Schweitzer for Christian Inquirers*, 88
23. E. P. Sanders, *Paul and Palestinian Judaism* (Philadelphia: Fortress Press, 1977), 462–63, 549; R. Barry Matlock, *Unveiling the Apocalyptic Paul: Paul's Interpreters*

and the Rhetoric of Criticism (Sheffield: Sheffield Academic Press, 1996), 40. For an account of Sanders's relationship to Schweitzer's thought on Jesus, see Robert Morgan, "From Reimarus to Sanders: The Kingdom of God, Jesus, and the Judaism of His Day," in Barbour, *Kingdom of God*, 80–139. For recent research on Schweitzer's Pauline studies and his academic conclusions, see also S. Westerholhm, *Israel's Law and the Church's Faith: Paul and His Recent Interpreters* (Grand Rapids, Mich.: Eerdmans, 1988); W. G. Kümmel, *The New Testament: The History of the Investigation of Its Problems*, trans. S. M. Gilmour and H. C. Kee (London: SCM Press, 1973), 235–44; S. Neill and N. T. Wright, *The Interpretation of the New Testament 1861–1986*, 2nd ed. (Oxford: Oxford University Press, 1988), 205–15; and A. C. Thiselton, "Biblical Classics 4: Schweitzer's Interpretation of Paul," *Expository Times* 90 (1979–1980): 132–37.

24. *MYST*, 147.

25. Ibid., 148.

26. George Bernard Shaw, *Pygmalion and Major Barbara* (New York: Penguin, 1957) p. 24.

27. *EDGE*, 11, 70, 124.

28. Schweitzer, sermon, "We Shall Be Exalted," Strasbourg (23 February 1902), in *RFL*, 22.

29. Schweitzer, sermon, "Creative Suffering," Strasbourg (14 May 1900), in *RFL*, 15.

30. Schweitzer, "We Shall Be Exalted," in *RFL*, 22.

31. Schweitzer, "Creative Suffering," in *RFL*, 16.

32. Schweitzer, "We Shall Be Exalted," in *RFL*, 22.

33. Schweitzer, sermon, "Christ in Our Life," Strasbourg (24 April 1904), in *RFL*, 35.

34. Schweitzer, in D. Roland Schutz, "Albert Schweitzer's Christentum und Theologische Forschung," *Rundbrief fur den Freundeskreis von Albert Schweitzer* 9 (1 January 1956): 13, quoted in Clark, *Ethical Mysticism of Albert Schweitzer*, 92.

35. Romans 8:13, as cited by Schweitzer, *MYST*, 169, 302.

36. Philip West, "Re-reading Schweitzer's *Quest*," in Barbour, *Kingdom of God*, 167.

37. Christopher Rowland, "Reflections on the Politics of the Gospels," in Barbour, *Kingdom of God*, 225.

38. *MYST*, 148.

39. *WWR*, 2:636.

40. Nietzsche, *Beyond Good and Evil*, 93 (Nietzsche's emphasis).

41. B. H. Streeter, "The Historic in Christ," in *Foundations: A Statement of Belief by Seven Oxford Men*, ed. B. H. Streeter (London: Macmillan, 1912), 77.

42. Grässer, *Albert Schweitzer als Theologe*, 79. See also O'Neill, *Bible's Authority*, 263.

43. *PC*, 245.

44. Ibid., 246 (my italics).

45. *PAUL*, 59.

46. *MYST*, 302.

47. Ibid., 25.

48. *PC*, 304.

49. *PAUL*, 59.

50. *MYST*, 387.

51. Schweitzer, in Schutz, "Albert Schweitzer's Christentum und Theologische Forschung," 14.

52. *MYST*, 388.

53. Ibid., 387.

54. Ibid., 388.

55. *IND*, 8.

56. Cooper, *Radical Christianity and Its Sources* (Philadelphia: Westminster Press, 1968), 139.

57. Ibid., 139–40.

58. *CRW*, 38.

59. *MYST*, 333.

60. Schweitzer, correspondence with Walter Lowrie (15 October 1913), in *LETT*, 37.

61. Schweitzer, sermon, "My Brother's Keeper," Strasbourg (4 April 1909), in *RFL*, 81.

62. Schweitzer, correspondence with the Paris Mission Society (18 June 1913), in *LETT*, 33.

63. Schweitzer, correspondence with his sister, Adele Woyttin (April 1913), in *LETT*, 28 (Schweitzer's emphasis).

64. Schweitzer, correspondence with Anna Schäffer (18 May 1913), in *LETT*, 30.

65. *OMLT*, 119.

66. *EDGE*, 168–69.

67. Erica Anderson, *The Schweitzer Album* (New York: Harper & Row, 1965), 169.

68. Schweitzer, "Compelling Hope," in *RFL*, p. 46.

69. Schweitzer, in Mozley, *The Theology of Albert Schweitzer for Christian Inquirers*, 90.

70. *MYST*, 388.

71. Moltmann, *Jesus Christ for Today's World*, trans. Margaret Kohl (London: SCM Press, 1994), 21–22.

72. *SOURCE*, 49.

73. Moltmann, "The Liberation of the Future and Its Anticipations in History," in *God Will Be All in All: The Eschatology of Jürgen Moltmann*, ed. Richard Bauckham (Edinburgh: T & T Clark, 1999), 267 (my italics).

74. Moltmann, *Theology of Hope*, 38–39.

75. Douglas Meeks, *Origin of the Theology of Hope* (Philadelphia: Fortress Press, 1974), 48, 49; Carl Braaten, *Eschatology and Ethics* (Minneapolis, Minn.: Augsburg, 1974), 121.

76. *MYST*, 384.

77. Schweitzer, "Philosophy and the Movement for the Protection of Animals," *International Journal of Animal Protection*, Edinburgh (May 1935), in Charles Joy, *The Animal World of Albert Schweitzer: Jungle Insights into Reverence for Life*, ed. Charles Joy (Boston: Beacon Press, 1950), 187.

78. Oscar Cullmann, *Salvation and History*, trans. Sidney Sowers (London: SCM Press, 1967), 31–32, 40 (my italics).

79. *CD*, 2:1:636.

80. Timothy Gorringe, "Eschatology and Political Radicalism," in Bauckham, *God Will Be All in All*, 93.

81. *MYST*, 297.

82. *REV*, 23.

83. *CD*, 3:4:355–56.

84. *ChrL*, 180, 175.

85. *ETHICS*, 13.

86. *CD*, 3:3:268.

87. Schweitzer, "Religion in Modern Civilization," in Seaver, *Schweitzer: The Man and His Mind*, 338.

88. John Webster, *Barth's Moral Theology: Human Action in Barth's Thought* (Edinburgh: T & T Clark, 1998), 93.

89. *ChrL*, 156 (my italics).

90. Ibid., 181.

91. Ibid., 266.

92. Ibid., 169.

93. Barth, correspondence with Hiderobu Kwada of Tokyo, 22 September 1964, in *Karl Barth: Letters 1961–1968*, trans. Geoffrey W. Bromiley (Edinburgh: T & T Clark, 1981), 88–91.

94. *ETHICS*, 513.

95. Barth, *The Epistle to the Romans*, trans. Edwyn C. Hoskyns (Oxford: Oxford University Press, 1968), 431.

96. *CRW*, 29, 30.

97. *PC*, 313.

98. Joy, *Animal World of Albert Schweitzer*, 11.

99. *CD*, 3:1:194.

100. Barth, *Holy Ghost*, 47 (Barth's emphasis).

CHAPTER 6

1. Don Cupitt, *The New Religion of Life in Everyday Speech* (London: SCM Press, 1991), 61.

2. Paul Tillich, in George Marshall and David Polling, *Schweitzer: A Biography* (London: Geoffrey Bles, 1971), 276.

3. The Albert Schweitzer Education Foundation (Chicago, Illinois) originally produced the program on 11 January 1959, and Jerald Brauer, dean of the Federated

Theological Faculties at the University of Chicago, conducted the interview. The Schweitzer Education Foundation of Chicago no longer exists.

4. Tillich, interview with Jerald Brauer, *The Theological Significance of Schweitzer,* 11 January 1959, transcript, located in the archives of the Albert Schweitzer Institute for Humanities at Quinnipiac University, 1.

5. Ibid., 2, 3.

6. Ibid., 6.

7. Ibid., 7.

8. Ibid., 11.

9. *CRW*, 84.

10. Tillich, *The New Being* (London: SCM Press, 1956), 11.

11. Tillich, *Systematic Theology*, 3 vols. (Chicago: University of Chicago Press, 1976), 3:12. Hereafter cited as *ST*, with volume number.

12. Ibid., 3:19 (my italics).

13. Jeremy Yunt, "Reverencing Life in its Multidimensionality: Implications in the Thought of Paul Tillich for a Deep Environmental Ethic" (Pacific School of Religion, Berkeley, California, May 1999), 34.

14. *ST*, 3:34.

15. Ibid., 3:36.

16. Ibid., 3:13.

17. *TEACH*, 47.

18. *ST*, 3:15.

19. *OMLT*, 104.

20. *ST*, 1:62.

21. *PC*, 310.

22. *ETHICS,* 192.

23. Ibid.

24. Tillich, *The Shaking of the Foundations* (London: SCM Press, 1954), 159.

25. *PC*, 237.

26. Ibid., 282.

27. Tillich, *Spiritual Situation in our Technical Society*, ed. J. Mark Thomas (Macon, Ga.: Mercer University Press, 1988), 115; see also *ST*, 1:34.

28. Tillich, *Perspectives on Nineteenth- and Twentieth-Century Protestant Philosophy* (London: SCM Press, 1967), 195–96, 197.

29. Tillich, *Theological Significance of Schweitzer*, 7–8.

30. Ibid., 8.

31. *ST*, 3:16.

32. Durwood Foster, "Afterglows of Tillich," *Newsletter of the North American Paul Tillich Society* 23, no. 1 (January 1997): 23.

33. *ST*, 3:96.

34. See Tillich, *Christianity and the Encounter of World Religions* (New York: Columbia University Press, 1963); see also *ST*, esp. 3:96–97.

35. *ST*, 3:97.

36. Tillich, *Theological Significance of Schweitzer*, 9–10.

37. *TEACH*, 25.

38. *REV*, 15 (Schweitzer's emphasis).

39. *PC*, 312.

40. *ST*, 3:54.

41. Tillich, *Shaking of the Foundations*, 81, 155 (Tillich's emphasis).

42. *PC*, 290.

43. Schweitzer, sermon, "Reverence for Life," Strasbourg (16 February 1919), in *RFL*, 112.

44. *ST*, 2:53; see also *ST*, 3:134–38.

45. Tillich, *Love, Power, and Justice: Ontological Analyses and Ethical Applications* (London: Oxford University Press, 1954), 66, 68–69.

46. Tillich, *Shaking of the Foundations*, 155 (Tillich's emphasis).

47. *MYST*, 384.

48. Schweitzer, "Philosophy and the Movement for the Protection of Animals," in Joy, *The Animal World of Albert Schweitzer: Jungle Insights into Reverence for Life*, 187.

49. *REV*, 23.

50. *PAUL*, 59.

51. *ST*, 2:96.

52. Tillich, *Shaking of the Foundations*, 139.

53. Ibid., 83–84.

54. Tillich, *New Being*, 176 (Tillich's emphasis).

55. *ST*, 3:383, 432, 433.

56. Schweitzer, in *The African Sermons*, "Preparing for the Kingdom of God" (30 November 1913), 15. Unpublished sermon located in the Albert Schweitzer Institute for Humanities archive at Quinnipiac University.

57. Schweitzer, in Mozley, *The Theology of Albert Schweitzer for Christian Inquirers*, 83.

58. Tillich, *Shaking of the Foundations*, 85, 86 (Tillich's emphasis).

59. *ST*, 3:422.

60. Ibid., 3:387.

61. Ibid., 2:97.

62. John B. Cobb, Jr., *Is It Too Late? A Theology of Ecology* (Beverly Hills, Calif.: Bruce, 1972), 49.

63. Ibid., 49, 53.

64. Ibid., 86.

65. Cobb, *Sustainability: Economics, Ecology, and Justice* (New York: Orbis, 1992), 99.

66. Charles Birch and Cobb, *The Liberation of Life: From the Cell to the Community* (Cambridge: Cambridge University Press, 1981), 148 (my italics). Hereafter cited as *LIB*.

67. Ibid., 149.

68. *OMLT*, 237; see also 204.

69. Schweitzer, in Anderson, *Schweitzer Album*, 162.

70. Nigel Biggar, *The Hastening That Waits: Karl Barth's Ethics* (Oxford: Clarendon Press, 1993), 12.

71. *PC*, 318.

72. *OMLT*, 158.

73. *EDGE*, 25.

74. PC, p. 312

75. *LIB*, 152.

76. Ibid., 153.

77. Ibid., 158.

78. *OMLT*, 235.

79. Jay B. McDaniel, *Of God and Pelicans: A Theology of Reverence for Life* (Louisville: Westminster/John Knox Press, 1989), 16. Hereafter cited as GAP.

80. Ibid., 21.

81. Ibid., 22.

82. Ibid.

83. Aldo Leopold, *A Sand County Almanac* (New York: Oxford University Press, 1949), 201.

84. Ibid., 224–25.

85. *GAP*, 58.

86. McDaniel, *With Roots and Wings: Christianity in an Age of Ecology and Dialogue* (Maryknoll, N.Y.: Orbis Books, 1995), 47.

87. *GAP*, 58.

88. McDaniel, *With Roots and Wings*, 47.

89. *GAP*, 60.

90. Ibid., 73.

91. McDaniel, *With Roots and Wings*, 73; see also *GAP*, 73.

92. *ETHICS*, 188.

93. *GAP*, 73.

94. Ibid., 79, 84.

95. Ibid., 84.

CHAPTER 7

1. Albert Schweitzer quoted in American Humanist Association, *The Humanist* Vol. 29, no. 3 (May/June 1969) p. 158.

2. Plato, *The Republic*, pt. 7, 518, trans. F. M. Cornford (Oxford: Oxford University Press, 1969), 232.

3. *PC*, 57 (my italics).

4. *ETHICS*, 188.

5. Pierre Hadot, *Philosophy as a Way of Life*, ed. Arnold Davidson (Oxford: Blackwell, 1995), 187.

6. St. Augustine, *The City of God*, 1.20, trans. Marcus Dods (Edinburgh: T & T Clark, 1877), 32.

7. St. Thomas Aquinas, "Summa Theologica," in *The Summa Theologica of St. Thomas Aquinas*, trans. Fathers of the English Dominican Providence (New York: Benzinger Brothers, 1918), pt. 1, question 64:1.

8. Ibid.

9. Aquinas, *Summa Contra Gentiles*, trans. Joseph Rickaby (London: Burns & Oates, 1950), bk. 3, 12.

10. Ibid.

11. Ibid., 72, 159, 164.

12. John Calvin, *Commentaries on the First Book of Moses Called Genesis*, vol. 1 (1:26), trans. John King (Edinburgh: Edinburgh Printing Co., 1847), 96.

13. John Calvin, *Institutes of the Christian Religion*, vol. 20, 1.16.6, trans. F. L. Battles (London: SCM Press, 1961), 204.

14. John Calvin, *Commentaries on the First Book of Moses Called Genesis*, vol. 1 (9:2), 291.

15. Martin Luther, *Luther's Works*, vol. 2, ed. Jaroslav Pelikan (St. Louis, Mo.: Concordia Publishing House, 1958), 132.

16. Ibid., 133.

17. *REV*, 24.

18. Ibid., 25 (Schweitzer's emphasis).

19. R. G. Frey, "What Has Sentiency to Do with the Possession of Rights?" in *Animals' Rights—A Symposium*, ed. D. A. Paterson and R. D. Ryder (London: Centaur Press, 1979), 108.

20. Peter Singer, *Animal Liberation: A New Ethics for Our Treatment of Animals* (London: Cape, 1976), 8–9; see also Singer, *Practical Ethics* (Cambridge: Cambridge University Press, 1993), 91.

21. *REV*, 24.

22. *PC*, p. 310.

23. Ibid., 11.

24. Ibid., 38, 39, 40.

25. "Religion in Modern Civilisation" in Seaver, *Schweitzer: The Man and His Mind*, 341; *ETHICS*, 181, 188.

26. John Burnaby, *The Belief in Christendom: A Commentary on the Nicene Creed* (London: SPCK Press, 1963), 40–42 (Burnaby's emphasis).

27. Ibid., 41.

28. James Gustafson, *Theology and Ethics* (Oxford: Basil Blackwell, 1981), 109 (Gustafson's emphasis).

29. Ibid., 96.

30. Ibid., 112–13.

31. Ibid., 99, 113.

32. Hans Küng and Jürgen Moltmann, eds., *The Ethics of World Religions and Human Rights* (London: SCM Press, 1990), 131–32 (Küng's and Moltmann's emphasis).

33. Schweitzer, "Philosophy and the Movement for the Protection of Animals," in Joy, *The Animal World of Albert Schweitzer: Jungle Insights into Reverence for Life*, 187.

34. Schweitzer, in Anderson, *Schweitzer Album*, 174.

35. *PC*, 310.

36. Stanley Hauerwas, *The Peaceable Kingdom: A Primer in Christian Ethics* (London: SCM Press, 1984), xvii.

37. See *MCY*, 37.

38. See *EDGE*, 112, 157.

39. Schweitzer, in Anderson, *Schweitzer Album*, 174.

40. Ibid., 47.

41. Richard Hays, *The Moral Vision of the New Testament: Community, Cross, New Creation* (Edinburgh: T. & T. Clark, 1997), 451.

42. *OMLT*, 237.

43. *SOURCE*, 49.

44. Anderson, *Schweitzer Album*, 37.

45. Free, *Animals, Nature, and Albert Schweitzer*, 40.

46. Schweitzer, in Norman Cousins, *Dr. Schweitzer of Lambaréné* (New York: Harper & Brothers, 1960), 195.

47. Albert Schweitzer, *Peace or Atomic War?* New York: Henry Holt & Company, 1958. p. 47.

48. Schweitzer, correspondence with John F. Kennedy (6 August 1963) in *LETT*, 383.

49. *PC*, 310–11.

50. *REV*, 32.

51. *EDGE*, 124.

52. Ibid., 124–25.

53. *PC*, 239.

54. Schweitzer in Anderson, *Schweitzer Album*, 64.

55. *OMLT*, 242.

56. *EDGE*, 125.

57. Dietrich Bonhoeffer, *Gesammelte Schriften*, vol. 2, 441, cited in Eberhard Bethge, *Bonhoeffer: An Illustrated Biography in Documents and Photographs*, trans. Rosaleen Ockenden (London: Harper & Row, 1979), 1 (my italics).

58. *REV*, 19, 20–21.

59. *EDGE*, 70.

60. *SOURCE*, 120; Moltmann, *Theology of Hope*, 206.

61. *SOURCE*, 50.

62. Schweitzer, "We Shall Be Exalted," in *RFL*, 22.

63. *OMLT*, 242–43.

64. *EDGE*, 70.

65. Schweitzer, in Anderson, *Schweitzer Album*, 162.

66. Moltmann, *The Crucified God*, vol. 2, *The Church in the Power of the Spirit* (London: SCM Press, 1992), 277; see also Paul Fiddes, *The Creative Suffering of God* (Oxford: Clarendon Press, 1992).

67. Schweitzer, in *The African Sermons*, "Preparing for the Kingdom of God" (30 November 1913), 15. Unpublished sermons located in the Albert Schweitzer Institute for Humanities archive at Quinnipiac University.

68. *REV*, 23.

69. Schweitzer, "Philosophy and the Movement for the Protection of Animals," in Joy, *The Animal World of Albert Schweitzer: Jungle Insights into Reverence for Life*, 187.

70. *PAUL*, 59.

71. Richard Bauckham and Trevor Hart, *Hope Against Hope: Christian Eschatology in Contemporary Context* (London: Darton, Longman & Todd, 1999), 128.

72. Moltmann, *The Coming of God: Christian Eschatology*, trans. Margaret Kohl (London: SCM Press, 1996), 132.

73. *MKG*, 183.

74. *CRW*, 16–17.

75. *OMLT*, 70.

76. Schweitzer, "The Conception of the Kingdom of God in the Transformation of Eschatology," in Mozley, *The Theology of Albert Schweitzer for Christian Inquirers*, 88.

77. Ibid., 89.

78. Letty Russell, *The Future of Partnership* (Philadelphia: Westminster, 1979), 102; Russell, *Household of Freedom: Authority in Feminist Theology* (Philadelphia: Westminster Press, 1987), 64.

79. Gustavo Gutierrez, *A Theology of Liberation* (New York: Orbis Books, 1973), 164.

80. Rosemary Ruether, *Sexism and God-Talk: Toward a Feminist Theology* (Boston: Beacon Press, 1983), 24.

81. James Cone, *A Black Theology of Liberation* (New York: Lippincott, 1970).

82. Xenophon, *Memorobilia*, trans. Amy Bonnette (Ithaca, N.Y.: Cornell University Press, 1994), 4:4:10.

83. *OMLT*, 242.

84. Schweitzer, *On the Edge of the Primeval Forest*, trans. C. T. Campion. (London: A. & C. Black, 1922), 21–22.

Selected Bibliography

WORKS BY SCHWEITZER

Christianity and the Religions of the World. Translated by Joanna Powers.
    London: Allen & Unwin, 1939. Originally published as *Das Christentum
    und die Weltreligionen* (Munich: C. H. Beck, 1923).
*Die Weltanschauung der Ehrfurcht vor dem Leben: Kulturphilosophie III
    Erster und zweiter Teil*. Edited by Claus Günzler and Johann Zürcher
    (Munich: C. H. Beck, 1999).
The Forest Hospital at Lambaréné. New York: Henry Holt & Company,
    1931. Originally published in 3 vols. as *Mitteilungen aus Lambaréné*
    (Bern: Paul Haupt, 1925; Strasbourg: Imprimerie Alsacienne, 1926;
    Strasbourg: Imprimerie Alsacienne, 1928).
From My African Notebook. Translated by Mrs. C. E. B. Russell (London:
    Allen & Unwin, 1938). Originally published as *Afrikanische Geschichten*.
    Leipzig: Felix Meiner, 1938.
Indian Thought and Its Development. Translated by Mrs. C. E. B. Russell.
    Boston: Beacon Press, 1936. Originally published as *Die
    Weltanschauung der Indischen Denker* (Munich: C. H. Beck, 1935).
    Also published as *Les Grands penseurs de l'Inde* (Paris: Payot,
    1936).
J. S. Bach. Translated by Ernest Newman. London: A. & C. Black, 1911.
    Originally published as *J. S. Bach: le musicien-poète* (Paris: Costallat,
    1905), and as *J. S. Bach* (Leipzig: Breitkopf & Härtel, 1908).
The Kingdom of God and Primitive Christianity. Translated by L. A. Garrard.
    New York: Seabury Press, 1966. Originally published as *Reich Gottes
    und Christentum* (Munich: C. H. Beck, 1966).

Memoirs of Childhood and Youth. Translated by Kurt and Alice Bergel. New York: Syracuse University Press, 1997. Originally published as *Aus Meiner Kindheit und Jugendzeit* (Munich: C. H. Beck, 1924).

More from the Primeval Forest. Translated by C. T. Campion. London: A. & C. Black, 1931. Published in the United States as *The Forest Hospital at Lambaréné* (New York: Macmillan, 1948). Originally published as *Das Urwaldspital zu Lambaréné* (Munich: C. H. Beck, 1931).

The Mystery of the Kingdom of God. Translated by Walter Lowrie. London: A. & C. Black, 1914. Originally published as *Das Abendmahlsproblem auf Grund der Wissenschaftlichen Forschung des 19. Jahrhunderts und der Historischen Berichte* (Tübingen: J. C. B. Mohr, 1901).

The Mysticism of Paul the Apostle. Translated by W. Montgomery. London: A. & C. Black, 1955. Originally published as *Die Mystik des Apostels Paulus* (Tübingen: J. C. B. Mohr, 1930).

On the Edge of the Primeval Forest. Translated by C. T. Campion. London: A. & C. Black, 1922; New York: Macmillan, 1948. Originally published as *Zwischen Wasser und Urwald* (Bern: Paul Haupt, 1920).

Out of My Life and Thought: An Autobiography. Translated by Antje Bultmann Lemke. New York: Henry Holt & Company, 1990. Originally published as *Aus Meinem Leben und Denken* (Leipzig: Felix Meiner, 1931).

Paul and His Interpreters: A Critical History. Translated as W. Montgomery. London: A. & C. Black, 1948. Originally published as *Geschichte der paulinischen Forschung von der Reformation bis auf die Gegenwart* (Tübingen: J. C. B. Mohr, 1912).

Peace or Atomic War? New York: Henry Holt & Company, 1958. Originally published as *Friede oder Atomkrieg?* (Bern: Paul Haupt, 1958).

The Philosophy of Civilization. Vol. 1, *The Decay and Restoration of Civilization.* Vol. 2, *Civilization and Ethics.* Translated by C. T. Campion. New York: Macmillan, 1950; reprint, New York: Prometheus Books, 1987. Originally published as *Verfall und Wiederaufban der Kultur*, vol. 1, and *Kultur und Ethik*, vol. 2, *Kulturphilosophie* (Bern: Paul Haupt, 1923).

Philosophy of Religion. Translated by Kurt Leidecker and appearing in Thomas Kiernan (ed.), *A Treasury of Albert Schweitzer.* New York: Citadel Press, 1965. Originally published as *Die Religionsphilosophie Kants* (Tübingen: J. C. B. Mohr, 1899).

The Problem of Peace in the World Today. Edited by Norman Cousins New York: Harper & Brothers, 1955.

The Psychiatric Study of Jesus. Translated by Charles R. Joy. Boston: Beacon Press, 1948. Originally published as *Die psychiatrische Beurteilung Jesu* (Tübingen: J. C. B. Mohr, 1913).

The Quest of the Historical Jesus. Translated by W. Montgomery. London: A. & C. Black, 1910; reprint, London: SCM Press, 1996. Originally published as *Von Reimarus zu Wrede* (Tübingen: J. C. B. Mohr, 1906). First complete English edition edited by John Bowden and translated by W. Montgomery, J. R. Coates, Susan Cupitt, and John Bowden (London: SCM Press, 2000).

The Story of My Pelican. Translated By: Martha Wardenburg. London: Souvenir, 1964. Originally published as *Le Pélican du Docteur Schweitzer* (Paris: Editions Sun, 1952).

The Teaching of Reverence for Life. Translated and edited by Richard and Clara Winston (New York: Holt, Rinehart & Winston, 1965).

WORKS CONTAINING ESSAYS, SERMONS, OR LETTERS
BY SCHWEITZER

Albert Schweitzer: An Anthology. Edited and translated by Charles R. Joy (Boston: Beacon Press, 1947).

Albert Schweitzer: Leben, Werk und Denken 1905–1965. Edited by Hans Walter Bähr. Heidelberg: Verlag Lambert Schneider, 1987. Translated by Joachim Neugroschel as *Letters 1905–1965* (New York: Macmillan, 1992).

The Animal World of Albert Schweitzer: Jungle Insights into Reverence for Life Edited and translated by Charles R. Joy (Boston: Beacon Press, 1950; reprint, Hopewell, NJ: Ecco Press, 1998).

Gespräche über das Neue Testament. Munich: C. H. Beck, 1994. Translated by Pierre Kemner as *Conversations sur le Nouveau Testament* (Paris: Brepols, 1994).

Goethe: Five Studies. Edited and translated by Charles R. Joy (Boston: Beacon Press, 1948).

A Place for Revelation: Sermons on Reverence for Life. Translated by David Larrimore Holland. New York: Macmillan, 1988.Originally published as *Was Sollen Wir Tun? 12 Predigten über ethische Probleme,* ed. Martin Strege and Lothar Stiehm (Heidelberg: Verlag Lambert Schneider, 1986).

Reverence for Life: The Words of Albert Schweitzer. Edited by Harold Robles (New York: HarperCollins, 1993).

Strassburger Predigten. Munich: C. H. Beck, 1966. Edited by Ulrich Neuenshwander and translated by Reginald H. Fuller as *Reverence for Life* (New York: Harper & Row, 1969).

Strassburger Vorlesungen. Edited by Erich Grä¢er and Johann Zürcher (Munich: C. H. Beck, 1998).

The Theology of Albert Schweitzer for Christian Inquirers. Edited by E. N. Mozley (London: A. & C. Black, 1950). See esp. pages 79–108.

The Wit and Wisdom of Albert Schweitzer. Edited and translated by Charles R. Joy (Boston: Beacon Press, 1949).

JOURNAL ARTICLES BY SCHWEITZER

"The Ethics of Reverence for Life." *Christendom* 1 (Winter 1936): 222–39. From a transcript of Schweitzer's Gifford Lectures made by Reverend Dwight C. Smith, edited and revised by Schweitzer.

"Forgiveness." *Christian World* (1 November 1934): 11.

"The H-Bomb." *Saturday Review* 27 (17 July 1954): 23.

"*Die Idee des Reiches Gottes.*" *Schweizerische Theologische Umschau* 23 (January–February 1952): 2–20.

"How Can We Attain the Kingdom of God?" *Christian Century* 72 (7 September 1955): 1021–22.

"An Obligation to Tomorrow." *Saturday Review* 41 (24 May 1958): 21–28.

"Philosophy and the Movement for the Protection of Animals." *International Journal of Animal Protection* (May 1935).

"*Das Recht der Wahrhaftigkeit in der Religion.*" *Christliche Welt* (1932): 941–42.

"Relations of the White and Colored Race." *Contemporary Review* CXXV (January 1928): 65–70.

"Religion in Modern Civilization." *Christian Century* (23 and 28 November 1934): 1483–84 and 1519–21.

"Reverence for Life." *The Animal Magazine* (October 1935): 3–4.

"Schweitzer Sees the End of Civilization." *Christian Century* LXIV (1 October 1947): 1165.

"The State of Civilization." *Christian Register* (September 1947): 320–23.

"The Tornado and the Spirit." *Christian Register* (September 1947): 328.

Index